From the Gulf

To God Knows Where

From the Gulf

To God Knows Where

MARION HOULDSWORTH

© Marion Houldsowrth 2006 - 2012

This book is copyright. Apart from any fair dealing for the purpose of private study, research, criticism or review, as permitted under the Copyright Act, no part may be reproduced by any process without written permission. Enquiries should be addressed to the Publisher.

All rights reserved.

First published in 2006 by Central Queensland University Press

Second published in 2012 by Boolarong Press, Salisbury, Brisbane, Australia.

National Library of Australia Cataloguing-in-Publication entry

Author:	Houldsworth, Marion.
Title:	From the gulf to God knows where : living in Australia's outback.
ISBN:	9781921920769 (pbk.)
Subjects:	Country life--Australia.
	Australia--Social conditions--20th century.
	Australia--Description and travel--20th century.
Dewey Number:	994.04

This book is published with the generous assistance of a RADF grant from Dalrymple Shire Council.

Front Cover photo: "The Build Up" Hugh Brown, Living Colours Photography www.hughbrown.com

Back Cover photo: Cobb & Co. leaving Cloncurry, Christmas 1900, courtesy John Oxley Library.

Cover Design by Jane Dorrington

Typeset by Watson Ferguson and Company

Printed and bound by Watson Ferguson and Company, Salisbury, Brisbane, Australia.

ABOUT THE AUTHOR

Queensland born and bred, Marion Houldsworth was educated at Blackheath College Charters Towers, Rockhampton Girls' Grammar School and the University of Queensland. She taught for many years in the Northern Territory and Papua New Guinea. With a life-time's interest in the history of the Australian Outback, especially of its women and children, her previous published titles include

Hearts Bright with Hope; A Grammar School Diary

The Morning Side of the Hill; A Townsville Childhood, 1939 - 1945

The Immigrant Boy; A Townsville Boyhood; 1911 -1918

Barefoot Through the Bindies;
Growing Up in North Queensland in the Early 1900s
(Central Queensland University Press)

Red Dust Rising; *The Life of Ray Fryer of Urapunga*
(Central Queensland University Press)

DEDICATION

To honour the memory of
Michael Edward O'Neill

Who, though critically wounded at the Siege of Tobruk,
Went on to become Senior Manager for Australian Estates Pastoral Company
And Manager, for over forty years,

Of Chatsworth Station, North West Queensland.
Esteemed and respected by all.

'Any man can do more than he thinks he can.'

Frontispiece: Charlie Rayment, mounted on Chocko, watched by his son Bruce and Wayne McCulloch, in the yards at Eildon Park, south of Richmond, Queensland.

FOREWORD

There's a difference between working long hours and working hard. Truck drivers, drovers, café owners, politicians and historians work long hours. Shearers and miners work hard, but for fixed hours. Men in jobs mostly gone now - wheat lumpers, cane cutters, timber getters – worked hard for long hours. Most of the men and women in this book worked hard for long hours at more than one of these jobs, and a dozen others besides.

Work is one thing linking them. The other is remoteness. Remoteness is itself hard work, and it demands long hours. An eight-year old girl starting a man's job, a woman manning home and station far from another voice, a ringer turning a rush back, a man or woman riding at night for help – that's hard work, and for these self-reliant people things like that always came up, the hours were always long.

Work is a comfort in remoteness. It's better to be doing something. Work makes years useful, and wears down remoteness until one day, like the Aborigines, people no longer feel isolated, but at home. They merge into the bush, never wanting to leave. That too links the people in this book, even if some have moved into town now.

From the Gulf to God Knows Where tells some of their stories. Most people in this book set out to make a quid, or at least an independence, and most succeeded. More importantly, they made a life. Outsiders often think such people are vanishing, because technology has softened both work and remoteness. But you still need guts and commitment to battle the bush. As in the past, and as here, every bush generation will have its epic stories.

Few stories have been or will be told with such vivid immediacy and disarming naturalness as Marion Houldsworth presents them here. Once they get going, bush people are good at story-telling. These are lives worth discovering, and a picture of the Australian outback worth preserving. It is a remarkable collection. Marion means it as a tribute to some wonderful people, and it is, but it is also a tribute to her work. Making things look easy is hard; letting others speak well is a rare skill. Make no mistake, hard work and long hours have gone into this book.

Bill Gammage
Australia National University

ACKNOWLEDGEMENTS

For the encouragement to begin work on this book I thank Professor Bill Gammage of the National University, Canberra, and writer and bush-poet Bill Simpson, for sharing their enthusiasm for recording the life-stories of men and women involved in the droving industry of Australia's north. The Gammage and Simpson Collection in the archive of the National Library has been a source of inspiration.

I have a special interest in the history of Australia's Outback, but I would not have had the chance to interview the people whose stories go to make this book were it not for the support of Ray and Betty Fryer of Tabletop station west of Townsville. Ray has an almost encyclopaedic knowledge of the people and places of the north and west. So with Ray's wife, Betty, and friends Bluey Ellis and Estelle Moody we had an interviewing team. For my purposes it was better to be part of a group of friends. Stories shared around a table are more relaxed, more filled with laughter and genuine recollection than those of a formally constructed interview situation. So, thank you, Ray and Betty Fryer, Bluey Ellis and Estelle Moody for the miles we travelled together meeting wonderful people.

And, as always, my grateful thanks go to lifelong friends for their support. In Sydney, Marion and Charles Jaggers, in Brisbane, Pearl Mahony, whose stories of her Callide Valley girlhood inspired me with a love for spoken history, and in Townsville, Ron and Beryl Quelch, always ready to provide a welcoming home-away-from home.

I am indebted to one of Australia's best loved poets, Will Ogilvie, for the phrase 'From the Gulf', the title of his poem which begins, 'Store cattle from Nelanjie, the mob goes feeding past…' I have taught 'From the Gulf' in schools across the Northern Territory and North Queensland, to the accompaniment of crows, corellas and clanking windmills, and it is always a winner. My hope is that the generosity of spirit expressed as 'But let them spread their thousand head, for we've been droving too' stayed in the children's memories long after much else that I taught them had faded.

But, to practicalities! Nothing that I have ever written would have made it safely into print were it not for my stalwart sons-in-law Kristian Kebby and Nick Wood. Their technical expertise with recalcitrant lap-tops is unfailing. My grateful appreciation also to Rachael Kallis for her art-work and to John James for expert advice and support. Thanks also to Dalrymple Shire Council for their generous grant towards publication costs.

Finally, writers and readers alike owe a debt of gratitude to Professor David Myers, A.M. Old Silvertail , publisher of Central Queensland University Press, for his inspired concept of founding the imprint Outback Books. His initiative in doing so provides a voice for Australian writers to preserve our bush and outback heritage in the teeth of a tsunami of overseas publications. Without David's tireless efforts much that is priceless in the social history of our Australian way of life would be lost to future generations.

INTRODUCTION

A rescue attempt! That is how Robert Graves once described an anthology. He said the purpose of any collection, stories or poems, is to include as much material as will fully represent the field it wants to cover, in essence, to rescue it before it is lost to all time. That is the sense in which I collect and present the stories of cattlemen, drovers, teamsters, tin scratchers and their wives and children in this book. The fortitude, the resilience, even the humour of lives lived 'from the Gulf to God knows where', provide glimpses in the rush of today's technological progress, of vanished realities, of work practices, attitudes and survival skills that have been important to the development of the north, and that if not recorded, will be as lost to future generations as stones tossed into a water-hole; lost for ever.

These life-stories are but representative of the many never given the chance of a written record. These people should be our heroes, not the ephemeratae of plasma-screen and cinema. We should value our own narratives and not allow ourselves to be engorged with overseas entertainment. For adventure, drama and sheer guts these stories of the Outback have it all. And what of sex and love, those all-important components of any present saga? Yes. There is love in plenty, but expressed rather as total commitment in the face of overwhelming odds than as trivialized commercial passion.

It might come as an eye-opener for today's reader, especially the young, to read of the work-practices of a yesterday not so very long gone. Men and women, now in their mid-seventies or early eighties, remember leaving school at eleven or twelve and taking their place in the work-force. They were apprentice-adults. 'Teenagers' had not yet been invented. You left school. You got a job. You off-sided, with the respect due to them, for working adults. You learned from them. You also learned to know your place. Bill Petrie, in the stock-camp at eleven, was 'booted up the back-side' by the head-stockman for putting jam on his brownie. 'Brownie is brownie. You don't put jam on it!' a philosophical principle akin to famously quoted Malcolm Frazer's 'Life isn't meant to be easy.' Bill never forgot. Similarly, ten year old Ann Brunner, struggling unaided with Grade Three Correspondence School lessons, decides 'I don't need this! I know how to work!' And she did. At an age when little girls of today are combing the hair of their Barbie dolls, ten-year-old Ann could 'knock up a feed' for her large family, off-side for her father in the mine, break in horses at ten bob a head - 'Good money in them days!' - and by thirteen was part of a droving plant. But despite their relentlessly demanding childhoods the people in this book went on to lead highly successful lives. Like Queensland's turtle hatchlings which must dig themselves out of the sand and struggle to the sea unassisted in order to survive, it seems that exacting effort early in the human life-cycle can be a vital stimulus to success.

We can only admire the spirit of men, women and children who had it tough but took fierce pride in not whingeing. We have to wonder at the skills of adaptation they used to survive. As a little girl Ellen Donnellen knew that to settle mud in a bucket of dam water you sprinkled it with ashes; William McDowall knew bleeding wounds could be plugged with cobwebs. Everyone knew, that lacking a wagon to transport your gear you could chop down a sapling, cut the fork out, invert it, and you had a slide for your horse to pull. Common wisdom was, 'Use it up. Make it do. Do without'. There was a lot of 'doing without'. The Edmunds family in the Gulf country never had beds. In their tent home they slept on the ground. But the children were brought up with standards of honesty and integrity far more rigorous than those of today.

There are not as many women's stories in Volume One as I would have liked. Women prove more elusive. Where are they when the tape-recorder reels are winding? Most often out in the kitchen seeing to the leg of lamb for lunch or bringing a batch of smoko scones out of the oven. Many feel that the story is the man's, not seeing themselves as the custodians of the saga. But without exception the men pay appreciative tributes to the women that have shared their lives, their steadfastness and their courage in the face of adversity. Charlie Rayment's, 'Pauline has always stuck by me,' perhaps says it for all of them.

The outback of Australia has been described as not so much a place as a state of mind.[1] The stories in this book support the proposition that the inland has produced a distinctive type of people. Recently, in Townsville, I was talking to an assembly of Year Ten students at a large secondary school. One boy, intelligent but reserved, wary of becoming involved in the cross-fire discussion, caught my interest. I sensed qualities in him that set him apart from his urban classmates. He seem to me to know a reality beyond the grasp of theirs, an ability to make judgments, assess risks, deal with practicalities in the natural world outside the range of the average teenager's experience. I asked, 'Whereabouts are you from?' He said, 'Stonehenge,' and I smiled. Stonehenge is about as Far West as you need to go to qualify for being 'Outback', a testing place for man, woman or child. Something about the pale blueness of eyes accustomed to looking into great distances made me recognize that this boy was far from his preferred environment, observing all, keeping his own council. He was accepting his chance of a modern education with the stoicism born of being bred to the idea that hardships are part of life to be taken in one's stride. He seemed to me representative of an Outback type that you would recognize and be glad to shake the hand of, on the streets of Mexico City, London or New York.

To me these people are wonderful. More than wonderful. Inspirational! I would like to feel that readers meet them as friends and are enriched and delighted by getting to know them. There is something of the Outback in every Australian. The Outback is a state of mind we all share.

1 Bruce Campbell, O.A.M., in his opening address of the Year of the Outback celebrations, Charters Towers, 2002.

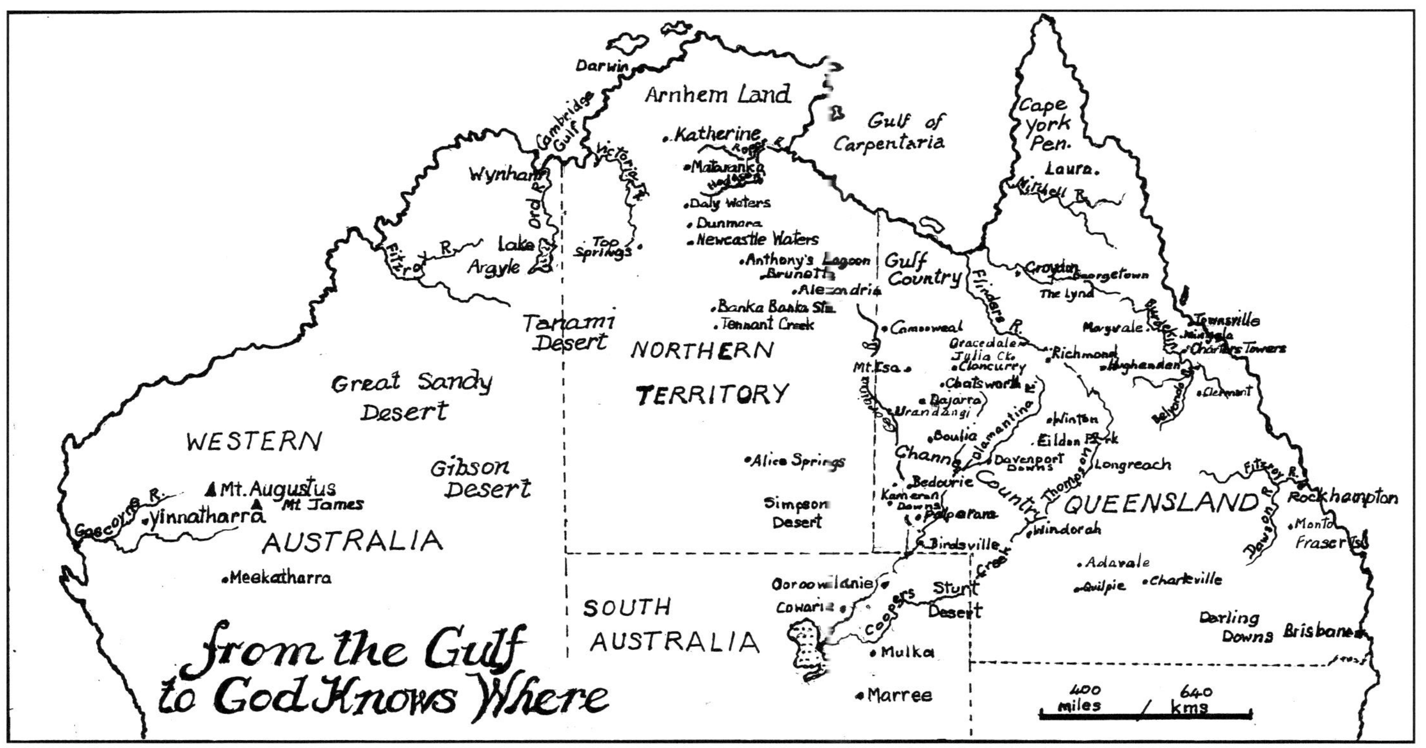
from the Gulf
to God Knows Where
Darwin
Arnhem Land
Gulf of
Carpentaria
Cape
York
Pen.
Laura.
Cambridge
Gulf
Wynham
Ord R.
Victoria R.
Lake
Argyle
Fitzroy R.
Top
Springs
Katherine
Mataranka
Daly Waters
Dunmara
Newcastle Waters
Anthony's Lagoon
Brunette
Alexandria
Banka Banka Stn.
Tennant Creek
Tanami
Desert
NORTHERN
TERRITORY
Great Sandy
Desert
WESTERN
AUSTRALIA
Gibson
Desert
Mt. Augustus
Mt James
Yinnatharra
Meekatharra
Alice Springs
Simpson
Desert
SOUTH
AUSTRALIA
Mulka
Marree
Cowarie
Stunt
Desert
Gulf
Country
Flinders R.
Croydon
Georgetown
The Lynd
Camooweal
Mt.Isa
Julia Ck.
Cloncurry
Chatsworth
Dajarra
Urandangi
Boulia
Richmond
Hughenden
Charters Towers
Townsville
Winton
Eildon Park
Davenport
Downs
Longreach
Bedourie
Kameran
Downs
Birdsville
Windorah
QUEENSLAND
Adavale
Quilpie
Charleville
Darling
Downs
Brisbane
Rockhampton
Fitzroy R.
Dawson R.
Monto
Fraser Isl.
Clermont
Maryvale
400
miles
640
kms

CONTENTS

Ann Brunner

Ann at her retirement home in Charters Towers. Aged eighty, she had been on the roof of the shed all day 'ripping the iron off.'

Introduction

If you go to visit Ann and Bob Brunner at their comfortable retirement bungalow on the outskirts of Charters Towers, you had better watch out for Pete, the dog. Pete, a well-set up Blue Heeler with a meaningful eye, might be the dog for whom the term Beware of the Dog was coined. Don't even lean on the gate or Pete will have your arm. Stand back respectfully and call, 'Y'there Ann? Y'there?' and wait, until, with the bright eagerness of a young girl, eighty year old Ann appears from somewhere out the back.

On the day we arrived to make the interviews that went into the recording of her life story, Ann greeted us with 'Hang on a bit 'till I slip this fella on the chain.' before letting us in the gate. She then led us to view the shed she was in the process of dismantling, adding, 'I've bin up on the roof all day. I've just about got all the iron off. But I've buggered my hands a bit. Look! ' And so she had. Her hands were covered with bloodied gashes. And, no, of course, she 'never wears gloves'.

Although Ann had little education, her life story, as she told it around the kitchen table, had the power to take the listener back to the early decades of the last century, to a time when, in the terrible years of the Great Depression, families knew the meaning of hard work, could live rough but still maintain standards of honesty and decency, and children could roam the bush, wild and free as the brumbies they pursued, captured and broke in for fun. In the hearing, our modern lifestyle, with its unlimited comfort, entertainment and security, seems pampered, effete and unchallenged. The heart longs to be off and away to the land beyond the northern ranges, to a simple home of bush materials, where a dinner- damper bakes in the camp-fire ashes, where nuggets of gold might brighten the gullies, where in the distance, a mob of long-tailed brumbies flies through the timber, and at night dingoes howl to a wild moon. It was in such a setting that Ann Brunner's family, the Edmunds children, eleven of them, grew up, all later to make their way successfully in life. Before retirement, Ann and her husband Bob owned four valuable grazing properties across North Queensland.

Of the constellation of remarkable people whose life-stories go to make up this book, I consider Ann Brunner a star. She is a truly unique, almost iconic, Australian bush woman. I was proud to meet her. One of my most cherished moments was when this wonderful lady, said to me, in parting, 'You come again. I like talking to you.' I will not receive a compliment I cherish more.

Joe Edmunds and his eldest son, Charlie, panning. The dish contains dark material, possibly alluvial tin, perhaps accounting for the relieved smile on the boy's face. Charlie was ten years older than Ann and would have been more aware of the family's difficult circumstances.

Joe Edmunds and his children at his dry-blower. Charlie is the tallest, back right. Ann, in hat, is centre left, with Snow on her right and Della, in hat, behind her.

Chapter 1...

THE LADY DROVER

Ann Brunner

Chasing the gold! My Dad was always one for chasing the gold. When I was born in Ingham, Mum took me straight back up the Mount Fox track to Dad's camp over the range. I'm in the middle of the family, fifth either way. And same when Joyce was born. Jimmy Woodhouse – he was on Valley of Lagoons – he picked Mum up coming home from hospital with a spare horse, and he put a pillow on the front of the saddle and she carried Joycie, a new-born baby, in front of her, twenty-nine miles out from Camel Creek, an outstation of Greenvale – a very rough ride through dense bush - to where Dad was camped. Mum battled!

Then they shifted to a goldfield called Balcooma, on Greenvale, and Dad and Charlie –he's the eldest - went away and they come back with this dry blower. It had big stampers, the arm would come over and dolly up the ore and then it goes through a ripple box that you had to put cyanide in, and quick-silver. It would bring all the gold together, and you wouldn't be losing any. The big kids, Della and Charlie and Ned, used to have to rock it all day. Talk about dust! But most times there would be a few pennyweights of gold and sometimes just a tiny little nugget. That would keep them going. If you got twenty-two pennyweights that was an ounce. Gold was fetching twelve pounds an ounce if you could get it, so it was good money, but they were only just living.

And when I was nine or ten maybe – I loved helping Dad at the mine. I always wanted to be with him because he used to have challenges all the time. And one time he was down the shaft, and he lit the fuse - he used to put one primer and two sticks of gelignite in it; and he used to put a little split in the fuse, and put a little bit of gelly in it to make it catch; it'd fizz - and he lit it, and he was climbing up and the ladder broke and he fell back down the shaft. And the fuse was going so he got his pocket knife and cut the fuse but it was still going and he couldn't stop it. So he grabbed the bridle reins and he was climbing up using them and singing out to me, 'Ann! Get away! Get away! Get behind a tree!' He just got to the top and fell over the edge and went maybe ten yards or so and she went! And didn't she lift! All the rocks was coming out! Rocks falling everywhere! But it done a good job! We got a lot of tin out of it!

Dad used to say to me, 'You collect all the specimens that was blown out.' There would be tin or antimony all through it. And I would go and find all them, and put them in a heap. And he would dolly them; put them through a screen. And then throw away all the no-good stuff, and the tin would go to the bottom. I used to love doing that with Dad. He used to pack it out on the pack-horses to Herberton to sell.

One time when Dad went to work he forgot his tobacco and matches and he said, 'Ann, you slip home and get my tobacco and matches.' It was about six mile, not that far. So I cantered off home and I got his tobacco and matches and I went back. And Dad was down the mine and he called out, 'Eh! You got my tobacco and matches?' And I said, 'Yeah, Dad.' So he says, 'You have a spell then.' And he went back down the shaft. And I thought to myself, 'Well, there's a good place to have a bit of a camp here,' and I put my head up against this big old iron-bark tree. And near it was a big mulluck heap, all stones and rocks. And I laid down against the tree and I went to sleep.

I had my legs crossed and I felt this funny feeling; something coming up over m'legs and coming up on to m' chest. And I woke up! And it was a snake! And it took two coils on m'chest and its tail was still back down over m'feet! And I was terrified. And he's waving his head in m'face and poking his tongue at me! And I yelled out, 'Dad!' And when I did, that snake stood up and he was going to have a go at me!

And Dad heard me the first time. He could tell by m' voice that there was something wrong. And he come up and he seen the snake laying on m' chest; two coils of him and the tail back down over m'legs! And he said, 'Don't you move, Ann. And I'll pretend to get a stick. When I turn m'back he'll go away. Don't move! Don't move!' And Dad went to walk away and I felt I just wanted to get up and get away. I was scared Dad would leave me there. But Dad was right. As soon as he turned his back and walked away that snake came out of his coils and went back down over m'feet back into the rocks.[1]

And I automatically stood up with shock. I was like a statue or a stick. And I started shaking. And I was shaking for about three or four days. I couldn't stop. I couldn't hold a cuppa tea. I couldn't sleep at night. I could still feel that snake. It was terrible. A couple of weeks later Mum took me in to Herberton to the doctor. She told him what had happened with the snake. He told her, 'That's shock.' And he gave her some medicine to settle me down. And that got me good again.

One time we were travelling across from Mount Garnet on a bush road. Dad had the wagon and five horses and Mum was following along with the buggy. Us kids were coming along behind with the pack-horses and saddle-horses. And here was this poor old man sitting at the foot of a tree; sitting up against it, sort've had it. For his swag all he had was a couple of bags. Dad says; 'Whoa! Whoa!' to the horses, and they stopped. Dad got off quick. He said, 'Are you alright?' And he said, 'Yeah. I'm alright.' Dad says, 'How y'off for tucker?' And all he had was this little old billy-can made out of a jam tin with a bit of a handle. And in it he had two frog legs. He said, 'This is all I got.' He used to cook these frog legs in this jam tin. Gee! It would make you sick!

1 The fact that the snake had come from the pile of rocks, and its length, and that it had coiled itself on Ann's chest and raised its head, seems to suggest that it was a rock python preparing to 'throw a coil' about her in the manner in which pythons are known to coil themselves around their prey, usually rock wallabies.

And Dad said to Mum, 'Mum, What'll we do?' And Mum said, 'Give him a feed!' So she got the tucker-box out. Dad said, 'Don't give him too much or you'll kill him!' So she got him some damper and some corned beef. He was just skin and bone! He'd never had much education and he was trying to survive to get across to The Lynd. But, poor old fellow, he just couldn't do it. It was sad to see him! We took him with us on the wagon. That old fellow thought a lot of Dad because he reckoned he'd saved his life. He'd say to Dad, 'I'm not leaving you, Joe!' Dad kep' that old man for about six months till he was right to move on.

Then later on Dad got an old Studebaker truck and he could get around better. So then Charlie and I had to fetch the horses back from Herberton to Mount Garnet and that was a wild trip! There was no track. We were just heading across country. Charlie was a good bushman. He knew where to go. I'd have been about ten and Charlie was ten years older than me. We only had a pack-horse; very little food. And at night time you would hear the dingoes howling! I used to get terrified! Charlie would tell me, 'You stop here. I won't be long. I'll check the horses.' I used to stand against the fire and I'd think to m'self, 'If a dingo comes I'll throw the coals at him!' I used to ride one horse all the time because it was a good one. And it knocked up. We had a lot of other horses there, but they were rough! But old Jimmy Onions, at Reedy Brook – he was a lovely old man - he said to Charlie, 'Charlie you can't take this little girl along no more. Y've gotta giv her a day's rest!' I said, 'No! I'll be alright!' But we stayed a day and instead of hobbling the horses out, he told Charlie to put them in a little paddock. He was a kind man.

During the years of the 1930s Great Depression there were families all over Australia who were forced to live like this. Despite the seemingly rough living conditions the Edmunds children were brought up to strict standards of honesty and hard work.

Then the next day we headed off. But we cut out of meat and we had no bread. We had nothing! And we were going past a big lake and I said to Charlie, 'Why don't you grab one of them calves and cut its throat and get a bit of beef?' Charlie said, 'You don't do that!' I could've ate anything, I was that hungry. It was ninety mile altogether, open bush and hilly. I was glad to get home again to The Lynd.

Dad kept those horses for a long time. Then a lot of people wanted to buy them off him. And he took them over to Einasleigh and sold them to a bloke at Kidston that wanted the two leaders. He would've giv about two pounds each for them. But not the harness; it's still up there on the place at Balcooma outside The Lynd. The wagon is still there and the buggy.

And down on the creek, a bloke from Conjuboy, old Mr. Arthur Wilson, he said to Dad, 'I got some horses here, Joe, for the kids. They can have them if they like to break 'em in and make 'em quiet.' And Dad said, 'Righto!' And he gets these horses over. And us kids had to tail these horses because they wanted to clear off back to Conjuboy.

And there was an old man camped on the spring on Balcooma, up at the head of Garbutt's Gully, and when we were tailing the horses, this poor old man, he had condensed milk, and I used to get hungry and I'd go and thieve a tin of condensed milk off him! It was the wrong thing to do, but I would be that hungry, and I would think, 'This milk will hold me.' So I would steal a tin. Anyway, he found out and he told Dad. He said, 'Them kids is breaking into my tent and stealing m'condensed milk!' And Dad put us all on the line, and he said, 'Who took the milk!' And when Dad said something he meant it! I put m'hand up, and I said, 'I did, Dad.' He said, 'What did you do that for!' I said, 'I was hungry.' He said, 'Why didn't you come home!' And didn't I get a lathering with his leather belt! I'll never forget it! Ooh! When Dad says one word we had to jump! We weren't to back-answer, or swear, or call anyone by their name; it had to be Mister or Missus. Dad was strict.

I never had no proper schooling. Mum taught us Correspondence when she had time; mostly for a while when we were on the Dry River, out from Herberton. There was a mailman used to come out once a week would bring the lessons. And Mum was helping Dad with the fencing, and couldn't teach us kids too. They'd be away all day. I got up to Third Grade, and I said, 'I don't need all this education. I can do all this!' I could work and I could make a damper or a cake in the camp-oven. I reckoned I didn't need any more.

Bush children. Despite the rigours of living conditions the children seem sturdy and self-reliant.

Dad used to do a lot of possuming. That was one way they used to get a living. Charlie, the eldest, used to go with him and he would carry a six-volt battery on his shoulder, to run a spotlight for shooting them. Times I'd go with them, because I liked it. They used to go all night until the battery went flat and then they'd have to come home. And when he got back he would put the battery on the vehicle to charge it up, and they would rev this old truck to get the charge up, to put the kick back into it.

Dad taught us all to skin. The same as you skin a kangaroo; down the front legs, up the neck, down the belly and back legs, and then just punch the skin and get it off. It wouldn't have taken no more than about two minutes. We used to peg the skins out on the ground. Bits of old fencing wire for pegs. Or if there was a tree anywhere we'd tack them out on the tree and then, when they got dry Dad would roll them up. But if he got a few at night, a dozen or so maybe, he would skin them himself out bush. He used to carry them on a sort of yoke over his back. He'd get a few roos of a night-time, too. I don't know what the skins were worth but it used to keep us in food. He used to send them to Herberton. When he couldn't get enough money to feed us he took jobs fencing and yard building on The Lynd and Lyndhurst, Cunjuboy, Greenvale, the Ninety Mile and Carpentaria; Mum and Dad worked on all those properties out that way;

One day, when Dad was working on the Wild River, a big storm come. I said, 'Can we go for a swim?' He said, 'Righto, but don't you kids go down near the junction, there.' It was the where the Wild River and another creek that came down from old John Lilley's place junctioned. So all us kids, away we go, in our knickers.

And when we get to the junction, I says to myself, 'Now, Dad says we can't go in there. Why's that? I'm going to go in to see what's there!' I had to see. It was a challenge. So, nothing surer, in I go. And Della is singing out to me, 'Don't go over there! Don't go over there! Then, 'Mum! Ann's going over!' But in I goes. And over on the other side, where that creek junctions in, there was a hollow in the water where the two streams come together and the water wound around and around and made this big hole in the middle. And I thought to myself, 'This looks cute!' I thought I could get a ride on it and go round and round like a merry-go-round. But it sucked me straight down. My legs and arms were fluttered around like a shirt. And I hit the bottom, and around it took me, two times. Lucky the bottom was sand. Not rocks. And I was out of wind and full of sand. And the third time round it picked me up and just shot me straight me out. Threw me out. And then Dad swum out and got me, because I couldn't swim! And didn't he lather me! And if you give me a million dollars there is no way you would get me into another whirlpool. It's about the worst thing that can happen to a human body. You got no control on what is happening to you. The worst moment of my life, that was.

We were terrible kids. Once at Clayholes, we were supposed to be helping Dad build a yard. And every time we could get away, we would get the horses and play the wag. Down from Clayholes was the Lynd River, and we'd get the horses and swim them. None of us could swim but the horses could. Della used to have a grey horse she called Teal Duck; it was Charlie's horse, but Della claimed it for swimming. And there would be Della and Snow and myself and Charlie, and away we'd go to see who could swim their horse across this flooded river. A lot of horses won't swim. They stand up and fight the water. We'd get them in alright, but then they would get up on their back legs and slip us off. And this one of Della's, this Teal Duck, she used to put him in and he would swim straight across. And we used to call out to her, 'Come back, Della, and we'll follow you!' We'd be thinking, 'While Della's going in we'll boot ours in too!' And they'd be rearing up and fighting the water, but we'd get them in, then we'd all end up half a mile down the river because of the flood. Us kids! We should have been dead years ago!

Once at Tinaroo there was a big rocky gorge with a flying-fox to get across. I think the government must have put it there because there used to be a lot of miners there after the tin. If you didn't have the flying-fox you would've had to climb down into the gorge and then up again. Then you'd have to walk a couple of mile around the hill before you got to where the tin was. The flying-fox would have been about seventy feet above the river, across this big rocky gorge. It was cemented into the rock at the ends. There was a box to sit in, and two pulleys, one on this side and one on the other side. A rope went from the pulley and you had to pull it from one side to the other. You get in and let her go! And then you'd get to the middle where it dipped down and after that you'd have to pull yourself up to the other side. Mum and I used to fit in it, with a dish of tin between us. Three kids could fit without the dish, but Dad had to go across on his own because he would always have a dish of tin with him.

I was always scared of the dingoes. Della and I used to have to go and get the horses, first thing every morning, about three miles. We'd get up about four o'clock. We'd have something maybe left over from the night before, curry and rice, or we'd cook a bit of steak and we'd go. And the way you'd go to get the horses went through this gap between two big hills. And these dogs used to meet us there; two of 'em, every morning. Dingoes always seem to hunt in pairs. These was two males, big fellows. They never missed meeting us there, and they started to get cheekier and cheekier. And the big one, it would get that close, you could hear its teeth going, 'Ngick! Ngick! Ngick!' And Della would have the bridle and she would lay into it with the reins. And I would be singing out, 'Get into it! Get into it!' And when she was swiping at it with the reins, it'd get back, but you could hear its jaws going 'Snap! Snap!' Della's name for me was always 'Jack'. And she said, 'Jack, I'm gunna put you up this tree.' And then she'd go and get the horses. And I'd have to be up that tree and the dingoes'd be there round the bottom of it. They wouldn't leave.

And Della would get the horses and she'd go like the devil and she'd pull up under the tree and she'd say, 'Hop on, Jack! Quick!' She used to double-bank me because of them dogs. So she told Mother about them. And Mother said, 'I'll come with you in the morning and see what's wrong.' So in the morning, we got breakfast and away we go. Pitch dark. And we gets to the same place, going through this gap where they'd meet us every morning. And I was always behind; I never knew to get up in the lead. And I saw the dogs waiting. And I said, 'Mum! Mum! Mum! The dogs are there! Mum! Quick!' And poor old Mum! She into it with the bridle reins. And a stick. And I'm hanging on to her. And she's saying, 'Let me go! Let me go! I can't get a good swing at him!' She fought him off and she said to Della, 'You go and get the horses and we'll wait here.' And she got me up this tree. She stood down under the tree with the stick. And Della gets the horses and away we go.

And when she gets home she says to Dad, 'You'll have to go out and do something about them dingoes. They're attacking these kids.' So next morning away we go with Dad. He had his rifle; an old timer. You push the handle down and it would reload itself, a Martini action. You'd push the bullet in the side if you wanted a single shot. And Dad had this and he was going along. I thought to myself, 'I'm going in the front this time!' So I'm padding along in front and all of a sudden Dad says, soft, to us, 'Whoa! Whoa! Whoa!' and these dogs are there!

We could see one but not two. One would come in to have a go at you and the other fellow would sit back. It was still too dark for Dad to see the sights on the rifle. He said, 'We'd better wait on!' So we waited and we waited and it started to come daylight. And Dad could just see him. Dad was one heck of a good shot. And he up and he barrelled the first one. And the other fellow went away a little bit. And I thought to myself, 'Gee, Dad! I hope you can get that other one!' It was still dark. But he up with his rifle and he got this other fellow. And wasn't it a pleasure to get the horses after that!

I really loved my mother. She was lovely. And Dad, too. He didn't just drag us up, but if he told you to do something and you didn't, well, he got his big leather belt, or his whip. And it was only that Mum and Dad was so strict that we turned out to be workers in what we could do.

When I'd have been about thirteen Mum would say to me, 'Ann, you go and get the meat.' And I would ride twenty-two miles, bareback, over to Greenvale station. No roads. Straight through the bush. Old Louis Secombe was looking after Greenvale then. I used to put the split-bag under this side and over that side of m' legs, and that holds you down and you can trot like anything. But I used to canter all the way because I had to get back before dark. Dad used to always tell me, 'You be home before dark!' They used to make me a cup of tea at the station but I didn't stop. I'd get the meat and go. I knew I had to get home by dark. And coming home I used to canter and that used to tear the split-bag. When it got dark the horse used to take me home straight across country. But I was frightened of the dingoes. And one time it got late and I'm riding along in the dark and crying and about four or five mile from home, next thing I hear this 'Cooee!' And it was Dad, out looking for me. He said to me, 'What kep'you!' And he felt the split-bag in the dark, and he said, 'It's nearly divided. It's nearly tore!' And he took it off me, and, oh! m'legs was that bruised from having that split-bag over the top of them! But he got the bag and held it in front of him; two sugar-bagfuls. He got it home and he said to me, 'Never you canter again when you pick up the meat!' And I said, 'I was frightened of getting a hiding for being late!' Because, Dad, if he told you to do something and you didn't do it, oh boy! Twenty-two miles; but it wasn't long, when you knew you had to get there and back!

But we had a lot of fun. If we had to go for the horses and we saw a mob of cows, we used to chase the buggers and reckon we were doing a camp-draft. And Jim Aitkenson had some cows and he told Mum that if we could break them we could milk them. We had about seven of them, over at a yard called Paddy's. And we'd go over there and camp the night on a greenhide bed that was there, with our boots under our heads for a pillow, and get up very early in the morning and milk these cows and then away we'd go and take that milk home in a four gallon tin on the saddle in front of us. And Mum would boil that milk every morning so it would keep; it wouldn't go off if she boiled it every morning. She'd stand it in another tin over the tripods and let it boil slowly, slowly, otherwise it would burn on the bottom. It would go pink, and that milk would last. And while we had it we were having all the puddings and custards! Mum was a smashing cook. She used to make yeast bread and all.

We were about thirty miles out of Herberton, right down on the Dry River. The way Mum and Dad set up camp was they had one them big Berkshire flies. Then they would get hold of some of them old sack-bags and sew them together, and that was where you would eat. We just had carbide lights or slush lights; a bit of rag in a tin of fat. They wouldn't blow out. The old candle and the carbide light would blow out but not the slush light or the hurricane lamp. We all slept on the ground, rolled up; Mum and Dad too. Never had a bed; none of us.

When I was about thirteen or fourteen, Snow and I used to break-in horses for different people that couldn't break-in their own. A lot of horses Snow broke in I couldn't ride. And horses that I broke in no-body could ride! Because I used to flog 'em! As soon as I got on them! Get into them and flog them straight away! All my horses, all along, I used to stand over them. Boot 'em hard and then they'd be frightened of you and take notice. And hold your reins out, so they could see them, and gees, you could feel them come together under you! We'd give them quite a few rides, bareback. We used to get about ten bob a horse; broken-in. That was good money in those days.

And when we'd ride over to Greenvale to get the beef; we used to ride them to get them used to carrying a split-bag on the back of the saddle. They didn't like that. And we'd ride along the telephone line from the Ninety Mile, across country, and put our horses over any trees that were down. And there was one big old ironbark; when it fell it fell half propped up; with a big forky part. I used to say to Snow, 'Here's my jump!' She used to jump over the bottom part, and I used to say 'No! Get him up there in the forky part. Then he's got to jump because his head's coming in!' She wouldn't take it on, but I never worried. I'd put mine through that forky part every time. I had no brains! I could've got killed, eh! But that horse turned out a good jumper! I never opened a gate.

When I was about thirteen, Lennie Smith wanted to take a mob of Lyndhurst cattle to Townsville and he couldn't get any men. He asked Dad to let Charlie, Della, Snow and me go with him. That was my first droving trip. It was a three week trip and we got thirty bob a week each. After that we got other jobs with George Towns, the Lyndhurst drover. Later on that same year in the Dry we were taking a mob of stores down from Lyndhurst to Charters Towers with Lennie Smith and a big electrical storm come up. With the thunder and lightning all round, the cattle took off and Lennie went after them, yelling at us to get round them. But we knew to get off our horses and hunt them and lie down flat. Dad always told us, 'Never you stay on your horse when there's a thunder storm! The sweat and the saddle brings the lightning to you.' But Lennie, he went after the cattle. The lightning was coming down all round. A big tree that was near to us got blown to pieces. And the next thing Lennie was struck! Him and his horse, both killed. That was a terrible thing to see.

We shifted camp to Lyndhurst station, fencing and yard building, and Dad got sick. It was raining and the creeks were running bankers and they'd backed up into this big swamp. All black soil; you couldn't get a horse through, the mud was that heavy. We made a bag stretcher and we carried him. It was heavy going in that black soil mud. We carried him half way and then the men from Lyndhurst met us and took over. Twenty-two miles he was carried. They had a plane waiting on a big claypan. When they were loading him on it Dad looked up at us and he said, 'Well, I'll say good-bye to you all. I won't be coming home again.' We were all crying our eyes out. They flew him to Atherton hospital and he died the next day. That was February 1940. When he was young Dad was famous at athletics. He broke the record in the hop-step and jump. He won the Halifax Hundred at foot-running; and he could do boxing and bullock-riding and shooting. He never stopped teaching us the things he knew. He was a lovely father.

When the alluvial tin or gold gave out the Edmunds family would shift camp to a more promising site. Ann recalls that 'they all slept on the ground' but there are stretcher-beds in the load. The sheets of iron would be for the wind-break around the cooking- fire.

After Dad died there was nothing for it but to finish the job building the big stockyard at the Twelve Mile on Lyndhurst. Then we worked on the boundary fence between The Lynd and Kidston. Snow and me were away droving at this time but when we got back we would give Mum and Della and Charlie a hand. It was a five mile ride out to where we were working on the fence. Ellen was about six or seven and it was her job to stop in the camp and look after the little ones and get a bit of a meal ready for when we got back. We had to cut the timber for the posts and then they had to be sawn and split. Della would get a harness on one of the horses and haul the posts along the fence-line and drop them in position. It was hard work digging the holes. It was that hot the crowbar would blister your hands. Mum and Charlie would shovel the holes out. Some days it was too hot to work and we worked of a night time with a carbide lamp to see by. There was nine miles of that fence to do and we finished it.

Then Snow and I were working at the mine at the Ninety Mile; underground with the men, down a hundred and fifty feet. We thought it was great. We used to load a four ton mine-truck with a shovel, spread it on top. The truck had a little trolley under it on a tram-line. It was on one of those big lair winches and I would winch it up and send it back down again. I was doing it just for the fun; not getting paid or anything. Then they started giving us five bob a load. In that mine they had to keep the pumps going to keep the water out. They took that copper across to Einasleigh and then from Einasleigh it went to Forsyth by train.

Mr. Jim Aitkenson, at Greenvale, he wanted some fencing done on Lucky Downs and a horse-paddock built on the Burdekin, and my sister Snow and I says we can do it. He loaned us a horse and collar and we cut a tree and made a slide out of the fork and we used to cart these posts with the horse and slide. We cut them and split them ourselves; ironbark, with bloodwood strainers, and three wires. Mr Aitkenson come out to look at the job and he said, 'I didn't think you girls could do it!' But we did it alright. We thought it was a chance for us to make a quid. We liked the work. And that paddock is still there to this day, at Paddy's Lagoon, down from the Ninety Mile. In our slack time, the two of us, we cut logs and props for the mine. I wasn't quite fifteen and Snow was two years older.

Then the Japs were coming into the war and things started getting serious. Manpower came and picked us up. They were short of men and they sent a constable out to get us. He asked us our age and we put our age up. He took us to Atherton to Mr Elliot at the Manpower office there. We wanted to go in the Land Army; I said, 'Well, I want to go transport driving.' He says, 'It's not what you want. It's what we say. You'll do what we tell you to! You're going in the Land Army alright. Back in the mustering camp and droving.' Mother was crying because she didn't want to lose us. And Snow and me, we were all the war years droving.

Our first mustering camp was on Lyndhurst. Laurie Shaw was the manager and George Towns was the Head Stockman. Those Lyndhurst horses were touchy, but we could meet them. We could do a bit of buck-jumping. Lennie Forman was running the camp. He was a good stockman. And one time, at the Ninety Mile mine, Lennie was shoeing his horses and he had this lovely little chestnut mare, Eau de Cologne; a beautiful camp horse. Lennie was an excellent horseman. But he didn't like me. He wanted to tail Snow. He wanted to get me a buster. And one time his horses had got away and were clearing out. He said to me, 'Here! Fly on to Eau de Cologne and get round them!' And this mare of his was a slippery ride! But I after them. And it was about a quarter of a mile before I got to the lead of the mob and turned them and hunted them back. And I thought to myself, 'Now, I've got this mare worked out! If I'm not watching, she is going to prop, and, bareback, I will keep going!' Which is what Lennie had planned. He wanted to get me a buster! But I just thought faster than both of them! And when I got back, he yelled at me, 'Get off that bloody mare or you will ruin her!' He was wild with me for getting the best of his mare. He thought she would pelt me. But she couldn't!

George Towns, he was the Boss Drover; a mighty man and a really good boss. He'd always explain to you where you were wrong, and if you were right he would say, 'You keep on going like that and you'll be right!' Besides us he had his son, Morris, a good stockman, and old Sid Lederidge; he was the cook with his camp-oven and about three or four billy-cans. Plenty of corned beef and damper. No butter. We had seven pack-horses and twenty-two riding horses. Beautiful horses. Very good night horses. On those trips we would watch the cattle all the way. There were no yards.

We'd camp in the same places, every trip. The horses used to get used to being hobbled out there and they would stop every time they got to that camp. They'd know, 'This is where we pull up.' Usually on a bit of a ridge. George would say, 'Well, the cattle will camp here.' He would try to make it a little bit of comfort for them. We mostly had timber camps. Hardly any open flat country through there. And in your swag, just one blanket on the bottom and one on top. No pillow. You had to put your clothes in the envelope in the swag, and that was your pillow, or it would have been too big for the pack horses.

It used to take twenty-four days to go down; down the Burdekin and through Blue Range, across the Star, then Dotswood and down the range. The buffalo fly had just broken out and we had to dip at the Star and at Blue Range; the horses and pack-horses too. The dip was arsenic and caustic soda. It was cruel to the horses. It used to take all the hair off them where the packs went. George swore that he wouldn't do it again!

We were mostly taking fats down. Five of us for six hundred head, but if it was a thousand he would get an extra man. It was about a two hundred mile trip and we'd do about ten mile a day. But sometimes, if they wanted to get the bullocks in early we'd have to miss a camp and go on to the next one; do a twenty mile stage. I used to go on watch at half-past two in the morning, after Snow come off, and I never got off until half-past six that night. I'd be with those cattle from half-past two in the morning until after seven at night. And even when we pulled up for dinner, I'd be watching them on dinner camp. It was a heck of a long day.

And there was one time when George said, 'Girls, we'll be on water today, if you want to wash your things' So we go to have a bath in the creek, but this was wintertime, and the water was freezing! Talk about cold! But there was a big flat rock with a hollow in it. So we boiled the quart-pots, and we poured the water into the hollow rock for a bath, and we got a hot bath out of it! When you're with those cattle all day, well, the dust! That was the worst part of it!

When we'd get down at Greenvale, there, at Miner's Camp, where the town is now, George would say, 'We've got to shoe them cows.' The cows used to get lame. They'd screw their foot as they walked, and it would wear out. So George used always to carry old worn-out horse shoes that he'd cut in half. He didn't throw the beast to shoe them. He would get up a tree and he would say to Snow and me, 'You get round that beast and bring it under the tree.' And he would have a rope up the tree and he'd say, 'Bring that beast up and as soon as I drop the rope on it youse grab it.' I'd say to Snow, 'You want the back leg?' and she'd say, 'No! You get kicked!' So Snow used to go for the front leg and I'd go for the back. George never missed with the rope and I got pretty good at getting the hind-leg rope on. I used to just put the rope out and give the tail a pull and pull the leg into it. Then Snow would get the head and I would get the tail between the legs and pull and the beast would go over. And then George tacked the shoes on.

You'd have to shoe a certain number of cows each trip, but only bullocks that had a broken toe, or something. You would have lost them otherwise. They wouldn't walk. They get too sore. George would tack shoes on them. The cow's only got the tiniest bit of hoof, and he'd tack three nails in and that beast would be right. Oh, he could shoe! The beast would go through to the Townsville, down the range, without any more trouble.

Once, we had to swim them over the Walsh River and it was pouring with rain and it was murder swimming them across. It would have been two or three hundred yards. What George used to do was he would keep them off water. Well then, once the lead gets in, you've got to drive the tail over. Push them through; keep them going, because once they turn, well, they can come over on top of you. We used to swim the horses up and bowl water in the cattle's faces to keep them moving; keep them from turning. George used to say, 'Don't let them come round on you! They'll drown you and drown your horse!' We had to swim about three mobs like that. There's only two things I'm frightened of; that's lightning and water. But George Towns was a great boss. One time we crossed by the weir on the Ross and it was pouring rain and we had nowhere to camp. George got some logs and put them up and we used our swag-cover up over the edge of it and lay in it, like a boat.

We had an experience once on the Clark River. We were camped on Red Ridge one night and an aeroplane come over and circled our camp. I was on watch, in the early hours of the morning, maybe two o'clock. I watched it go round. And then later on I heard this voice calling, 'YoYo! Yo Yo!'

I raced back to the camp and said, 'Quick, George! There's something wrong!' And George said, 'It's the Japs! The bloody Japs have landed!' and he said, 'Go on, Girls! Go for your life! Hide down the creek!' Snow got out of her swag and away we went. We went down to where the horses were, not far. We were going to get the horses ready for the men to get away. And we waited there. But, George found out that they were Americans. They'd jumped out of their plane in parachutes. And he yelled out to us. 'Come on, Girls! It's alright!'

That plane went over the Clarke River and rammed into a gully on the north side and cut off trees a good ten to fifteen inches through, and tore itself to pieces. It folded the wings right back and the engine went up into the gully. The seven of them parachuted just before it hit. The navigator and the wireless operator landed one on either side of the cattle. But one of them, his parachute was caught up in a tree. And so one of them ran right through the bullocks to help his mate and the bullocks only jumped up. They ran a bit, that's all. They didn't rush; just sort've rattled a bit and stopped. And the Americans pulled this fellow out of the tree and brought him into camp.

All those men were all OK. None of them was killed. They were coming back from bombing up in New Guinea and they got lost and ran out of fuel. They were following up the Clarke River to where it runs into the Burdekin, and they came to Clarke River station. They were going to land in the creek because they could see the white sand but there were too many ti-trees. And then they saw our campfire, but then they cut out of petrol and they were just parachuting out and down she went. And they weren't sure if our fire might have been the Japs or the blacks. That's why they were calling out, 'Yo! Are you black or white?'

Anyway, George rode into Ewan that night and reported it. And he left us with the cattle. He said, 'Girls, youse look after the cattle.' And next morning a convoy of army trucks came out to rescue the Americans. And they were taking photos of us. They took those airmen to Townsville. We never found out even their names.

And another mob we were taking down, they rushed twenty nights out of twenty-four! They were cocky-cattle from Kidston and they'd never been mustered or tailed enough. The first night they took out the yard at the Five Mile at The Lynd. We had a devil of a job all the way with them. And after we came down Riley's Range and left Keelbottom those cattle were thirsty and we had no water for them. And George said when we got to Hughie Langdon's place, 'We've got to water them here.' There was no water in the creek, just a sort of little tank they had, sunk in the gully. So George put together two lengths of trough and then he brought down two four-gallon tins with handles in them. And he said, 'You'd better get in the tank and bail out it in turns.' We all had a go at it. We had to dip it out of the tank in the creek and carry it up the bank and tip it into the trough. We watered six hundred bullocks like that. Took us about three, maybe four, hours. We were working alright! But after they had that drink those cattle all settled down and they just walked out and wanted to feed. One thing about fats, they settle down to feed pretty quick.

It was a bit risky getting down Herveys Range. George told us, 'When you start, don't let the bullocks stop, see! Keep pushing them down.' You had to have your girth as tight as it would go so your saddle wouldn't slip over your horse's head. Them northern horses wouldn't stand a crupper. George didn't break his horses in to a crupper. I don't think he believed in them. And that track, you could go down, but you couldn't get back up again. And sometimes a bullock would hit a rock and it would go down with them and they'd be trying to get away from it. You had to push them down that range track, a couple of mile, it would be, and steep. If they broke and tried to come back up again you could've got broken legs or had them go over the side. We also experienced a lot of trouble getting the horses down that range. You had to put the loose pack horses in the front and keep them going. Not let them stop. But we met some nice people around there; the Fryers on Tabletop and the Moodys at the Eureka.

And when we get down to the flat near Dally Holden's, we were holding them there, about four or five miles out of Townsville, and it happened that I was on watch, about four o'clock in the morning, and a big plane took off loaded in bombs. Just where that big beacon-light on the hill is. It hit the hill, and the bombs and the whole lot went up. It was that bright it was like daylight and you could see bullocks and horses and horse tracks, and it lit up Townsville.

The bullocks rushed and we couldn't block 'em. It was so dark. We got most of them but seven got away. Then George said, when we got them together, 'Now listen, Girls. You'd better get back and track where them seven bullocks went. But hurry them up, Girls. Hurry them up!' So we went back and we found the bullocks and got round them and we're cantering along and we bring these bullocks into the mob and settle them down. And we cross the river and we're coming along nicely - I'm in the lead; George used to always put me in the lead because I was the little one - and we come to this army camp and there's some MPs - Military Policemen.

And this MP comes out, and I've got these bullocks behind me, and they're stirry and they won't stop and one of them wanted to rip my horse. George yells, 'Don't stop! Keep 'em going! It don't matter what they say!' But this MP had a gun and he shook it at me. He sings out, 'Halt!' I thought to m'self, 'How am I gunna halt when I got seven hundred bullocks behind me!' But he's got this gun and I thought, 'Gee whiz! I'm going to get shot!' So I'm singing out, 'Don't shoot! I can't stop! These bullocks are coming!' And he's shaking the gun at me. And next thing, this big bullock tore out of the mob and took after this bloke. I sing out, 'Look out!' And this MP he threw the gun to the devil and dived into his little sentry box.

He yelled at me, 'You'll stop next time!' So when we get to the next gully, there's another MP. And the first one must have told him that we wouldn't stop. So this fellow comes out and he yells, 'You'll stop this time!' But the bullocks are ready for this one because they're getting hotter! And this MP shakes his gun. And he yells, 'Halt!' I yell,

'I can't! I can't stop them!' He said, 'Halt! You'll halt when I tell you!' And anyhow, this bullock comes out at him. And this fellow throws his gun to the devil and he dives into his little sentry box, too! And didn't that bullock lay into that little sentry box! With the fellow inside it! Horns it over! Rolled it! And him inside! And I didn't care because he knew I couldn't stop, I'd kep' telling him. And I was frightened of my horse getting horned. But, anyhow, we got the bullocks to the meat-works and we delivered them. During the war the American camps was all through that country; airstrips all through that chinee-apple scrub.

Another time, just after we had swum the cattle over the Ross and got to where Lavarack Army Base is now, there was a big Flying Fortress swept in and landed.[2] They were going to pull the gun on him because he didn't circle like they were supposed to. He just smacked her down on the strip, and run along and didn't come to a halt. She run into the rubber vines at the end of the runway and stopped. And they rushed down and when they got down there they found every man on board that plane was dead. They'd all been shot and the pilot just landed the plane and then died himself. There were holes in the plane, and parts of it shot away. It was a terrible thing to see.

So I was five years droving, right up to the end of the war. And then I went rodeoing. One time, in Ingham, I got thrown, saddle and all, off a big bay horse, Napoleon. Straight into the ground! The fellow had done the girth up in the wrong hole. I used to get a bit too anxious rodeoing so I took up show-jumping. The highest jump I ever put a horse over was six foot six. That was in Cairns. Later I heard that under that showground there used to be a rubbish dump and that put a bit of spring into it. I never had any bad falls high jumping but I broke all m'ribs once, in the team jumps. There were six jumps in the circuit. First you did them single-file and then double and then ended up in fours. You had to do the complete circuit in fours, four horses jumping together. One time, Kevin Bacon was on his horse, High and Mighty, a big brown fellow, and he took off too far back and hit the hurdle head on. He come right over and it sort've knocked me out. I woke up in hospital a couple of days later. I had a headache for a week. I had a few falls but

2 Possibly present-day Duckworth Street which was an important wartime airstrip.

not many on my own horses; mostly on other people's. I didn't care as long as I was going round the ring.

I took a job on the Inlander, from Townsville to Mount Isa, waitressing in the dining-car, and one time, in Prairie, I seen this good looking fellow that had the mail-run, twice a week, down through Aberfoyle and Lammermoor and Uranda, and I thought to myself, 'I think I could get on with this fellow! He don't smoke and he don't drink. I could just fill his shoes!' And that was how Bob and me started getting together and got married. I used to run the mail and cart the wool with him. We've been best mates ever since.

We've always had horses. The best were Captain and Abdul. Beautiful horses, they were, both of them. Could jump anything. But we lost Abdul in his stall in Longreach. We thought he'd been got at with poison. We got the vet in and he did an autopsy but we couldn't prove anything. After that I always slept in my swag in the stall. I was top Lady Rider for two years in the 'fifties.

Bob and I had four properties out west. First we bought Poseidon, outside of Hughenden. It was named after a racehorse, Posei. A Chinaman had it before us. The story goes that this Chinaman wanted a property and he never had the money. And he was a punter. They had a sweep and this old man drew a horse named Poseidon and this Poseidon won the cup. And that's how the place got its name. We had it forty-five years.

One time on Poseidon my sister Della came out to give us a hand get round some scrubbers in some bad prickly scrub we had. Bob's idea was to throw in some syrup tins filled with sand with a plug of dynamite in. It didn't shift the scrubbers. They were wily old buggers, five or six years old. Cunning! Della said, 'Here! Give me that lot!' She stuck the rest of the dynamite under a big box tree with a long fuse. It went up like a bomb! There were bullocks clearing out of that scrub in every direction. They were wild! But we got round them and got a good price for them in at the sale yards.

As a young woman Ann competed successfully in ring events across North Queensland, winning many trophies. She was invited to train for the 1956 Olympic team. She is shown here with her sister Della.

We had a lot of wild pigs on Posie messing up the water-holes and dams and one time Della and me were out shooting pigs and she took off after this old man kangaroo she'd shot. She had him bailed up and she went to finish him off with a stick. But he grabbed her and ripped her real bad with his hind claws. Those big old-man fellas can be savage when they're cornered. She was bleeding bad. I just got her back to the Jeep when this fellow rode up and starts foul-mouthing us. I told him, 'Listen, Mister. I don't know who you are. And I don't care. But you'd better start clearing off or I tell you what, smoke's gunna start coming out of this gun.' He took off pretty quick.

Bob and I bought another place, Nindi, about ten mile from Poseidon. And then the dingoes got badder and badder, ripping the sheep open, and we were badly droughted-out so we bought Leslew, outside of Richmond, so we could move the sheep up there. And we were stuck with the cattle so we bought another place outside of Richmond, Emlyn. We ended up with about three thousand head of cattle, mostly Droughtmaster. I liked them. In the end we were mustering by helicopter. It used to cost a quid but, god! I liked that helicopter mustering! I liked the challenge!

The dingoes were thick on Nindi. One afternoon we were up Sawpit Creek where the sheep were. Bob was riding his good horse. He said, 'There's a dog!' I said, 'Get it!' And he stood up in his stirrups and shot it dead! First shot! It went head over tip! We used to always carry our rifles over our shoulder when we went out, except when you were galloping you had to bring them around in front on your hip a bit. There would always be dogs about. Some of them would be cross-breds. There was one big fellow; real big, and cunning, he'd have had Alsatian in him. He had the markings. You'd get his mate this time and next time he'd have another one. But we could never get him. As soon as he smelt that trap he would take off and go down another creek or another gully. You couldn't get him. And Bob said, 'If we don't get that dog, Mate, we can't do the Shows.'

We'd do the Show Jumping circuit; Hughenden, Longreach, Charters Towers, Cairns, Ingham, Innisfail, Atherton and back to Tully. We'd send the horses on the train in an IC wagon and we'd camp with them. It was coming up Show Time and I wanted to go so bad; my horses were really ready. And I thought to m'self, 'That dog's not going to beat me! I'm gunna get him! He'd not gunna stop me doing the Shows!'

I used to make m'own decoy for dingoes. It was a secret in them days but I don't care now! It was Tom Edmunds'. I used to do a lot of trapping with him. The bounty was about five pounds a scalp in them days when Tom and me was trapping. It was good money. When you shot a dog you took the liver and the gall-bladder out and put it in a syrup tin and when it blew the lid it was ready. The way I'd set a trap was; I used to put the jump-trap down, and I'd get a tiny little bit of cotton wool and put a tiny bit of that decoy on it; if you put it strong the dog won't go there. He's cunning. You put just a tiny little bit to make him find it. You put it under a little bit of dirt or a stone; just enough to make him hunt round for it. When you see a dog walk up to a tree, when your dog is that distance, where his feet'd be, that's where you put your trap. If you put your trap back a bit you'll get him.

And where Sawpit Creek came round in a bend there was a log with a fork, and a kangaroo pad. I thought to myself, 'I'm gunna tie this trap to that log.' I poisoned it with strychnine and opened the jaw and put a layer of rag around it, and put a wire round it, so that when he bites it he will get the strychnine quick. They always bite the leg that's caught. And this dog came cantering along the kangaroo pad and he put his foot, his front off-side leg, in the trap. And he took the strychnine and he was dead alright! But he'd he bit all the limbs off this dead gidgea log before he died. But I got him! And, God, he was a big dog! He cost us a lot of money, that dog! The sheep he had killed!

You hear people say, 'Oh! Save the dingo! You gotta protect the dingo!' But we used to go out in the morning to the sheep and you would see the poor buggers with their udders ripped out! The dingoes would tear out their udders and then leave them to die! They wouldn't eat them and then they'd come back in the evening and kill again to eat!

We had good waters on those four places. We put a flowing bore on Posiedon, and when we bought Nindi we got a flowing bore there. Then we bought Leslew and we put down a bore there and got another flow. There was a flow on Emlyn when we bought it.

And that old Flinders; you could bank of her for a while, but you couldn't depend on it in all seasons. You'd get a dry year and there would be nothing to see you through. You had to have the bores. But it cost us a lot of money to put those bores down.

Sawpit Creek had a flowing bore up in Burinda that came down onto our place and it used to bog all our stock. I had an old black horse I used for jumping and I used to go out and pull the cattle out of the bog with him. I'd hook the cow on to the horse's tail with a rope and make sure the cow would come when you pulled it, and tell the horse to git-up. And when he was pulling and the cow's starting to come out of the mud I'd be getting ready to sit on her head as soon as she was clear. If you didn't, she'd have got up and hooked into both of us, me and the horse too. They get so stirred they rip into the nearest thing, even though you've been trying to save them. You've got to fly on to your horse and get out of there quick.

During one drought I was pushing gidgea scrub for stock feed up on the rocky ridge. I'd drive up in the Jeep. And the cattle got used to the sound of the tractor and they used to come round as soon as I started the engine. You could see them bellowing and cantering up, they were that hungry. And this morning, I got there early, and I thought to m'self, 'I'll get a few trees down before they get here! I'll make a start on that good bushy tree. That'll hold them till I get a few more down.' So I backed off and I hit this bunchy gidgea with the blade and what I didn't notice was that there was a big dry tree growing up in the middle of it.

And when I hit it, the dry one come back over the top of the bushy one and it come down across the tractor and whacked me on the head. Lucky, when I fell forward I must have knocked the lever out of gear. And when I come to, after a bit, the engine's revving, and the cattle were all round feeding, everywhere but in the tractor with me! I thought, 'Where in hell am I ?' I never knew where I was for a while. And this dry tree is all over the top of me. The green one was down, but the dry one was back over the top of the tractor and me underneath it. I thought, 'Gee! How am I going to get this tree off the tractor?' And I thought, 'If I pull it and it rolls down it will bend all my levers and the oil pump.' But you ought to've seen the driver's seat! It was solid steel but it had one hell of a dint. But I got that tree off.

I hooked on it with the Jeep and pulled. After that I went and pushed some more scrub for the cattle. But I had a good look to see there were no more dry ones up in 'em. I had one hell of a headache, and runny eyes, for a good few weeks after!

And at Nindi, once, I was doing some fire-ploughing, towing a big heavy wagon wheel we brought from Poseidon, along the fire-break. I'd said to Bob, 'I'll do some fire-ploughing today.' Because he could do jobs that I couldn't do. I was pulling the wagon-wheel with the sixty-five tractor, hitched off the power-take-off on the drawbar at the back. And I'd bored a hole with the welder through the rim of the wagon-wheel; more than an inch thick that wheel was, and six inches across – and I had a chain through it and I'd pushed the chain through and had a shackle to hold it.

And I did one section and I thought, 'I'll turn around and go along a bit faster. I'm not crawling along in low gear like this all day.' So I was going along a little bit too quick, and the rim of the wheel hit this rock with a smack! And the chain broke off and come over like a whip and it struck me on the head. Smacked me a beauty! It knocked me right out to it. And when I come round and got m'knowledge back, there was all blood everywhere. And I thought, 'Christ! Where did I get this from!' There was blood running down my face. And I was ropeable, too. But I backed the tractor and I hooks on to this wagon-wheel and I made sure I got it away from that rock. And I went home steady, steady. When I got home Bob and another bloke was there. And he yelled out, 'Ann! What's wrong with you! What've you done to yourself!'?' And he had a look at me and he said, 'Christ! I'd better get you in to the hospital!'

It was about forty-four mile in to Hughenden. The doctor had a look at it and patched me up a bit and said, 'You'll be right!' He said it had split the bone, but good job it didn't get the brain part, eh! I've got a lump there on m' head to this day! And another one on the other side from the tree coming down!

But it was really good country and we could shift our stock around between the four places. We had Flinders and Mitchell grass. And a bit of timber. Each of those places had a set of yards. We put the yards on Poseidon and Nindi ourselves. But there was a set on Leslew and Emlyn when we bought them.

I never opened a gate while I was on Nindi. I used to jump all my horses over the fence; take 'em up and show it to 'em and then take 'em back and get 'em in stride, three paces off. If you're right you've got to bore him into it, and if you're wrong you've got to pull him back and get him into step. I never got a fall out of it; touch wood. It just come natural to me since I was a kid. All of us could jump. We knew that if the horse wasn't in the right step he couldn't jump the fence. We could do it bareback. Thought nothing of it.

And one time they had an Equestrian School at Hughenden. Bill and Ann Allingham was there. A bloke come up from Brisbane and he was putting us through this course; two days. And he put a mark on the ground in front of the jump and he would say, 'Now, look! I want you to have those horses' feet right on that line before you jump. If you're over it you've got no connection with your horse. You must have his front feet on that line.' I thought to myself, 'I've never done this in my life.' But I knew where a horse should be to jump. And where that instructor put that line was just the place where the horse had to be! And he said to after, 'Ann! Do you want to train for the Olympic Games?' But I said 'No'. I would have had to leave Bob and it was just when we had all them dingoes in the sheep, and I just couldn't leave him. So I pulled out of it. But that Kevin Bacon and John Pheyse; they went on and they did alright! They were good blokes!

I rode in the shows for many years and then, after I gave it away I went judging for ten years. They used to fly me out to Mount Isa to do the judging out there. I'd be mainly looking for conformation. If you're judging hacks you're looking for the horse that's got good points; a good head and a good neck and a nice rolly rump; good back; good shoulders, and a good eye. If a horse has got a pig-eye, well, you can't place him in front of a horse with a good eye, even though he does the work. I did a fair bit of judging with old Ted Cunningham from Strathmore. He was a terrific old judge.

Bob and I were on Poseidon forty-five years. We built the homestead ourselves; a two-storey place; upstairs and downstairs. No-one would believe that we built it, but Bob had the skill and I off-sided for him. But in all the years of my life I never knew what town-power I was until I was in m'sixties. Never knew the comfort of 240 volt power. We always used to have the 32volt!

Bob Forster

Bob Forster at his retirement property Kapunda, west of Charters Towers.

Introduction

Bob Forster has one of the best smiles! It radiates warmth and humour, as does this, his life-story, recorded at his retirement property, Kapunda, a half an hour's drive west of Charters Towers, where, in keeping with his life-long passion for racing, Bob breeds 'a few thoroughbreds'.

I first met Bob at Outback 2002, in Charters Towers, when he was one of the staunch supporters of that memorable occasion, the finale of the Year of the Outback. We delivered Ray Fryer's horses to Bob's place for paddocking and were made warmly welcome. Bob is one of those men who make your day seem better for having shaken hands with him and, if you are a lady, being given a welcoming hug.

Bob's story of five generations of life on his family's property, Gracedale, forty miles north of Richmond, has all the elements of saga. His grandfather, Thomas Forster, overlanded 'a mob of thoroughbreds' north until, 'beyond the Flinders' he came across the land of his heart's desire. He built a hut, fenced paddocks and, two years later, returned for the girl, Grace Pegler, who had promised to wait for him, and after whom, in the tradition of the day, he named the property Gracedale.

The Gracedale story is almost the 'happy ever after' version of Mary Hannay Foote's 'Where the Pelican Builds'. But Gracedale's pastures were, in fact, 'wide and fair, to be found past the sunset's glow', without the melancholy of the poem's lost love and lost hope. Many a reader will smile that newly-wed Grace insisted on taking her piano on the wagon-journey north. Many a male reader will snort,'Women!' But this strength of purpose not only enabled twenty-year-old Grace to live six months entirely on her own in the station hut when her husband went south to buy his flock, but sixty years later, to bring her flying out of bed in her nightgown, an octogenarian with a garden hose, to fight the homestead fire. What a spirit!

Of particular interest to the social history of North Queensland are Bob's recollections of the period during World War Two when All Souls School, Charters Towers, was commandeered by the army for a hospital and the boys were moved to Dalrymple Crossing on the Burdekin to continue their education 'under canvas'. That they took the rough and ready conditions in their stride and, when the time came, passed their examinations 'with flying colours' is a tribute not only to the hardihood of the boys themselves but to an entire generation of North Queenslanders who knew how to 'do it tough' when times were hard without complaining.

Chapter 2...

FIVE GENERATIONS ON GRACEDALE

Bob Forster - Pastoralist

I have had a few close shaves in my life but the closest one I ever had was when I was a young fellow on Gracedale. There was a two-thousand gallon tank on one of the mills and where the pipe came from the bottom of the tank there was an elbow, and it was leaking. We wanted to fix it and it didn't have a turn-cock to turn the water off. There hadn't been any wind for ages but just the night before there had been enough to fill the tank. If we didn't fix the leak we were going to lose that tank of water. So I thought, 'OK. I'll get up and I'll dive in with an old pair of trousers and I'll stuff them in the down-pipe and that'll stop the water and then we can undo the fitting and replace the elbow'.

The tank was full right to the very top. I got in through the manhole, took a decent breath and dived. I felt round at the bottom for the opening of the pipe and stuffed the trousers in. I was just about out of breath by the time I'd made a good job of it so I headed for the surface. But what I didn't remember was that the manhole was not right at the edge. It was in about six inches away from the edge. And I was running my hand around the edge at the top trying to find the manhole. But I couldn't find it because I was feeling right against the wall of the tank. By this time my lungs were nearly bursting and I looked up. I reckoned I could see the sun; see daylight. But because it was bore water it was a bit murky and I couldn't be sure. And because the tank was full to the top there was no space to breathe under the covering.

But there was another fellow sitting on top of the tank and he's thinking to himself, 'Christ! He's been down there a long time!' And he put his arm down through the manhole, and felt the top of my head. He grabbed me by the hair and he pulled my head out. By God! I took some deep breaths, I can tell you! So I might have just been born a bit lucky.

Our family has been on Gracedale for five generations. Old Tom Forster, my grandfather, started off on the Murray River and he was given a contract to take a stallion to Marlowe station, a very big property near Adavale. So he set off with this big stallion and thirty-six thoroughbreds of his own and a string of pack-horses. He went up the Murray and then on to the Darling. From there he went across to the Bulloo and across to Marlowe station, which was being managed by A.H.

Pegler, who had thirteen or fourteen kids. They gave him a job as an overseer on the outstation so he stayed there to help put the shearing through. He finished up putting in five years there and during that time they shore six-hundred and seventy thousand sheep in one shearing. During the 1900s strike they had a straggler shearing of fifty thousand. All with blades.

And then he put in for a block on Cambridge Downs up near Richmond. He left Marlowe with a mob of thoroughbred horses – he would never ride anything but a thoroughbred - and a dray and a few pack-horses and he followed up the Diamantina and he struck across and hit the Flinders where Hughenden is now. Then he followed the Flinders down, past where Richmond is now, and he saw all this open downs country north of the river, and he went out and set up his camp on Flagstone Creek, which is about twenty miles north of Maxwelton.

The first paddock he built was a horse paddock. There were ten thousand acres of gidgea scrubs on the block and he used to go there with his dray and cut gidyea posts for fence-posts.

He didn't have a wife at this stage, but when he was working at Marlowe, he had fallen in love with one of old A.H. Pegler's daughters, Grace. And she had told him that she would wait for him until he got established. So after two years, when he had built a bit of a hut and some more paddocks, and had got a bloke to work for him, he set off for Marlowe again with his pack-horses, and she was still there, waiting for him, and he married her. They had a big wedding in Adavale and then their honeymoon was getting back from Adavale. And she wanted her piano so he had to buy another bloody dray and he put this piano on it and took it all the way up there for her. It took them weeks. I'm damned if I know how they got the piano off the dray! And he called the place Gracedale after her.

After a few years, he left her there, while he and the fellow working for him went to Isis Downs where he bought five thousand ewes and one hundred and fifty rams. And all the time he was away, for the best part of six months, she was there on her own. She would have only been in her early twenties. He left her a lot of salt beef and a couple of big dogs. She told me in later years that she knew when the men were returning because the dogs started to bark. They could smell the sheep before she could even see them. She was a good horsewoman so she rode out to meet them. And that was the start of his flock. And even when I left school he was still shearing twenty-four thousand.

Grand-dad and Grandma had four sons and a daughter, all born in Richmond, about forty-two miles away. One of them was born during the Wet, and they had to make a sledge and hitch a couple of draught-horses to pull it through the sludge and the mud four miles down to 'the frontage'. The frontage was where the forest starts, and once they got on to that sandy, forest country they were out of the black soil it was good going. So they followed the sand-hills right round to Cambridge Creek, and from there she went in a buggy from Cambridge Downs into Richmond.

Then Grandad started to build a homestead, and gradually built on more and more. As more kids came there would be another room added on. Then he got some carpenters from somewhere, real craftsmen. The old homestead at Gracedale was beautifully built. It had a verandah all the way round and a great big billiard-room in the middle and bedrooms all over the place and a huge dining-room. In those days they didn't build the kitchen on to the house in case of fire. It was built separately and connected to the main house by a long landing with a curved roof over it and the kitchen-girls used to rush the food across to the dining-room from there.

Neil and Bob Forster and Allan Crowther drafting sheep on Gracedale about 1950.

Gracedale has always bred thoroughbred horses. Old Tom, my grandfather, wouldn't ride anything else, and any thoroughbred that couldn't be ridden and worked was used in the buggy. He had two big black thoroughbreds called Satan and Sin in his buggy. And when they got their first car, an old T Model Ford, whenever Old Tom was driving it and wanted to stop, he would say, 'Whoa!' When he came to one of the wooden gates they had in those days, he would 'Whoa back!' and go through the gate and smash it. And the boys got sick of having to fix up the gates so they nominated my Dad, Murray, as Grand-dad's driver. Every time he wanted to go somewhere Murray had to drive him.

One day they had to go to Wongali, a property outside Hughenden, to inspect three thousand wethers. It took them all day to get there, and they got there late in the evening.

Now if old Lex Thompson that owned Wongali and old Tom Forster were standing side by side, you wouldn't know which was which. They were exactly the same build. Very similar in appearance.

And in the morning, Old Tom always had a shower. And the bathroom was off the landing from the kitchen to the house, halfway along. So Old Tom is having his shower and he's left the door slightly ajar and he's just finished and got his leg up on the stool drying himself, and Mrs Thompson and the maid come along the landing carrying the breakfast things – the maid's got the tray and Mrs. Thompson's got the teapot. And she looks through the door and she sees this leg up on the stool and this purse dangling down between the legs and she grabbed it between her thumb and finger, and she gives it a bit of a squeeze and she says 'Breakfast's ready! Ting-a-ling!'

And she goes on along to the dining-room in the big house and puts the teapot down and there's old Lex, her husband, sitting at the table. And of course, she realized! And she went as red as a beetroot. And about ten minutes later Old Tom comes in, very sprightly- looking and pleased with life! But, of course; nothing was said! And driving home Old Tom says to my Dad, 'Now, Son! Don't you tell Jenny!

(Jenny was my mother) If you tell her it will get over the whole district.' Well, of course, he did tell Jenny and, of course, it did!

But, anyhow, they bought the wethers. And the boys had to take a plant and ride over and walk them all home. It took them about ten days.

I was born at The Rocks, a private hospital on Melton Hill, in Townsville, in 1928. My father was Murray Forster, the eldest son of Tom Forster. My mother was Jane Crowther. Her father was Commissioner for Railways in Townsville.

When I first started school we did Correspondence. Mum used to teach me and my older brother, John. And then, when my sister Janice came on stream, they decided it was time to get a governess. She was Nancy Garbutt of the Garbutt family in Townsville[1]. She was there for years, a very good, very strict teacher. One day I said, 'I gotta go to the toilet.' She said, 'You don't say, I gotta go to the toilet.' You say 'I have to go to the toilet.' 'He has to go to the toilet.' 'We have to go to the toilet.' I said, 'Cripes! Are you sure there's gunna be enough paper for us all?'

Not long after this I was sent to All Souls School in Charters Towers. I was ten, and I was there five years. I was at Souls when the school was commandeered by the army for a hospital and we shifted out to Dalrymple Crossing. There were rows of big marquees that a lot of the boys lived in, but anybody who had their own tent could use it. My brother John and I had a tent that we brought from Gracedale. We pitched it on the river side of the camp underneath a big ironbark tree. One night there was a huge electrical storm and it hit the tree and limbs came down everywhere. Missed our tent but flattened the tent next door that belonged to a fellow named Sandy Brodie from over near Winton. Luckily they didn't get hurt.

At this time the northern stations in the Gulf were doing the scorched earth policy and shifting all the cattle down so that the Japs wouldn't have tucker when they landed. So these mobs of cattle were coming between the school camp and the river; continuous mobs of cattle moving past. And the drovers would leave behind any sick horses, or horses that had split a hoof, and we used to nurse them back to health and ride them. By the time the end of the year came we had about thirty horses!

There were no objections from the teachers. We gave old 'Johnno' Johnson, the Latin teacher, a very quiet sort of a bloke, one of the horses and he would ride it everywhere. He used a corn-bag as a saddle-cloth, and he had an old saddle he'd got from somewhere, with half the counter-lining hanging out the back. Us boys only had the one saddle between us. We used to ride bareback.

We'd chase wild pigs and run them down along the river. We were all pretty fit. If you see photos of the school at that time we were none of us carrying any spare weight. We'd get these pigs about porker-size. We built a pig-sty and we put all the pigs in and we fed them all the scraps from the dining-room and fattened them up and killed them for the kitchen. We had to do the butchering ourselves because none of the masters knew how to. But we were all bush boys. We'd clean them, cut them up and take the meat up to the old cook, Stan. He'd been a gardener when we were at the proper school, but this was war-time and men were being called

1 Pioneer pastoralists after whom Garbutt Air Force Base in Townsville is named.

up. But he was a shocking cook! There was another one, Old Jack. Whenever you saw Old Jack there would be a big swarm of flies around him! We got lots of stews. We used to call them 'Deep-sea Stews' because you got a lot of water in them and not much meat. And for puddings it was nearly always 'Burdekin Mud'– chocolate blancmange with custard. All on tinned Sunshine milk.

We used to use the tins to set traps on the end of a line to catch black-bream and perch in the river. The tins were the marker-floats. The traps were made out of old wire-netting lying about, because Dalrymple had been an old station. The building we used for a dining-room was a big old machinery shed of galvanized iron and bush timber.

There was a lot of old material lying about the place that we made use of. Four of the boys built their own hut out of logs; Freddie Tritton and Stuckley Davidson and a couple of others. There was a storm one night and the whole thing fell in. We used to get big wild storms and the run-off would flood through the camp. We didn't have duchesses, or anything like that. Your things were in your port under your bed. And in a storm you threw your port on your bed to keep your clothes dry.[2]

There were no showers or bathrooms. When the bell went in the morning, the first thing you did was jump out, strip off, strip your bed, grab your towel and head for the river. And you were supposed to put your towel around you and run. But you can't run with a towel wrapped around you so you carried your towel and away you went for a swim. There were four or five ladies on the kitchen staff and they would always be out on one side of the kitchen watching this peep-show as the boys ran for the river. Then when you came back you got dressed for breakfast.

I don't remember that anybody actually supervised this early morning swim to make sure that if seventy-eight boys went into the river seventy eight came back out again. I know I nearly stayed there one day when there was a bit of fresh in the river. It was alright during the normal time of the year when the river wasn't running swiftly. But when the river was in flood – well, there was a rock about fifty metres out; and we used to swim out to that rock. And this time there was only a little bit of the rock sticking out of the water and a fair current, so I missed it. I swam like hell to try and get back and I was just about all in by the time I did. No-one was aware of it. That was another one of my close shaves.

The year that the school was out at the river I was in Scholarship class and our classroom was one of these big marquees. When we sat for our exams in the December, officials came out from the Education Department and supervised us. They also supervised the Junior and Senior exams. In spite of the tough sort of life the school got some of the best passes in exams that year that it ever got. I passed my Scholarship, flying colours.

And then, at Christmas time, the whole school got washed away in the big flood so we shifted into the race-course at Charters Towers; three boys to a horse-stall; two along the sides and one at the back. All the ports under the bed again.

2 'Port' is traditional Queensland usage for 'suit-case', presumably derived from 'portmanteau'. Other terminologies specific to Queensland include; 'duchess' for 'dressing table'; 'double' for what in southern states is called 'dinky'; as in 'Giv's a double on yer bike,' and 'ging' for 'shanghai.'

They built a dining-room that is still there today. But it wasn't as much fun at the race-course as out at the river. Next door was a big American air-force base called Breddan Base. During the Battle of the Coral Sea there'd be planes coming and going over day and night, with big holes shot in them; some of them on two engines. They used to come right across those stables where the school was so you didn't get much sleep. In between the race-course and the air-base were all these rubber-vines.

We were always hungry. A couple of mates and I had tunnels through the rubber vines that we used to sneak out through. We'd head for the American canteen and get frankfurters and tomato sauce, which we thought was God's food, after the stuff we'd been eating. And this day we were crawling through this tunnel we'd made and we ran smack into a huge American negro military policeman, with a bayonet on a rifle. He said, 'What are you guys doing here?' We said, 'We just wanted to see the aeroplanes. We thought we might join the air-force!'

He marched us up to the Commanding Officer. And here's this Squadron Leader sitting there, with all his pips on, and all these flight lieutenants and pilots coming in and getting their orders and saluting him and going out again. And he's just writing away and writing away. He didn't even look at us and we're standing over in the corner with this big negro with this rifle and bayonet guarding us. And eventually there was a bit of a break in proceedings and this Squadron Leader looks up at this big negro fellow, and he says, 'Yes! What is it?' And this fellow says, 'Sir! I caught these intruders on the perimeter.' And the Squadron Leader starts writing again, and he says, 'Shoot 'em!'.

And my mate Freddie says, 'You can't shoot us! We just wanted to see the planes! We thought we might like to join the air-force.' And the Officer says, 'So! You think you want to join the air-force? Righto! Come outside and hop in my jeep.' So we get into his jeep and away he takes us down the airstrip. And there was this big bomber. It had just landed ten minutes before, just back from a raid. And here they are, hosing the rear gunner out of his turret on to a sheet. Oh my God! And this Commanding Officer looks at us and he says, 'You still want to join the air-force!' And we tell him, 'We think we might join the army.'

Anyhow, he took back in us in his jeep to the school and pulled up in front. Old Bidge Mills, the head-master, was there. And Bidge comes out, and this Squadron Leader says to him, 'Do you own these?' And he pointed at us three. And Freddie whispers to me, 'I hope to Christ he says "Yes".

Anyway, Old Bidge claimed us. We got six of the best with the lawyer cane for breaking bounds. But as we got out of the jeep the old Commanding Officer gave us a whole tin each of frankfurts and tomato sauce, and at least Bidge let us keep them.

And then the Japs were right at the door and were expected to land at any time and the north was declared a war zone. So they were training all us young fellows in the Cadets to defend the country. We used to go out on to the Burdekin River and do manoeuvres; and to Selheim where all the soldiers were camped. They gave us three-ought-threes and we'd do manoeuvres in the dark-time with dummy bullets, shooting all over the flat. We handled Lewis guns and Bren-guns and towards the end of the war we trained on bofors for shooting down planes. When we were doing these night manoeuvres the fellows from the Observer Unit would plant gun-cotton in the sand and every now and then there would be a huge explosion and it would be this gun-cotton going off. It would frighten the hell out of us. It made it pretty real.

And one time they made us dig a latrine trench because there were fifty AWAAS – Australian Women's Army Auxiliary girls - arriving on a train. There were little latrine huts to put over the trench, one beside the other. And one of the fellows that had us digging this trench was in Signals and he put a loud-speaker down in the trench with a wire running back though the grass into the trees with a microphone on it. And when all these ladies came off the train, they were busting, and they headed straight to these latrine huts. And when they all got squared away, this bloke gets his microphone and says in a booming voice, 'Hey! Steady on, girls! There's still blokes down here working!' And these latrine doors flew open and out shot all these girls like horses coming out of a barrier!

Then one day at school Old Bidge sent for my brother John and me and called us into his office. He was looking pretty serious. He told us he had bad news for us. Our Uncle Les had been killed. He had been taking a load of chaff into Richmond for a bloke that had some horses in town, and a spark from the gas-producer got into the chaff. Everything in those days was rationed because of the war; tea, sugar, butter, clothes; everything. And because petrol was rationed, to get the station work done they bought an old utility run on gas made out of carbide in a gas-producer on the back behind the cabin. A spark from the gas-producer had got into the chaff and caught fire.

Les didn't realize at first because while the vehicle was moving all the flames were streaming out behind. But he smelled something burning and when he pulled up, the flames came right over and engulfed the entire cabin. He got out and only burned his hand on the door. But he had his mother-in-law and his sister-in-law with him and he tried to get them out. And when he was trying to get his mother-in-law out, his sister-in-law on the other side panicked and was trying to pull her the other way. So he raced around and pulled his sister-in-law out and then he got the mother-in-law out. But by the time he had done this he had lost all the flesh on both his arms. And he carried those two women about a hundred and fifty yards and got them under a tree and then he walked eight miles to Richmond. The first house he came to, old Ernie Fontaine's, they couldn't recognize him and they had known him all his life. But they got him up to the hospital. The ambulance went back out and got the women. They both died that night. But Les hung on until they got his wife in to see him and then he died the next night. The three of them are buried in Richmond cemetery.

When old Bidge was telling us about this, well, my God! We were shocked. Les was such an active man, full of life and energy. He was only thirty-two. And then my father died when he only forty-six, just at the end of the war. The doctor seemed to think it was from over-work.

After I left All Souls I went to Gatton College and started a course in Vet Science. You also had to do a trade so I did leather-work. Then because man-power was getting a bit short at home my brother John and I went back to Gracedale to start running the place. We were only young fellows. We weren't twenty.

As well as the main homestead on Gracedale there was a brick home that my father had built when he got married, about three hundred yards away on a high knoll on the bank of Flagstone Creek. That's where I grew up. Between the two houses there were sheds and stables and ringers quarters. And when I got married I took my wife to the house that my father had built because my mother had moved to Sydney. My uncle Neil and his wife lived in the old homestead with my grandmother, Grace.

I met my wife when I had bought a mob of cattle in from Segal's Creek in the Northern Territory for Fred Clifford. We trucked them at Kajabbi and came down with the plant to Maxwelton. I'd been on the road for months and I had a big black bushy beard. And this young woman and her mother got off the train. And I said to one of the blokes, 'Who's that beautiful young woman?' And he said, 'That's Ann Kennedy from Merriula, south of here.' She'd been away nursing and she'd come home and her mother had come in to pick her up off the train. I knew her mother, Mrs. Kennedy, so I went over and said Good Day to her. She introduced me to her daughter. And in later years Ann always said that she thought, 'Gee! What a scruffy looking fellow!' But I shaved my beard off and she and I met at different functions and parties, and at the Townsville Amateurs, I asked her to marry me. We were married in St. James Cathedral, Townsville.

And one night, not long after I was married, Ann shook me and said, 'There's something going on over at the old house. I heard a big bang. Or it's in the stables or the ringers' quarters.' I said, 'It's probably one of the horses knocked his feed tin down and rattling it around looking for more feed.' But I thought 'Oh, Well. I'd better have a look.' And I opened the door and here is a huge glow. It looked like the old homestead was on fire. So away I went, flat-out!

Killing day on Gracedale, about 1950. Bob cutting-down the carcass while Neil Forster steadies it.

The ringers had gone for Christmas, and my uncle and his wife had gone south for the Christmas holidays, so my grandmother, Grace, was on her own in the big house with only two old house-girls in the quarters next to the kitchen.

But it wasn't the main homestead on fire. It was the big garage and workshop building. When I got over there I went racing around the side of the house to get Grandma out.

I said, 'Nannie! Get out! Get out! Quick! Grab what you can and get out quick while you can!' She said, 'Get away with you!' But anyway, she got out, and in her nightgown, the first thing she did was grab the garden hose. For Christ's sake! The flames are roaring twenty feet high! All the store-rooms, the work-shop, the garages; they were all on fire. And she's got this old garden hose and she's trying to squirt it on to the flames.

The first thing I did was to roll all the forty-four gallon drums of fuel out of the way. They were all lined up outside the garage. And the things you do on your own when you have to! It's amazing! I loaded the fire-fighting plant on to the back of a truck. I wouldn't be able to do it on my own any other time. But I got it on. Got the tank on filled with water. And I thought, 'Well, there's nothing much I can do except stop the fire spreading to the main house, and the main kitchen and the men's dining-room.' So every time sparks flew over I'd put them out. The other buildings were too far gone to save.

The mailman had come the day before and put all the stores in the storeroom. There was a big old weighing scale, and right in the middle of it he'd put a big demijohn of rum. The sealing wax melted and the cork flew out and all these pretty green and blue flames were shooting up. And where the cold-room was there was a big cylinder of gas and it went up like a rocket; straight up into the air and landed over in the horse yards!

One of the sheds had a fifty years' collection of tools and equipment. And in the store, well, it was not only the grocery store, but the most remarkable collection of memorabilia; old side-saddles, muzzle-loaders, gear for making bullets, all the gear and equipment that Old Tom, my grandfather, had when he started off. We lost the lot. And it was all started by mice! Mice chewing the wax matches in the store. Flick! And away it goes! Wax matches! That's why they banned them. They were too much of a fire hazard.

Grace's two old black house-girls cleared off up the bore-drain. It frightened the life out of them. We never saw them again for two days. But they sneaked back again after a while when they got hungry. Grace would have been about eighty-odd at the time. She lived till she was ninety-five.

Gracedale is undulating downs country. It had a big creek, Flagstone Creek, flowing through the middle of it to the western boundary and into the adjoining country. There was a bore which used to run into it all year round. It would chuck out a million gallons a day. When we were kids we used to swim in it, catch yabbies in it, catch pigs in it and in the water-holes we'd catch sleepy-cod and perch and black-bream. It was muddy-bottomed

The wool leaving Gracedale, about 1950.

but with flagstone in a lot of places. In some places the flagstone was just like paving. You could walk right across the creek. We used to use those places for crossing cattle. Anywhere else and they would bog.

About 1951 a lot of us young fellows in the Maxwelton area got together and decided we would start a race club. We didn't have much money and we had to build everything right from scratch. It was all voluntary labour and all the materials were donated by the stations round about. And when we were building the jockeys' room somebody suggested we should all put in five quid each and build them a urinal. Five quid was a lot of money in those days. And the bloke sitting next door to me– he'd spent all his life in the bush - leaned over and he says to me, 'What's a urinal?' So I told him what a urinal was. And he thought it was a great idea. And he said, 'I reckon we ought to chuck in a tenner each and build them an arsenal as well.'

And then somebody reckoned that was too much money and suggested we just sink a six inch bore-casing down into the sand and get an oxy-torch and cut a hole in it for them to use and let it all drain away. And we all agreed, Yeah. That was a good idea. And so we did this. And the oxy-welding fellow we got to cut the hole was a big tall fellow. And he cuts the hole and then he sings out to us little blokes that are the jockeys, 'Here you little short-arse lot. Come over here and have a try at this!' But he was about six foot four and he had cut the hole to his own convenience. It was up to our chests! So this urinal was never used and if the jockeys wanted to go to the loo they had to get one of the stewards to accompany them down to the public Men's.

As well as Gracedale we also had another property twenty-two mile away, called Trivalore. Then twenty-four mile on was Euthella, another place we had. Sandy, the youngest of old Tom Forster's sons, was there, and Neal was managing a place over near Corfield called Buna. He came home too, so Sandy and Neal and John and I were running the whole box of dice until John and I eventually bought Neal and Sandy out and they retired. And then when John and I split the blanket our sons grew up and we thought we'd better do something about it. So he took Trivalore and Euthella which are about the same area as Gracedale, and I took Gracedale. John is still on Trivalore, and his son, Geoff, is on Euthella. And my son David is on Gracedale and his son Miles is the fifth generation. In all things I have always tried to be fair and square with every man I've ever dealt with. I believe you should be able to look any man straight in the eye.

When we first decided to change over to cattle we had Santa Gertrudas. But after a while we noticed that we weren't getting good calvings with them and we changed to Droughtmasters, and it is still a Droughtmaster herd. We also introduced a bit of Limousine into them. That puts a bit of weight into them. We get our bulls from several different studs, but mainly Kerry Pastoral Company down near Emerald. I used to do the buying but now my son David has taken over. The first thing to look for is a nice, quiet docile animal; and then length. It is the cattle with plenty of length that weigh. You have got to get plenty of weight into your cattle because that's how you sell them, by the kilo. And plenty of depth in the brisket and a good even back line. A full-developed hind-quarter and well let down; the muscles coming well down the hind leg. And a good tidy underneath; not a big sheath that collects grass seeds. And a real masculine head. We go for the reds mainly because the herd started from a shorthorn base. Droughtmasters handle the heat well.

Droughtmasters were developed by old Monty Aitkensen of Mongala near Ingham and Valley of Lagoons. He imported what they used to call zebus in those days from America and he crossed them with shorthorns and then crossed them back again and kept going until he finally got a type and he bred to that type. We pay about four to five thousand for our herd bulls and keep them about five to six years. You don't want them back over their own heifers. So then you put them in the sale yard and some breeder might buy them. And if they don't then the meat-works buys them and they are made into hamburgers. The bull-carcass will absorb its own weight in meal and that's what they use for hamburger patties. That's why they like to buy bulls. We've had this Droughtmaster programme in place since the late 1970s or early '80s.

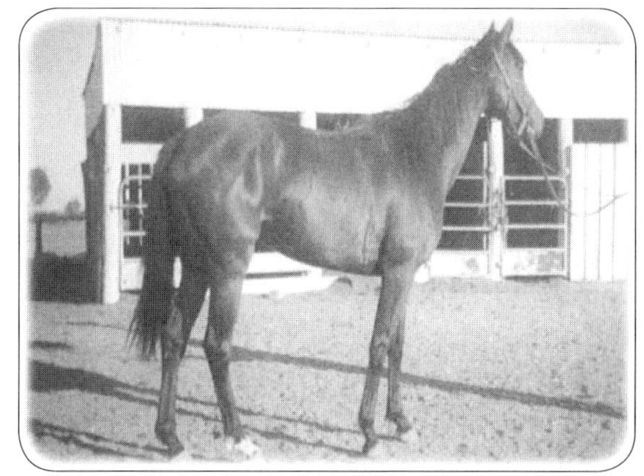

The Forster family were noted across the North for their love of racing. This is 'Gliding Star', Bob's wife Ann's favourite.

I bred a few limousines here at Kapunda and sent them out to Gracedale but limousines can't seem to handle the heat, so I gave it away. Limousines can be extremely stirry cattle. Part of the breed can be extremely temperamental. I had one bull and his stock were beautiful. But the next bull's stock were shocking. They'd put you up the rails all the time!

Old Tom was a very good horseman and all his sons were the same. They used to race horses and the set of colours I use today, pink with silver stars and a pink cap, were registered at the turn of last century in 1902. I've got three sets, one each in Townsville, Charters Towers and at Richmond. Each trainer's got a set. They are the same colours that were registered in 1902 under the name of Thomas Forster. It's harder these days because you can't use colours that anybody else has registered. No-one else in Australia could register pink with silver stars and a pink cap. You pay a renewal fee every year to re-register your colours.

So Old Tom bred thoroughbreds; he sent mares to thoroughbred stallions. A lot of the big company properties like Australian Estates had very good thoroughbred stallions, and he would send his mares to them. All our stock horses were thoroughbreds. And any that were exceptional he would put into training. We had our own race-course and a line of stables. Before any race meeting in Richmond we would have trials which other stations brought their horses to. The men would camp in the wool-shed and the married couples at the homestead.[3] Tom's sons

3 Kent, Nancy; 'The Forsters were the great racing people of the district. At race-time shoals of men would put up in the Gracedale wool-shed, while forty or more married couples and girls stayed at the homestead.'

started off doing the training and then they had an old fellow called Tommy Yuel, a real down to earth Australian trainer. He taught the Old Tom's sons how to train, and they in turn taught me. I started riding in races when I was seventeen and I won my first ride in Richmond on a mare called Tracey. And then I had a trainer's licence and a jockey's licence. I raced at Julia Creek, Mount Isa, Cloncurry, Richmond, Hughenden, Charters Towers and Townsville, and at odd times down to Winton and Corfield. They were old dirt roads in those times, a bit rough.

When we used to first take horses in we didn't have horse-floats or trucks. We'd ride one and lead two, all the way to Richmond. There'd be me and one of the ringers. We'd leave early in the morning about four o'clock and we'd get to Richmond about sundown. Usually the meetings were for two days; some races corn-fed some grass-fed.

There'd be a dance at night, a big dress-up job; penguin suits, the whole lot. The worst part about it was having to ride home on Sunday if you hadn't won a race.

One time, we got to Cambridge Creek and the water was churning down. I thought to myself, 'Gee! This doesn't look too good.' I went in myself and depthed it. By that time we had a big five-horse float, pulled by a Toyota. I thought to myself, 'Suppose I take the horses out of the float; unload them and lead them across?' So I dropped the tail gate and unloaded the horses and we waded them across. I had three and Ann had two. The horses thought it was great! They were pawing, and splashing and carrying on. Then I went back for the Toyota and the float. When I got to the middle I could just feel the float starting to lift. But we got over! And we won a couple of races that time.

Cambridge Creek is a hundred yards or so wide. It is really the Stawell River which flows into the Flinders. It comes from up in the ranges around that basalt country, where the old gold mines used to be, north of Richmond, a run-off area they call the Woolgar. A lot of hilly, rocky country. When it rains up there it can roar down overnight.

My grandfather told me that years ago there used to be a big blacks' camp at Cambridge station. They'd camp in the shade of the big tea-trees against one bank of the river bed where there was nice soft sand. The station homestead was on the Richmond side. And one night there must have been a cloud-burst up in the Woolgar and the water came down and swept the entire blacks' camp away and only about four or five of them survived. That would have to have been sometime in the 1890s because Grandfather got there in 1898. There is nothing left of Cambridge homestead today except a fortress built of flagstone that they built to protect themselves from the wild Aboriginals that would raid the homestead now and then.

My wife Anne chose a lot of the names of the horses I raced out west. She was very keen on racing. She loved horses. She would always come with me to race meetings. She'd bring the swags and all the clobber that you had to wear to the ball at night. I built a crate on the back of a truck and we used to carry three horses abreast. One time they were playing-up like mad and I said, 'I'll get in the back with them. It's the only way to settle them down. You'll have to drive.' She was terrified but she did it anyhow. There was nobody got more excited than Anne when our horses were winning. And she would come in when the horses were being decorated in the saddling paddock and stand beside them and receive the trophy. One of our most successful horses was Advantage Receiver. He shared the honours with two others for Richmond Horse of the Year in 1990. I was active in the racing industry and president of the Richmond Amateur Race Club for a good many years.

Anne and I had three children. We lost a little daughter, Linda, in 1958. She was born with a hole in the heart. The doctor gave us a bit of hope that he might be able to save her, but she died when she was six months old. My son David was our first-born, and after we lost Linda we had Kate. When Kate was married I led her on my arm down the aisle in St. James Cathedral in Townsville where Anne and I had been married all those years before. I lost Anne from Alzeimer's in 2002. My word! That was hard, because she and I always went everywhere together. We meant everything to each other.

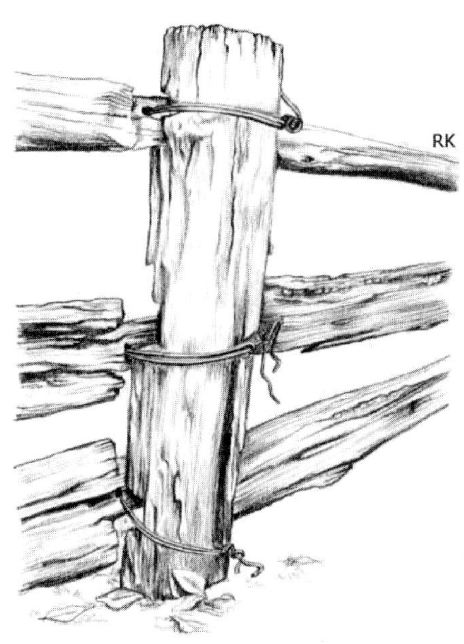

Bluey Ellis

Bluey Ellis feeding the horses at Tabletop station.

INTRODUCTION

Given a homestead verandah filled with visitors laughing and talking, Bluey Ellis will always be the quiet one in the squatter's chair, not missing anything but not offering much of a contribution to proceedings until someone calls out, 'Well, what do you reckon, Bluey?' Only then will Bluey deliver a well-considered opinion quietly and with conviction. He will have thought deeply about the matter under discussion, is never judgmental, always fair-minded, and as a result, his opinion is listened to with genuine admiration and respect. Bluey could be deemed something of a bush philosopher, the very type of Mrs Aeneas Gunn's Quiet Stockman.

However, my personal admiration for Bluey stems from a snake story. On one occasion when we were both guests at Ray and Betty Fryer's property, Tabletop, on Harveys Range, west of Townsville, a neighbour had electrified us all with a story of having been angry with her little dog for growling continuously at her bedside the previous night. On investigating she had found a large brown snake in bed under the doona with her. So, later, when Bluey came in from feeding the Tabletop horses and mentioned casually, 'There was a snake out on the landing, but it went up the mop handle into the ceiling,' I convinced myself that this snake would waste not a moment of time in insinuating itself from unpromising ceiling, into the dark security of the cupboard of the bed-room where I slept, and as the door of this would not quite would latch, would then not hesitate to venture forth during the night intent upon sharing the warmth of my doona with me. My unfeigned alarm at the prospect was the subject of much hilarity, but Bluey went off quietly, fetched his tool-box and without a word went and fixed the cupboard door, ensuring not only my peace of mind but my unqualified gratitude. That is the way Bluey is. If something has to be done, you get on and do it; no fuss; and you do it well.

Bluey is a not only a skilled hand at manning the tea-towel at washing-up time after dinner at night, but, like most men who have spent time droving and are not afraid of the sound of their own voice, will sing along in manly fashion while the task is done.

A man of wide reading, Bluey gives us a memorable account of his boyhood and youth, working on Western Australian sheep properties, of the rigours of ensuring the water supply for stock, of life as a stockman on Argyle station, of Darwin after the wartime bombings, and of that ultimate challenge to the seasoned cattleman, crossing the Murranji with 'thirteen fifty' head of store cattle for the Barkly and the Queensland border.

For many years, Bluey and his wife Judy ran a successful Security Company in Sydney. Now retired, he travels regularly north to outback Camooweal where he is involved with the biennial Drovers' Camp Festival. Bluey is the sort of man to be relied on when there is a job to be done.

Chapter 3...

THE QUIET STOCKMAN

Bluey Ellis

A horse of my own was all I ever wanted when I was a kid. And I wanted my Dad back, too. I knew I couldn't have Dad back. He was dead. He died when I was about six. He'd been a POW in the Great War and got TB. Then he went to hospital and died. I tried to look on the bright side of things, thinking there might be another Dad somewhere. But there never was. A horse of my own would have been a great help. I used do odd jobs in the local vineyards so I could save up to buy one. A horse of my own was the first step in the plan I had to escape from civilization. Civilization included school.

During the war years there were no young teachers. They'd all been called up. So at school we had this old Pommy fellow by the name of Marshall. He'd put;

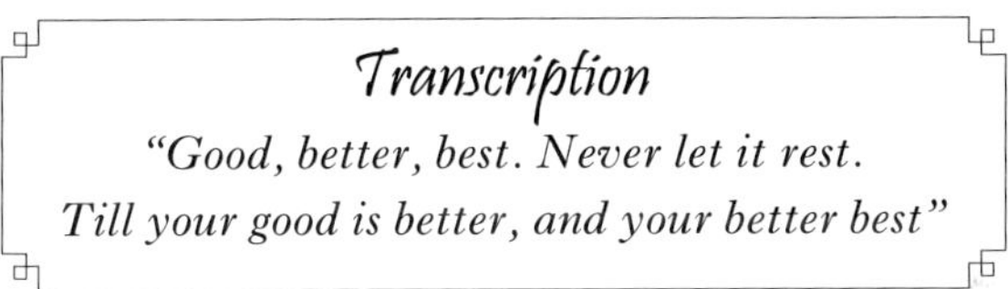
Transcription

"Good, better, best. Never let it rest.
Till your good is better, and your better best"

on the blackboard for us to copy. No biros; push pens and ink wells. While we were writing, two to a desk, he'd be walking up and down swishing this bit of needle-bush with a handle on one end, for a cane. It had no spring in it, either. It was like getting hit over the head with a piece of railing. If he got you on the arm your pen would go 'Skkittch!' across the page and when you went out to the table to get marked this old bugger would say, 'How did you get this mark in your book!' If you said, 'That was where you hit me, Sir!' he would say, 'Well, I wouldn't have hit you for nothing, so bend over and get another one!' The only good thing about Transcription lessons was that you could dip the end of the girl in front's pigtail in your inkwell and if she got a bit snooty and started tossing her head around she'd get ink across her face.

We lived on a property about ten mile out from Midland Junction west of Perth. My great-grandfather had come out from England with a boatload of boys, called the *Parkhurst* Boys, who were all convicts under sixteen, for pinching two pairs of shoes. Because our Dad had died, Legacy did a bit for my sister and me. I remember going for dental treatment once and getting a split lip out of it, and one time they sent a crowd of us over to Rottnest Island on a fortnight's camp. It was all army-style; sleeping on palliasses that we had to stuff with straw, and lining up for meals with our mess-tins. I'd have been about twelve and it seemed like a big adventure, being away from home like that.

Then we left the property at Midland Junction and moved closer in to Perth to an area known as Dog Swamp. On the week-ends I used help the local dairy man move his cows, and I'd help a drover who lived near us, moving sheep and cattle from the paddocks to the meat-works. This drover had had a son my age, about fourteen, who was hit by a car and killed, so he was looking to get away and go shearing. He must have promised the contractor that he would bring a rouse-about with him; so I became one.

We went by truck all the way up to Meekatharra then out on to a station called Mount Padrey and shore there; four shearers and four rousies, picking-up, tar-boying, and sweeping. The rouse-about is employed by the station, so if it rains the rousie still gets fed and paid. We used to reckon, 'More rain; more rest.' But the shearer is on contract to the station and he has to fork into his own pocket. The bloke who does the penning-up is usually one of the station employees. We finished that shed off and moved to Mount Seabrook. That was about the time the price of wool went to a pound a pound and we all got a rise in wages to about eight pound a week and tucker, which was pretty good money. So we shore a few more sheds and I was picking-up for eight men. That brings the blood blisters to your heels, I can tell you! Then we went on to Yathroo.

In a lot of eight-stand sheds the board is four stands on each side of the table so you are only running a short distance. But Yathroo was an old place and the shearing board was outside the original stone barn. The barn had been made into the wool room and was two steps up from the board. Number eight would be the learner's stand and you had to gallop from him the full length of the board, throw the fleece and then race back and pick up two fleeces at once to keep up. You're on the gallop. It was an eight hour day; two hours, then smoko. You'd give the board a quick cleaning-up and then go and get your smoko. Then two hours' work and an hour for lunch; another two hours then afternoon smoko.

There was a shearer's cook and mutton three times a day. One of us rousies would get paid for killing the sheep. You'd get rib flaps for lunch – fat and bone and a bit of meat. You'd get roast meat and spuds, onion and pumpkin, at night and the following day you'd get it in sandwiches for smoko.

Yathroo was originally heavily timbered with red gum but they'd cleared most of it. Doing this made the water table rise and a lot of springs came to the surface in that light sandy country. On the 25 000 acres there were only two windmills and they were both at the house. The rest of it was just dams fed by springs. One of these springs sourced just up above the men's quarters and in the early days they'd built a stone-walled reservoir there and the overflow from it used to turn a flour mill. The early settlers went north along the coast to avoid the areas heavily timbered with tuart, a timber which is impossibly hard to fell, until they got far enough north to head inland past the line of coastal sand dunes and salt lakes into more arable country.

Yathroo was owned by the Australia New Zealand Land Company and had an English feel about it. The perimeter fences were stone walls. The homestead and out-buildings, the store and cow-yards and bails and ram sheds and horse stalls, all with hay lofts above them, were all stone. The original settlers came from England and built what they knew. Of course none of the workers ever got invited to the homestead. Not even on Christmas Day. In fact on Christmas Day everyone was standing with an eye to the sky for smoke. The manager had a morbid fear of fire; fire-breaks everywhere and nobody was allowed to smoke. Or supposedly. None the less we did.

Bill Ingalls was the boss. He always wore a tie and had his sleeves buttoned at the wrist, though on a very hot day in summer he might roll them up to his elbow. And polished boots and always had the smart, snappy brimmed hat on. We had to call him 'Sir.' On one occasion we had a new bloke there, and we were going out to poison rabbits. He just happened to say to Mr. Ingals, 'Hey! Bill! Can y'save some weed for me? I'm runnin' out.' Mr. Ingals said, 'What did you call me!' This bloke says, 'I said would you save me some 'bacci, Bill.' He gets told, 'When you speak to me, you call me Mr. Ingals! Do you hear!' This bloke tells him, 'Ah! And you can stick your flamin'job up yer arse!' and walked off. He was a returned soldier and he wasn't putting up with that tripe.

I stayed at Yathroo about eighteen months until I'd got the hang of the fundamentals; horses, cattle and sheep. Then came the day when I thought, 'Bugger this! I'll pull out!'

I answered an advertisement and went up to Yinnathurra in the Gasgoigne. The station agent paid my fare when I signed up. The mail plane got into Gascoigne Junction on the Friday, and Friday afternoon the mail truck from Carnarvon arrived. The road was just a dirt track. There were only two stations along the way, Brickhouse and Dirawarrie. The mail-man was always called 'Clive On-time'. He drew my attention to the fact that every kangaroo we saw was hopping towards the north as if they knew something. Late afternoon we got to Yinathurra station. That night it started to rain. It rained eight inches continuously over the next ten days and that was the most rain they had had over the past twelve years. There was water everywhere.

Yinathurra was considerably bigger than Yathroo. That year after the rain had gone they sent about five thousand sheep away with the drover. The manager had won a ballot for a block down south which was why he was leaving but he was held up because of all the rain and the new manager couldn't come for the same reason. Everything was in limbo until people could start to move around. There were big stock losses but there was never an accurate count. There were still 15 000 sheep to be mustered. The new manager was Dudley Farrow, a tall man and an excellent horseman. I began to look on him as a father figure. When you lose your own father young you always seem to be on the look-out for a dinkum sort of a bloke for a new one. But of course, it's a gap that can't be filled.

I shore on Yinathurra but only on stragglers; sheep that had been missed in the shearing muster. Sometimes they'd have a fleece that was double or even triple. They'd be pretty wild and woolly. Sometimes they would be what was called a rosella with only half the fleece on them. The rest would have fallen off. But you have still got to shear them. In many cases if they had missed the lamb marking they would be rams. They weren't inclined to be grateful for the experience.

The homestead was made out of hand-cut stone; building it they had to burn their own lime. It had been in the same family for a couple of generations. The old station diaries were written in the most beautiful handwriting. 'Joe Blow arrived from the Port.' 'Played bridge.' 'Joe Blow left for the Port.' And for all these years the ink hadn't faded and there was no scratching out. They must have been very well educated. They must have come out from England expecting to found a dynasty but with the rise and fall of prices and the two World Wars and the shortage of labour it just hadn't happened.

There were some interesting mountains around. About sixty miles away there was Mt. Augustus and near to it was Cobra, which was composed almost entirely of white quartz. It glittered as though it was covered in snow. In the old days there had been a bit of a gold rush to the area. And on a clear day you could see Mt Seabrook which was way over on the Murchison. And Mount James.

In that area they've got a relation to gidgea called snakewood which grows along the ground and comes up and curls around. But it burns well like gidyea and you can cut posts out of it even though they do have a bit of a curl to them. There was a man there named Doug Miller who was exceptionally good at working that type of timber. He was the windmill man and yard builder. I off-sided for him a couple of years. You could learn a lot from a man like that. The management treated him with great respect. Any man can learn to be a musterer but a good windmill man is key to the whole operation.

There were about thirty-eight windmills on Yinnathurra, all on wells; some of the worst water in the world there. Some of it you'd need your pants down before you drink it. It goes straight through. You could be perishing for a drink and have a drink of this stuff and then wish you were still perishing. They had a ram paddock and the rams would suffer it. Then they put horses in and horses wouldn't touch it. Then they put a bore in the other end of the same paddock and got good soft water like rain-water. Beautiful. It depends which underground stream you hit.

They had wells there over a hundred feet deep, dug with pick and shovel in the early days. They were logged in round the top with a rod going down from the windmill into the pump with a foot-valve at the bottom. Most of these wells would only have about six or eight feet of water in them. At one stage another chap and I got a contract on Dirawarrie station to clean one of their wells and put a new cap around the top. The original timber had rotted and was falling to pieces. It would have been there seventy to eighty years. It was a circular well, and about six feet from the top the clay started and went down to a hundred and seven feet. In the bottom where I had to clean it out, it had been timbered in with sawn timber, squared. All I had was a twenty-four gallon kibble, or bucket. My mate on the surface was pulling the bucket up with the jeep. All I was digging out was very fine water-washed gravel like the stuff they make that pebble surface on concrete with.

After a while the water was coming in that quick I couldn't dig any more out. It was the actual stream-bed, underneath this hundred foot of clay.

You can feel a bit claustrophobic if you let it get to you but I'd been down wells when I was a kid, diving for pumps and foot-valves and so on. You just have to talk yourself out of it and overcome it. You don't get any danger money. You're doing it for a price, a contract. I'd go down on what they call a bosun's chair, a bit of wood on a wire. You need to be able to trust your mate up the top. You need somebody up there who's not going to get tired halfway through and quit and go home. The bloke I was with was always up top. He was a lot heavier than I was, and a lot older. His name was Roy Dix. Anyone that called him 'Dorothy', well, if they couldn't fight, they didn't.[1]

Because the surface was sand we had to put the new collar in before we did anything else so I swung on the bosun's chair and gouged holes in the wall to put bearers in and then put a floor on that. The bearers have to be six inches square so you have to gouge a hole to fit. Then on the other side you gouge out another square level with the first one and scarf the top in so you can bring the other end of the bearer down and slide it in. It has to fit because if you've got slack to slip and slide too easily, it might slip and slide when you don't want it to and drop the lot.

For the collar at the top, we had two sections of galvanized-iron tank we put in. We blocked up all the gaps at the bottom edges with bags so the wet cement wouldn't drop down the well. Then you start shovelling and mixing cement and pouring it in. That's a heavy job because you've got to keep mixing and shovelling and pouring, working round and round quick enough so that the section you've finished is not too dry for the next batch to stick to. That collar goes down about six feet all round on a six foot diameter well, so you're working!

In bad seasons some of these wells would go completely dry then you had all the trouble of shifting all the sheep, taking them to another water. But they would keep coming back to that same well. If you didn't shift them again they would perish there. So if a well went dry you had to work out whether it was worth while deepening it to try to get water. There were numerous underground streams depending on the run-off in that very flat country. But no reliable rain.

In a bad year when the water level gets low in waterholes and creeks and starts to disappear, the station horses and brumbies would get down into the creek beds and start digging, making a soak. They would dig until they were completely out of sight, using their front hoofs and scraping the sand back behind them until they hit water. They'd take it in turns to scrape sand and drink. That's common all over the back country. Kangaroos and dingoes will stand back and wait till the horses are finished drinking and then they'll take their turn. Once the horses are convinced there's no more water at that place then they will move somewhere else.

I was on Yinathurra about four or five years. I'd go south at Christmas. I'd have saved about a hundred pounds. One year, another young fellow that was there said, 'Why don't we go to Darwin?' I said, 'What for?' He said, 'Just to have a look.' So we got on the old *Kalinda* and went to Darwin.

1 An allusion to a noted Lonely Hearts columnist of the 1930s and '40s, Dorothy Dix.

This was in '52 and Darwin was still getting over the war and the Jap bombing. Though it was pretty-much a man's town the cops would come down hard on anyone that didn't have a shirt on or at least a singlet. You couldn't walk around bare-topped. The main street had no glass in the windows, just chicken-wire. The New South Wales Bank was just a skeleton pock-marked with bullet holes. The Japs had bombed the Post Office because that was the centre of communication. There were a lot of temporary buildings everywhere. Before the war Cavanagh Street was the China Town area. The Japs had flattened it. They didn't touch Paspaley's Hotel. They probably wanted to keep that for themselves. They were very selective about what they bombed. They bombed the ships in the harbour, twenty-odd of them. The American ship the *Neptune* was only about fifty yards off from the wharf. Every time the tide went down you could see about half of it lying on its side.[2] Salvage people had recovered a lot of the propellors off the ships out in the harbour for scrap. They used to chain a buoy to the prop and cut it off with an oxy torch and wait for the tide to lift it then they'd float it in. There's a thirty foot tidal rise and fall in Darwin harbour. They'd keep doing this, working the tides until they'd get these props close enough to the wharf to pick up with a crane. Then they'd cut them up for scrap.[3]

There were no cafes or restaurants in the town. We stayed at the Vic hotel, one of the original stone buildings from the early days, which the Japs had not bombed. You couldn't get a meal there but there was an old Greek chap, George Fortiades, running a dining room not far along the street. Every dinner time and night time the place would be crowded.

My mate and I got a job at the uranium mine Rum Jungle, which was just starting up. Northern Drillers was doing the exploration work. They had one shaft down to 150 feet and another down to 100. They had just started to put a drive at fifty feet into the Number Two shaft for a 'winse' – a ventilation airshaft. One of the problems with Rum Jungle was that it was a very wet mine. They had to pump continuously day and night. That was one of the factors in deciding to change from deep shaft mining to open cut, about 1953. Then Northern Drillers didn't have the finance to convert to open cut and they called in Australian Zinc, a subsidiary of BHP.

It's a strange area geologically. Not far from Rum Jungle was a bottomless pool known as Crater Lake; about three or four hundred yards across with very steep banks with thick stands of bamboos growing around. Nobody knew how deep it was. It was supposed to have been caused by subterranean subsidence.

The workers at the mine lived in rows of company tents. Some of them had wooden floors and fly-proof windows. Others were just tents with a fly over them. Ours was one of them. And when the rain tumbled down, the fly got mildewy and the tent got mildewy and your gear got mildewy and your brain got mildewy. If you wanted to get into Darwin you had to make your own way in. I parted company

2 The Neptune had been sunk, with the loss of forty-five lives, in a surprise attack by Japanese aircraft on the morning of 19th February, 1942.

3 Sprague, William; A Personal Memoir; Sprague, a signalman on the USS Corpus Christi which visited Darwin during the war, recalls, 'As the tide receded we saw the tops of bridges and the smoke stacks of ships appearing all over the harbour. When the tide was dead low the whole superstructures of merchant ships were visible.'

with my mate. He was just out for a good time. I'd been warned about 'having too much of a good time' – I didn't have those strict old Presbyterian grand-parents for nothing! And this bloke didn't seem to have a good attitude towards work. He'd turn up late and didn't give a damn. So with another mate I decided to head off down The Track and make for Adelaide.

We got as far as Dunmara and met a bloke who was breaking-in horses. He told us about a friend of his, Geoff Nixon, who was going on the road with cattle and needed a couple of men. We contacted him and he took us on. He'd been told that there were five mobs going off that year and that he'd get the fifth. But as it turned out we got the first mob. We had a truck and a plant of horses and we cut across country from an out-station called Birrimba on the Dry River road towards Willaroo. Geoff was the Boss and Fred Heard was driving the truck and there were two blackfellows, Charlie, who had a bit of a clue, and Harry, a myall from Phillip Creek, an old man who could only just ride a horse and couldn't speak English. They came from down the Centre so they weren't too happy about being away from their own tribal area.

Geoff told me to ride on ahead with Charlie and Harry and look for a track. So we kept going and we came to a road at right angles to the way we were travelling. I climbed up a nearby hill to try to get our bearings. Away off, there was this red cloud rising straight up into the air in a column. I judged it was from cattle yards about fifteen mile away. We kept going along the road and by dark we could hear blacks corroboreeing. Charlie and Harry got very nervous. We came to a gate and went through. I said, 'You two blokes hobble the horses and get a fire going. I'll go down and see what's up.'

Where the sing-song was going on there was a homestead, a two-story corrugated-iron place with a lot of corrugated-iron buildings around it. I tied my horse up to the fence and went round the back and knocked on the kitchen door. One of the house-girls came and she turned pale to see a strange white man standing there. She went and got the boss. He wanted to know whose outfit I was with and I told him Geoff Nixon's. None of the other outfits had arrived. He told the girl to give me a feed and then he gave me some tucker to take back to the Charlie and Harry.

In the morning he came down to where we'd camped with a four-wheel drive and we back-tracked along the road and found Geoff and Fred. They'd bogged. I'd seen a wet part on the road and I'd broken off a branch and chucked it on the track to warn them. They'd noticed it and done a detour but they hadn't detoured far enough. So they had unloaded the truck and carried all the gear across to the other side - a forty-four of petrol and two forty-fours of water and all the pack-saddles and all the tucker and swags. They were in the process of endeavouring to dig themselves out but the truck was right down to the chassis. The station manager hooked up his Dodge four-wheel drive weapons-carrier and pulled them out.

I had told Charlie and Harry to muster up all the horses and to hold them until we got back. We went straight out to where the yards were at a place called Brandybottle. It was just like a big English park, except it was gum trees instead of oaks and pines. A beautiful place. They were inoculating the cattle against pleuro for the trip ahead. We made camp and took over tailing the cattle and then a couple of days later, took delivery; thirteen fifty, all shorthorns, big bullocks, five or six years old, forward stores in pretty good condition. Some of them had been on the road before. You could tell because they had stumpy tails. It often happens that when they were inoculating into the tail with a needle and woollen thread, called a seaton, if they hit the bone it can go poisoned and swell up. Then it rots and the bottom part of the tail falls off. So if you see a beast with a stumpy tail you know that he has been on the track before and given them the slip and headed back home.

The abandoned Junction Hotel at Newcastle Waters, NT, once the end of the historic Murranji Track from Top Springs. The Murranji stock-route, in use from about 1904 onwards, played a significant role in the development of the cattle industry of the north-west. Stock routes from several directions converged at the Junction Hotel.

Then we started out with the mob. There was a big bullwaddy scrub that we had to go through along a bit of a two-wheel track. Bullwaddy is bad news; terrible stuff. When it gets to about nine or ten feet high it bows over and forms a barrier of interlacing tunnels that cattle can push pads through but not a man on horseback. It's impenetrable rubbish. It's very hard and sharp and if you get a splinter of it into you, it festers and causes poisoning. It's unique to that part of Australia. It defeated John McDouall Stuart's first attempt to cross the continent in 1861. The Government had bull-dozed this track through but only wide enough for a vehicle; no ten chain road. The cattle had to string out so we sent old Harry up in front and the cattle followed, strung along for about a mile behind him, to get through this bullwaddy.

We got through at last to Binda and camped. The cattle were a bit toey. They splashed a couple of times that night; just run-ups, where they take off for a couple of hundred yards and then stop. You hear a lot of talk about cattle rushing. They jump up and run and it's bingo and they're gone. But it might be that if you get after them too quick that keeps them galloping. Sometimes they'll 'splash'; just go for a little while and then stop and you can ride up round them and bring them back on to camp. And if as sometimes happens they refuse to come back, you just settle them down where they are. That can happen two or three times in a night. The more you watch them and the more they get used to being watched, the more they start to form a pattern of how they will camp, some on one side, some on another, then they will stick to the same pattern once they start to settle down . We had one bullock that always came right up and camped next to us. He liked us. He was an intellectual among bullocks.

Then we started down the Dry River road. With thirteen-fifty bullocks to water there were a couple of places, a water-hole and a creek, where you've got to spread them out to water them. Eventually, doing nine or ten mile a day, we got down to Pussycat bore. We met old Bill Crosen and his son there. Bill had just won Montejinnie station in a ballot and he was moving his gear out there. So we had a bit of a yarn before moving on.

We were always conscious of keeping bush cattle out. We kept old Harry in the lead because we could watch him from there, but the problem was you could never catch his attention and block him up. You'd have to anticipate what might go wrong up and canter up and stop him. But if any cattle came up that had been bang-tailed then you would put them in. Most of the time they'd have been Vestey's cattle, anyway; Manbulloo, Willaroo and Delamere; they were all Vestey's properties at that time.

On one occasion old Harry was up the front and these bush cattle were trying to come in on one side. I galloped up at an angle to keep them out although you had to be careful galloping or you'd stir the bullocks up and they would string out and run up the road on to one another. So I hunted these cattle out. They ran round the head of the mob, heading bush. Old Harry eventually heard me and saw them coming. I'm singing out, 'Let 'em go! Let 'em go!' but he was taking off after them to bring them back. And he put his hand up on his hat to hold it, and just at that moment his horse put its foot in a hole and did a complete head over heels on him. That was all yellow gilgai, melon-hole country through there; full of holes. The ground had given way under his horse's hoof. I thought, 'Jesus! Oh, well! Poor Old Harry! He died with his hat on.' But he got up, OK, still with his hat on. It must have been a premonition that made him hold on to it.

Being early in the season we were doing pretty well as far as feed was concerned. When we got down to Nine and Ten Murranji, they had corrugated-iron tanks that had to have pumpers on them constantly pumping to keep the tank full. You're in the middle of the Murranji and there's a concentration of cattle behind you and the windmills would never keep the water up to them. The capacity of the tank is not much more than a drink for thirteen hundred head of cattle. If it got empty it would take about six to eight hours to fill again. At that stage the next mob was about two or three days behind us. We were meeting drovers that were still going out; at Pussycat Bore, Eric Rankin and Eric Griffith.

They had their two plants together and were just on their way out. They wouldn't be back for a few months. Bruce Simpson was on his way to Willaroo. Ray Turner; he had his family with him. They used to have a cow with their plant, and chooks. His daughter was bringing the horses along. But you don't have much time to socialize with people going past when you've got cattle in hand.

So doing the Murranji Track was like this every day and every night until the trip was over. Then the cattle were delivered at Morestone and I went back to Dunmara and took over running the camp. But it wasn't satisfactory. I ended up footing the tucker bills for the camp out of my own pocket while the management would be off and away to Brunette Downs races and so forth. By that time I had turned twenty-one. I'd had my twenty-first birthday at Daly Waters when I got drunk on a bottle of Drambuie. I couldn't stand the smell of it for years after. So I decided to head up to Darwin. I met up with a bloke there I'd known at Rum Jungle. He'd been down working on the Snowy and he'd lost an eye in a brawl in a pub. He wanted to get back to Wyndham but he was a bit of a drinker and down on his luck. So I shouted him his plane fare and we went to Wyndham.

Bluey Ellis and Aboriginal drover Tommy Saville, at Camooweal, 2004. Bluey got on well with the Aborigines at Argyle station because he was interested in their culture. Tommy Saville had been a drover from the age of four. He recalls that he was so little at the time that he had to be lifted on to his horse.

Wyndham was just the one pub in town and another pub out at the Six Mile. The Six Mile was where they used to tail bullocks waiting to get in to the meat-works. A bloke named Bill Finlay had the contract to cart supplies out to the stations. I got talking with him and got a lift with him to look for station work. We went out to Alice Downs, the station owned by Diamond Jack Dickson, but I couldn't get a job. When we got back into town, this Bill Finlay said to me, 'I'll leave my shed open and you can camp in there. You can get to the tap there but roll your swag out on the back of the truck. The crocodiles come up of a night time and they'll get you. You can't leave a dog chained up of a night time or they'll come up and take it.' His place was about fifty yards from the edge of Cambridge Gulf. He told me he'd had a race-horse in a temporary yard made of timber and forty-four gallon drums and the crocodiles came up and ate him; no problem. But I was safe enough on the back of the truck. As long as I didn't fall off.

I got a job at old Des Gee's pub. One Sunday night we were all just sitting round in the lounge-room talking and the manager of Argyle, George Schultz, was there. He said to me, 'You looking for station work?' I said, 'Yeah. It'd come in handy, alright.' He said, 'I could give you a job out at Argyle if you want it.' I'd heard of Argyle but it wasn't as famous then as it is now. It's become a household word since then.

So four of us went out to Argyle in a Jeep they sent in. There was Billy Crane the cook, who half the time was in the DTs, the old saddler, this other bloke and me. The Ord River was going down after the end of the Wet and at Ivanhoe crossing there was a concrete causeway that had been built in earlier times when they didn't have concrete pipes. They'd used forty-four gallon drums with the tops and bottoms cut out instead. They'd laid them five in a row and there were fifty-two rows of fives and then they'd concreted rocks over the top of that. And they are still there today, pouring water through.

Because of water coming over the causeway we had five people wading alongside the Jeep on the down-river side and the driver and old 'DT Billy' in it. It took the five of us holding against the pressure of the water to keep the vehicle on the road. The crossing was about a hundred and fifty yards across and built on a curve but only wide enough for the vehicle, and pretty slippery. The wheels would start slipping sideways. You had to take it steady, steady. If you'd tried to go fast you would have slipped over the edge. There were little concrete blocks along the edge and when things were looking hairy we could get our feet against them and brace.

The cook at the station was called Jimmy. He had false teeth and his top plate was always dropping and he'd have to 'Sssssslllllppp!' to suck it back as he talked to you. It was a bit unpalatable but you ignored that. You mix it up with custard! He'd be telling the gins to hurry up and do something and at least fifty percent of this 'Ssssslllpp!' went back in, but you had no way of telling where the other fifty went.

The homestead was built by the Duracks last century. It was made out of stone; flag-stones from the river for the verandah all round. It was on the Behn, a tributary of the Ord. There was a big old croc, a freshie about twelve foot long, that the gins used to feed on all the offal, that lived in that creek. And if you're thinking, 'A twelve foot freshie! Get out!' well, all I can say that it was an estimation based on fear. They had a bit of a punt there and I was paddling it along the creek one day and I got to the western end where there were rocks where the old road used to cross. I didn't see this croc sunbathing up on the rock. And as the paddle hit the side of the canoe he went, 'Swwishhtt!' into water. He could have just as easily come the other way in on top of me. He hit the water and swam away, and if I tell you he was twelve foot, by gee, he was twelve foot from where I was sitting! Believe me!

Across the river there was a drover named Tommie Wilson that had a permanent camp. The gins used to wade across and visit Tommy's missus. They would walk down to the water and they'd pick up their dress and as they waded out it got higher and higher and higher until they were in the middle and then it just got lower and lower and lower as they came back out on this side. They didn't seem to worry about the croc or any mates he might have had in there.

Argyle was a beautiful place but too much reliance had been put on watering stock from the river so that the country was flogged out along both sides of the river when there was still good untouched country further out. They should have put more bores in out there to use those good areas. It was beautiful country. Now they are ploughing it up for the Koreans to grow melons and cucumbers and sugar-cane. It's lend-lease. We lease it to them and they have a lend of us.

The camp on Argyle was three or four hundred yards up behind the stockyards. The humpies were just waist high. That way they didn't have a great deal of air-space to warm up on cold nights. They didn't need to build them any higher. They were only for sleeping in. If they want to stand up and stretch they go outside. The humpies were made out of bits of old corrugated-iron but the traditional ones would have been made of sheets of bark. The Duracks might at one time have built them better style huts but over the years when somebody died they would have been burnt down. That was the Aboriginal way of doing things. But now they've started thinking, 'You don't have to burn the hut down. You can just smoke it. That will chase the debil-debils away.' But in those days if someone died they got rid of the hut as quick as they could.

Some of the old people, Old Biddy, the cowgirl, and Old Jessie her off-sider, lived in proper huts closer to the house. They looked after the house cows. Then there was Old Daylight and Old Grasshopper. Old Daylight had been around the world with Durack. He'd say, 'Him good boss, that Old Man! You feelim' my head, Young Fella! You feelim' lump? Old Boss, Him bin hittim' me wit' hobble. An' stick! Ah! Good Man! That Old Man!' When we were mustering those two old fellows used to do nearly all the tailing. They'd both have been in their seventies or eighties. They'd have been on Argyle since before Mary Durack was born. There were also a few old girls there that I didn't get to know the names of; all Judy's and Ruby's and Trixies and Daisies. Argyle was their home. They'd all been born there. They had a tribal name. It sounded something like, 'Meangala'. They told me once it meant 'river reeds'. Daylight told me, 'Young Fella! You look long that reed. That name we-fella. Suppose we go town, they tell us, we same name longa that reed, Meangala.'

But they had hardly any kids in the camp which seemed a bit odd. Other places with a camp that size would have had a mob of kids running round, but on Argyle there were only four; a couple of kids about ten or eleven and two little fellows. Nowhere near enough kids. Other stations had at least two or three kids a year coming on all the time.

The Argyle Aboriginals were very interesting people to get to understand. But first you have got to get their confidence. Then you can talk to them and ask questions. Daylight said to me one time, 'Hey! Young Fella! You like see pretty stone?' I said, 'Yeah! You got a pretty stone? You show me.' It was winter time and cold. He had an old army overcoat on. He dug in his pocket and he come out with this stone that had been washed smooth in the river with a dark, olivey-green colour about it. I said, 'By Chrise, Grasshopper! That's a pretty one! You got any more?' He said, 'Oh, yeah, Young Fella! I got planty!' And he fishes them out of his pocket. 'I got this one! And this one.' So we were having this big conference about these shiny stones. But just then he starts getting into finger-talking [4] with Old Daylight over on the far side of the cattle, and he says to me. 'Cattle he bit come up now.' Daylight was telling him he had seen the movement of the mob the other musterers were bringing in, about five mile away. We had to get out round our lot so they wouldn't bolt. We didn't want the other mob to come through ours. But the end of that story is that, years later, of course, they discovered diamonds on Argyle! Old Daylight could have been showing me a pocketful of diamonds that he'd found in the river, for all I knew.

We were mustering once and I got pelted at top speed. My horse got tangled-footed over some rocks and we went down together and he rolled on top of me.

4 finger-talking; ancient Aboriginal sign-language used when hunting.

From the pain I thought I had broken my back. My horse got up but I couldn't move. The other fellows came up and they wanted to move me. They were genuinely concerned because they'd seen what happened. But I said, 'No way in the world. You can build a shade over me but I'm staying here.' They said, 'But we got to get you to a doctor.' I said, 'You could get me some water but I'm staying here until this pain goes. If there's any real damage it'll still be there. But if I get up now it might make it worse.' They said, 'Aw! The ants'll eat yer!' I said, 'There's enough of me. They can have a go.' So they made this bit of a shade over me. They broke off some branches and stuck them in, and then covered it over the top with bushes. It makes a piebald shade. I stayed there the rest of that day and then the following day. And on the day after that I got up. Forced up by water. It was very painful but I could move. They were going to get me a horse to get me back to camp. I said, 'I reckon I might just walk.'

Friends are part of having a life. If you are not making friends then you are doing something bloody wrong. All people are different, and you have to learn to live with them and get on with them. Sometimes you have to needle them to make them perform a bit better, and sometimes you've got to give them a lot of support. It's got to be give as well as take. You've got to be able to receive as well as give. It's reciprocal. And the thing that I've always stuck by is this; once I say I'll do a thing for a friend, or for anyone, for that matter, then I make sure I bloody-well do it. I always stand by what I say and what I do.

With Persistence and Determination

John Nicholas, of Payne's Lagoon station, with his grandson William.

INTRODUCTION

Since John Nicholas took up Payne's Lagoon station as a Returned Serviceman's block in the early 1960s, the road across Herveys Range from Townsville has been upgraded from inaccessable army-vehicle track to seamless bitumen. Driving west is now as smooth as low-flying. This road connects through to the Lynd Highway from Charters Towers to Georgetown and the Gulf. From the comfortable Payne's Lagoon homestead slightly north of the road there are views across drought-seared paddocks to pale distances of ranges.

John Nicholas could be described as an autocrat with a down to earth sense of humour. On the day we arrived John had not long been to the hair-dresser in town. He told us 'The girl asked me, 'Been having any fun lately?' I told her, 'Not a lot since I broke my hip.' A fine-looking man in his early eighties, with a shock of unruly silver hair, John does not let confinement to a wheel-chair prevent him from being the dominating force of any gathering. In his electric chair he zips around the property taking command of every situation. Nor is he satisfied with earth-bound activities. The hangar beside the airstrip has not one, but two aircraft, a Cessna 182 - in John's words 'the Mercedes among aircraft'- and a strut-based ultra-light Drifter. He shakes his head in puzzlement that more 'young fellows' are not similarly enthusiastic for the delights and challenges of ultra-light flying.

Wynifred, John's wife of over fifty years, had a very welcome smoko spread on the long silky-oak dining table when we arrived. We were joined by six year old grandson, William, wearing a hat as big as himself, which with old-fashioned courtliness he removed on entering the house, before coming to drape an affectionate arm around his formidable grandfather. The bond between the two was obvious. William was wheel-chair-bound Grand-dad's 'right-hand man.'

But our pleasant smoko was suddenly shattered by thunderous bangings and hammerings followed by the ear-shattering 'NNGNNnnngnnggnnngs' of an electric saw immediately outside the back door. With the calm of one who has accepted the unexpected for over fifty years of married life, Wyn told us, 'It's just the carpenters putting on a new back verandah for us.' As if to get into the act, the two-way radio on the sideboard crackled briskly to life with the morning's traffic. Feeling decidedly challenged I began setting up my recording equipment, thinking several very indelicate words and could only hope for the best.

Chapter 4...

WITH PERSISTENCE AND DETERMINATION

JOHN NICHOLAS

Dad was in the artillery at Pozieres on the Somme and after the war when this big English estate called Silsoe outside Longreach was cut up in a land ballot, he was lucky enough to draw the homestead block. So I grew up at Silsoe, seventy-five miles outside Longreach. For those days Silsoe had a damned good homestead. Dad must have thought he'd won the Golden Casket when he saw it. Mum had come straight out of Sydney and had never done a hand's turn in her life. But there was no water on the property. There was an overshot dam[1] on Silsoe Creek not far from the homestead but it only lasted about ten or eleven months of the year if it rained. Water was always a problem. But Dad got top wool cheque one year; nine-pence a pound!

My little brother Bill and I used to get Barcoo rot sores from vitamin deficiency. The Old Man tried to grow fruit trees and vegetables but they would all die. One of the methods of dealing with Barcoo rot was to get a corn bag and wet it and spread seeds on it and eat the shot grain, much the same way as you buy sprouts in the supermarket today. They probably got the idea from the Chinamen. It's a very old cure in desert countries round the world.

At the age of seven or eight one of my jobs was to drive the Model T Ford to the mail box to collect the weekly mail. Dad used to get it started for me by jacking up the back wheels to take the drag out of the engine. When it fired over I would put my foot on the reverse pedal and then the second gear pedal a couple of times so that she would rock backwards and forwards and fall off the jack. Then while I did a few slow circuits round the mail box, Bill's job was to jump out - I couldn't pull up in case she stopped altogether – grab the mail-bag and any goods that might have been left there and then scramble back in.

Longreach summer temperatures were high. But in winter when a south-westerly was blowing it would go right through you. Billy and I used to get out in a warm possie facing the sun against the end of the storeroom. We didn't mind the dogs sharing it with us.

1 A holding dam scooped by horse-delver and scoop at the side of a creek and connected to it by a pipe which filled the dam when the creek ran after rain without silting it up.

Mum tried to teach me on Correspondence while Billy did pothooks. But she couldn't handle us. In the end she gave up and we had a governess named Eva Casey. We used to give poor Casey a hard time. We'd bolt from the house and go down swimming in the creek. Casey would come down and she'd have broken off a bit of stick. She'd appear over the creek bank and threaten us with telling our father. That would get us out. Another time she told me to do something and I bailed up on her. Mum called out from the other room, 'You do what Casey tells you to do!' I said, 'Bugger Casey!' and dived out through the window. And there was Dad right outside with his razor-strop in his hand! He gave me a good flogging and wheeled me round by my collar to the door with, 'Now you get back in there and apologize!' Casey can't have minded all this too much because later she married my Uncle Chip and became part of the family.

But we had a lot of fun. We'd go shooting kangaroos or cats which were thick along the creek. I had a Winchester 25/22 and rode no saddle or bridle with the rifle across my legs, Indian style. We'd range far and wide from home. And Mum would go to a lot of trouble to arrange birthday parties for us, and others around did the same. These parties were conjured out of thin air as everyone was poor. Wool prices were well below the cost of production. But those parties gave people the chance to dress up a bit and put on a bit of spit and polish. In those times western women always seemed to be able to cater for unexpected visitors and produce a meal out of nowhere. No visitor ever went away hungry. Dad spent most of his time trying to keep his sheep alive in the five year drought. When the rain did come it broke with dust storms. Bill was about five years old and had never seen rain. He went flying under the bed with the dogs to hide.

In 1928 the first aeroplanes were starting to fly into Longreach to refuel on their way from England; Bert Hinkler, Amy Johnson and others. I was immediately attracted to the idea of aeroplanes and have been ever since. Once a year we used to go into Longreach in the Model T and it was a tremendous occasion. Weeks of preparation were involved; maintenance on the engine, patching all the old tyres that had a mile or two left in them, tying a week's tucker on the running boards and the swags on the back and finally tins of water and petrol.

There was a stretch of the road that was known as the Desert where the hard narrow tyres of the Model T didn't run too well in the deep sand. One method of getting through was to let all the tyres down low and sneak through. The disadvantage was having to pump them up again. We would all be pretty glad to get to Longreach at last. We would stay at the Imperial for a couple of days. There'd be plenty of unlimited boiling hot water that stank of sulphur from the artesian bore. They used to pump it into tanks to cool it off so you could have a mix of cool and hot water. We would have a couple of days at the Imperial before it was back to salt mutton, spuds and onions again.

As soon as we got to Longreach I would make a beeline for the Qantas hangar to look at the aeroplanes. Willie had to go with me. I had to look after him so he didn't have much choice. I would stay half the day there, talking to the mechanics, asking questions, fingering the sides of the aeroplanes and getting in the way. There was one old bloke there who'd been a wagon builder in his day and he had the job of making propellers for Qantas. He'd rough them out with a tomahawk and then a spoke-shave and rasp; all hand tools. He had a series of propellers all at different stages and when he got sick of doing one process he would move on to another.

I was always on the look-out for a free ride in an aeroplane but the only ride I ever got was once when Mum and Bill and I had been to Sydney, and coming, home, the Darr River was in flood and looked like being impassable to wheeled vehicles for months so Dad arranged with Qantas to fly us over. No doubt it cost him more money than he had but there was a great roll-up of people on the Darr to greet the plane when we landed. They'd got a smoke fire going so the pilot could gauge the direction of the wind.

On another occasion when Billy and I were at the aerodrome, a big storm many miles wide with severe lightning and wind was blowing up in the west. The mechanics told us to go back to the hotel. About halfway the rain started coming down in buckets and suddenly it was raining fish! They were only about two or three inches long and they were coming with the rain, flipping into any running water and were soon swept away.

When I was about twelve we had to leave Silsoe. During the long drought Dad had been keeping his sheep alive by scrub-cutting. In 1930 the dry spell ended with thirteen inches of rain in 48 hours. That effectively destroyed the rest of the sheep. As a last resource Dad had got the 2000 sheep he'd been able to save in a black soil paddock beside the road ready to go on the track and follow 'the long paddock' with them[2]. After that rain most of them bogged in the black mud and died where they were. Dad spent days pulling sheep out and scraping the mud off them. They would stagger a few yards and bog again. He lost 90% of his flock. The bank declined to fund restocking and in the end there was nothing he could do but walk off. The bank was in possession. Dad scraped together just enough to finance getting on to a dairy property outside Monto.

Mum and the little kids went to Monto on the train and Dad and I drove the Model A Ford. It took us weeks because of floods around Clermont. We had to dodge flooded creeks and the Dawson River in flood. I had a cage in the back of the car with two pet galahs that I wouldn't leave behind. Dad was happy about that.

The new place was called Berry Park. It was about 25 miles south of Monto along the Eidsvold road on the Burnett River, a block of a couple of thousand acres off Langley station. It was big for the area because it was right at the far edge of settlement. The closer you were to town the smaller the blocks were. The homestead was just a three- room weatherboard cottage. Mum burst into tears when she saw it. But there was a beautiful set of cattle yards and an old original puddle-dip. A puddle dip was first slabbed-in with a timber framework and packed in behind the framework was a thick layer of good quality clay, rammed down. Done well, it would hold like a bottle.

Dad had bought the farm from the family that had been dairying there. Old Jim Smart, the father, used to keep his wife and three daughters on the go at the hand-milking, morning and afternoon milking, every day. He would walk around

2 To 'long paddock' was to take sheep on the road as a last resort when feed on the property had run out, in order to let them graze on whatever feed was available along the way.

belting them across the shoulders with a shillelagh. The youngest boy was about my age and his legs had all bruises on them. I said to him, 'What happened to your legs?' and this kid looked all around him over his shoulder and he said, 'M'Old Man got me with the stock whip.' And I said, 'By the look of your legs you cop a flogging pretty often.' And this kid said, 'Any time the Old Man can catch me!' The eldest Smart boy's name was Allan and he was about twenty-three. He rebelled at one time. He got the manure shovel and when Old Man Smart had his back to him he brought it down on his head and dropped him cold as a maggot. Poor old Mrs Smart said, 'You've killed him! You've killed him!' Young Jim said, 'Good enough, too! The bastard!' Old Jim recovered and sat up but he never laid a hand on Allan again.

Dad wasn't having hand-milking. He had milking machines installed. The day they stopped hand-milking, the cows were transferred to the new set up. It took about a week to break them in. At the start they wanted to kick the milking cups to pieces. We were milking about ninety cows, not for milk but for cream, which was picked up every second day to be sent to Monto to make 'P.C.D', 'Port Curtis Dairies' butter. The cream would keep pretty well in the cool room, a twelve by twelve ventilated hut, built to Department of Primary Industries specifications, on a concrete slab with weatherboard walls. The ventilation gap at the top and bottom was covered over with wire netting to keep the possums out. We had about sixty pigs on the skim milk. The pigs used to go to the bacon factory in Maryborough.

There was a one teacher school called Langley Flat about three or four miles from the house. Us three kids had a worn out push bike and a worn out grey horse that was also used to work the spring cart. We used to take it in turns to ride the bike or the horse. My little sister Jill was always a passenger on the horse. We had to cross Splinter Creek but if it was running more than waist deep the rule was we could go home again. The local Parents' Committee rigged up a flying-fox over the creek for any emergencies and if the creek was running a banker after rain, some of the neighbours would be there to make sure kids didn't get washed away.

There were about eighteen kids, all ages, in the one room. The teacher was Joe Tierney who believed in frequent doses of the cane. If you were cheeky or not paying attention, six of the best was what you could expect. You didn't forget for a day or two either. From there I went down to Gatton College for twelve months. But Gatton decided I wasn't very promising material so they sent me back to the bush. To my mother's great sorrow.

Towards 1938 it was obvious that the world was drifting towards war again. A Light Horse troop was formed in Monto for defence against potential enemies. It seemed to me natural to join the Light Horse and the training did me, and thousands of other young fellows like me, a good turn. Training was at the weekends with a fortnight's camp in Area Head Quarters on pay. To a farm boy three shillings and sixpence a day was very welcome. Many of us had fathers who'd served in the First World War and when these old fellows got together and started yarning we listened enthralled.

We learned to use a .303 and to fire machine guns and a World War One Lewis gun; also to use a sabre. We used to go into camp once a year. We'd load our horses on the train and the army paid us five bob a day for each horse. So we were on good money, getting three and six a day as a trooper and five bob a day for the horse! The horses had to meet army specifications of course. A lot of the officers were Old Diggers from the First World War. We would do manoeuvres and cavalry charges. I could spear a packet of cigarettes on the ground at full gallop, no trouble at all.

When war was declared they formed a mechanized cavalry unit that was supposed to have tanks, and Light Horse men were given priority. I got my discharge from the militia in Gympie and went down to Brisbane to join the 7th Divvie of the A.I.F, on the first of July, 1940.

We did all our initial training at Redbank. We got our issue of uniform in dribs and drabs because they never had enough to give it out in one go. You'd get a pair of long-johns and a pair of khaki pants this time, and great coat and a hat the next. We were in long wooden huts, about eighty or ninety men to a hut, a row of bunks along each side. They'd give you straw to fill your palliasse, but after about three weeks the straw would turn to dust. No sheets of course; three blankets initially but after a while they gave us four; it was that bloody cold that winter. We moaned, of course. That is the way to keep the officers on their toes. If men don't moan the officers get slack. We were on parade once and the officer said, 'Gentlemen of the cavalry! Men of other ranks!' The men of other ranks said, 'What sort of a dick-head have we got here?'

We went overseas on Christmas Eve, 1940 on the *Queen Mary*. Our outfit was in F Deck, Aft. There were no fittings. It was about the equivalent of Boggo Road Gaol. I used to listen for the torpedoes coming. I had the feeling that down there we could die like rats in a trap. With a light cruiser as escort, we left Sydney Harbour at about four o'clock in the afternoon in drizzling rain. There were people on the harbour in small boats waving good-bye. It didn't cross my mind that I mightn't ever get back. When you are nineteen that always happens to the other fellow. We went south around Tasmania because the Germans had a submarine in Bass Strait, but we never saw so much as a seagull, all the way to Fremantle.

In Egypt the weapons we were promised when we left Australia never materialized. If you went on guard duty you were issued with five rounds of ammunition which had to be accounted for at the end of guard duty. We were to be sent to Greece but were side-tracked to Cyprus where we were warned to keep away from the girls for medical reasons and from there across to Palestine and north to Syria. Somewhere in an olive grove outside Tripoli I celebrated my twenty-first birthday. Over Christmas it was so cold the poor were dying in the streets. They would be found frozen in doorways. It was while we were on the Turkish border, on shocking rations of horse and donkey meat, that we heard that the Japs had bombed Pearl Harbour. Rumours started flying round that the 6th and 7th Divvies were going home to defend Australia. It was while we were at sea actually heading for Singapore that we heard it had fallen. We landed in Adelaide on the day that Darwin was bombed.

The 7th Divvie was sent north to New Guinea to help drive the Japs back at Kokoda. We then took part in the Buna/Sananandа campaign. We were flown to a forward position, Popandetta. There was a shortage of carriers; those poor buggers had been decimated going over the Owen Stanleys, so we each had to carry a 200 pound load of supplies in for about fourteen miles; knee-deep in mud half the time. They gave us a five minute break for a smoke every hour. With that load on you couldn't sit down or you would never stand up again. All you could do was stand up against a tree for a bit of a spell to ease the load. When we got closer to the front line they told us, 'It would be a good idea not to smoke now. The Japs'll smell the tobacco.'

We got to Saputo just as it was getting dark and filed past and dumped our load at head quarters. Then they told us we could camp just anywhere in the grass. Next morning we were sent in behind the Jap lines on a fighting patrol. We got a few hundred yards along the track and came under fire. We got behind the main Japanese defences in an encircling movement and got slaughtered. In the first half day we lost about 30 killed. There wasn't anything we could do to retrieve those bodies. They just had to be allowed to lie there in the jungle to rot. Later when we were mopping-up I came across a Jap that had a dixie with a chunk of steak in it. He'd cut it off one of our fellows. I shot the bastard. I had no compunction about killing Japs for the way they treated our people. Wherever they fought they behaved with utter callousness. They deserved to be treated the same way. There is no humanity in war.

The survivors of our unit were flown back to hospital in Port Moresby and then sent down to Sydney in a hospital ship with the lights on all the way which didn't make us feel too safe. By international agreement hospital ships were safe from attack but then the Japs sank the hospital ship the Centaur off Bribie Island and proved themselves incapable of abiding by such ideals. So I spent six weeks in Concord Military Hospital in Sydney with malaria. After a spell of leave on the Atherton Tableland our cavalry unit was disbanded and we were used to reinforce other units in the Ramu valley in New Guinea where the fighting on Shaggy Ridge was going on.

By this time my father was too sick with asthma to run the farm any longer and I applied for compassionate discharge and got it. I found it pretty hard to settle down again to farm life. It all seemed a bit petty. My brother Bill also returned about the same time after surviving the fighting at Shaggy Ridge. I didn't get involved with any of the local girls at Monto because I had met the girl I wanted for my wife, Wynifred Wilson, in Brisbane. We corresponded and our romance grew. In due course I went to Brisbane to ask her parents for her hand in marriage and our wedding was celebrated at St. John's Cathedral, followed by a honeymoon at Coolangatta, before returning to the farm. I would not have achieved what I have in my life without Wyn. She has been a wonderful wife to me. In due course we had three daughters and later, a son.

I learned to fly at Monto in a Tiger Moth, an Auster, and later, a Victor. One day at the Aero Club one of the fellows had a bundle of material from the Lands Department advertising a land ballot including a block called Payne's Lagoon which was reserved for ex-servicemen. He said to me, 'Here, John. Look at this. You ought to have a go at it.' So I put my name in the ballot for this Payne's Lagoon. There were only ten others in it and the upshot was that I won.

I was over at the milking shed when Wyn got the telegram. She walked over with it in her hand. She said to me, 'What's all this about?' She didn't even know I had entered the draw so it was a bit of a shock to her. I thought it was as good as a win in the Golden Casket but when I went to see the bank manager he said, 'Well, John, I don't know whether to congratulate you or to give you a sympathy card. The bank will not finance you, y'know.' I said, 'In God's name! Why not?' He said, 'Because you are not allowed to sell it for five years and so it is not worth a thing to us.'

So I started to look for finance elsewhere, through the stock and station people and private finance companies but got the bum steer every time. None of them would touch Payne's Lagoon with a forty-foot pole as there were no improvements, no boundary fences and no income coming in. I put the Monto farm up for sale but it took twelve months to sell. After I had paid off all I owed I only had a couple of thousand left.

Then the Lands Department started getting restive because I hadn't 'taken up residence' at Payne's Lagoon. I got a stay of occupation from the Minister for Lands, chartered a plane for fifty pounds - it would be five thousand today - and hot-footed it up north to my raw ballot block. I was bitterly disappointed when I first saw the drought-stricken condition of the country, but my brother, who had gone with me, said, 'Never mind the country. Look at the cattle! They're all sleek and contented-looking. That tells you what the country is like.'

So I drove the Blitz from Monto to Charters Towers and drove out next day to Payne's Lagoon with thirty sheets of corrugated-iron tied down with wire on top and built myself a humpy, thirty by twenty. I used new iron for the roof and covered the walls with bits and pieces I scavenged from an old miner's hut on the place that the white ants had eaten the timber out of. I built it in the shade of a wind mill that had been put on the original Dotswood station in 1930 as one of the first improvements after Angliss bought it. But I knew I couldn't bring Wynifred and the four children out to live in a humpy under a windmill so I got a flat for them in Townsville so the children could go to school. I used to go down and get a few grits every three or four weeks and come back out to the salt mine. You get used to poverty. Poverty is only a state of mind.

Then out of the blue A.M.L. & F came to the party with limited finance. They bought

John Payne's first camp on Payne's Lagoon. John recalls that, as a Soldier Settler he arrived with thirty sheets of roofing-iron and scavenged the rest from abandoned mining camps in the area.

me a mob of cattle at Clermont which included cows, calves and heifers. They were trucked from Clermont to Garbutt trucking yards in Townsville and my friend Ray Fryer, the 'Boss Drover', picked them up. I'd met Ray when I first came up Herveys Range. I'd stopped to ask him the state of the road out to Payne's Lagoon on the Star River. He told me, 'You'll never get through. You'd better come over home to Tabletop and have a feed and we'll see you right.' He introduced me to his mother who was a wonderful old lady. She knew the history of the entire district.[3]

BASIC PLANT – PAYNE'S LAGOON – 1963

1943 Ford. Ex Department of Supply. Condition excellent.

One portable pump; 1 and one quarter inch, centrifugal,

Villey's engine and hoses	£50
Concrete mixer, new	£40
Chain saw	£80
Tools, forge, drill, etc	£200
Battery charger	£50
Two Way Radio	£150
Two saddles, bridles, halters, hobbles, etc	£75
Caravan camp	£100
	£1,245

So Ray and I dipped my first lot of cattle at Langhan's at the foot of Herveys Range and then started to push them up the old bullock-wagon track. A few went over the side but there wasn't much we couldn't do about that. We spelled them a couple of days at Ray's place and then dipped them again. Ray said to me, 'We'll have to brand these calves. You're not taking unbranded calves out to the Star! They wouldn't last five minutes!' I said, 'I haven't got a set of branding irons.' Ray told me, 'Look, I've got every brand in the district here. I can make you up a set, no trouble.'

So Ray and I had dipped and branded the calves and set off. I was driving the blitz with the camp gear. I had an Aboriginal stockman named Eddie and he went with Ray and the cattle. We crossed Keelbottom Creek and headed on towards the Argentine, a deserted gold-mining township. One of the drums of fuel on the blitz kept rolling off - the track was pretty sketchy – and the gear on the back kept shifting. Ray and Eddie pushed on with the cattle towards a wide open red ridge where we arranged to camp that night. When I caught up with them I said to Ray,

3 See 'Red Dust Rising' , Marion Houldsworth, CQU Press, 2004, which describes the lives of the Fryer family of Tabletop station and their legendary hospitality to all comers.

'How do you like camping beside a fire?' He said, 'It's alright. I've done it before.' I said to him, 'Well, you'll have to tonight if you want to keep warm. I've lost your swag.' It must have worked itself loose off the back of the blitz. I'd circled back to try to find it but never did. So I gave Ray a couple of blankets out of my own swag and we made do.

The next day we got the cattle to the old yards at Payne's Lagoon and left them there. That was how I brought my first mob of cattle in. It was in the early sixties. Because of the requirement to turn them over as soon as they calved they were then sold again and this way you could trade your way out slowly. Then I was able to buy a few culled cattle and bring them home. They were in terrible condition because they were drought stricken. I took a punt on early storms and for a change the rains came. After about three or four weeks of keeping the cattle alive on hay we got more rain and the country went ahead and so did the cattle. We gradually bred the numbers up. We were able to sell a few cattle to keep the company quiet and I was able to employ a family from Monto, the Carmodies, to come up and work on the property. There was still no help from the bank. The cattle bred up and we had a number of steers ready for sale when the beef market collapsed. That was the 1974 cattle crash. Cattle were being sold at give-away prices. The Rurul Reconstruction Scheme gave me two years' carry-on finance to pay outstanding bills.

At the end of two years I had bullocks to sell but could not afford to truck them into the sale yards in Townsville. We decided to walk them in ourselves. Wyn drove the Toyota, which did as the cook-house, and the kids and I did the droving. We had a mob of 400 and I expected to get $145 a head for them. Before we reached Herveys Range the stock agent came out and he said, 'Don't be in too much of a hurry to get them down to town. Things are starting to happen on the market. I can't tell you what it is but you will be better off.' By the time we reached town, prices had risen to $400 a head. That was the break-though. It was the key to us getting established. It enabled us to pay off the Rural Reconstruction loan and we had young cattle coming on for the following year. Prices held and the next year's sale cleared the debt. Since then we have never been in debt to any bank or finance company, or anyone else.

One of the first things I did was to build an airstrip. With the blitz, a pick, a shovel and an axe I cleared and burnt off a 1500 foot landing-strip and I was able to charter a plane. It proved very handy for emergencies, urgent business or just to be in town in a very short time. To go by road took five hours in a wide loop through Mingela, with the Star and the plenty of creeks to cross, which at that time had no bridges, and the Burdekin only had the low-level bridge, and we could get held up.

I supplied all the measurements of the aerodrome to the Flying Doctor Service and they used it quite a few times for accidents and medical emergencies around the area. There were seven airstrips within a twenty mile radius of Payne's Lagoon and every one of them except mine was unserviceable because they wouldn't control the re-growth on them.

We had the Flying Doctor out once to young Susan when she was pretty sick with pneumonia. They told us on the two-way to give her a shot of penicillin so I pumped some into her. Then the doctor's plane called in on their way back from a trip up to one of the missions in the Gulf and picked her up and took her back with them into hospital in Charters Towers.

Over the years we developed a degree of medical skill here ourselves. Old Bob Morrison was here once and Mum had this big old tomcat that was making a nuisance of himself. Bob volunteered to castrate him for her. So he's got his cutting-knife out and he's put a bit of extra edge on it and he's got this cat wrapped up in a sugar-bag and the cat's not enjoying it very much, and Mum comes out and she says, 'Now Bob! Did you wash your hands before you started?'

We had to get the Flying Doctor out to me once when my horse fell in the pig wallows where they go rooting up the nut grass down the Star River. I was mustering and when he fell the saddle got me right in the small of the back. I was paralyzed from the waist down. I had two black boys with me and I wouldn't let them touch me. I said 'We're not going to let these cattle go. You two boys get them up there and get them in the yard. The car's there at the yard. You can bring the car back after you've got the cattle in the yard.' So back they came about an hour later with the car. I was fairly uncomfortable lying on the ground. One of the boys said to me, 'Ah! Boss! You got dirt all over y' face! I get a rag and wash y'face for yer. Might make y' feel better.' So he pulled his dirty old singlet off and took it down the river and gave it a bit of a swish and brought it back and wiped my face down. It was a bit rankish but he meant well. The two of them had a bit of a conference then. They pulled the car up alongside me and opened the back door. Then they said, 'Ah! We dunno how we're gunna get yer in there, Boss, but leave it to us, eh! We'll work it out.' So then they pounced on me. They grabbed me and threw me straight in on to the back seat, like throwing a bag of spuds in. They said, 'More better one big pain. Git it over quick!' I bit all the buttons off the seat on the way home.

I reckoned I'd be alright in the morning but I wasn't. A couple of the Dotswood fellows came over and gave Wyn a hand to feed me on cups of black tea and so on and the Flying Doctor came out at daybreak the next morning. They brought the stretcher in and put it alongside the bed then lifted the stretcher out through the window. That was an interesting experience. Then they took me out to the airstrip in the back of the blitz. I was in hospital in Charters Towers a couple of months. There is nothing they can do for you, just x-ray you and then feed you on pain-killers. You can't roll over. If you try to move the pain kills you. You just lie there and let nature take its course. The worst part about it is you can't go to the toilet. It's not possible. I told the doctor I was a bit worried about it. He told me, 'Don't worry about it! You'll be like a sheep after a while.'

For their schooling the girls went down to St Margaret's in Brisbane and to St. Gabriel's in the Towers. David, our son, our 'last man and last shilling' didn't take too kindly to this getting an education business. He used to do his Correspondence lessons at the dining room table but he'd always be wanting to be outside. Every chance he got he used to bolt. 'I got something I got to do!' he'd say. He did School of the Air with the two-way and he became a highly competent radio operator. Later on he went to All Soul's in the Towers for a couple of years.

I continued putting in improvements on the place, watching my fences. For pasture improvement I decided to try what was then a new grass, *secca stylo.* Once it gets going the cattle spread it well. But the greatest development of all in my opinion is the solar-pump. Slow-yielding bores equipped with sun pumps can water a hell of a lot of cattle. When they first came out they were very expensive. They are made of highly refined and very expensive silicone; which we gave to the Japs for as good as nothing, $50 a ton, and we pay $30 000 a ton for it refined. The pump is very expensive to install, but properly installed they work like a charm and do everything for free.

For the one down the river, I didn't get much change out of fifteen thousand. It involved cutting the river bank to bury the pipe below flood level, and excavating the bed of the river down to bedrock then back-filling it with graded gravel over the screen, which is twenty-four feet below the low level of the river. That had to be done in a very dry time. Theoretically a big flood won't disturb it, though it hasn't been tested yet.

The other solar pumps are all on low-yielding bores. They are all sealed and can't be interfered with. You've only got to check them every two or three days, maybe once a week. Even then it's not the pump you've got to check; it's cattle getting caught in the trough.

I've only lost a pump once, a conventional pump. The Air Pageant was on down at Smithy's at Woodstock and I'd flown down to it. My son David's wife was to go and check the pump and start it again. She went back up to their house and she told him 'There's no pump there! But the ground's still wet where the water ran out of the pipe.' It must have been pinched that morning. That pump was well back off the road so whoever thieved it had been looking for it.

I had an old blackfellow working for me once; a very good stockman; a good worker. He had a couple of sons back on Palm Island. I said, 'Why don't you get those two boys of yours over; start teaching them a bit of stock work?' He looked at me sorrowfully and he said, 'Ah! Boss! You wouldn't feed them two boys o'mine! Useless young buggers! They don't know how to work.'

I myself have always put a lot of store by what Reg Ansett, the founder of Ansett Airways said; 'Nothing in the world can take the place of persistence and determination.' I agree with Reg. I always reckon that if there's something someone wants to do, and wants to do it badly enough, then they will do it by persistence and determination. That's all it takes. There's no such thing as can't. You just get on and you do it. And a bit of rum doesn't hurt, either.

Ethel Donnellan

INTRODUCTION

I searched for the story of Ethel Donnellan in the archives of the National Library in Canberra and was delighted to find it in the Gammage and Simpson Collection. Many of the people I interview have made reference to this wonderful old lady in their stories. For example, Pauline Rayment, in 'Facing the Wilderness' describes Ethel Donnellan as 'the best friend I ever had.' When I shared my pleasure at having found Ethel's story with Pauline, she told me that she and her husband Charlie had sat by Ethel's bedside in the hospital at Charters Towers in 2002 and tape-recorded some of the memories of the years that they had been neighbours in South West Queenland's Channel Country - neighbours separated by fifty miles of rugged bush terrain and bad roads but in constant touch by Outpost Radio.

No-one reading this account of Ethel Donnellan's life, can doubt that this wonderful lady must have been 'the best friend they ever had' to many an Outback man, woman and child. Who could read the story of the laying-out of the fencer's baby without being moved to tears? Certainly, I couldn't, in writing it; the compassionate bathing of the little body and the practical common sense of ensuring protection of it 'against the ants and the flies'. In a land of intolerable heat and fearsome isolation, where the very sand-hills were capable of picking themselves up and marching in formation upon unwary homesteads, Ethel Donellan brought to the situation the down-to-earth wisdom of many a bush woman before her, of seeing what has to be done and doing it.

Ethel starts her story matter-of-factly with 'I have spent all my life in the Outback'. As we share her memories of the hardships she underwent and over which she triumphed with womanly dignity and courage, we can only marvel at the resilience, fortitude and strength of character of such women and celebrate with pride that they and the Outback they loved are integral to our national story.

Chapter 5...

RED SANDHILL COUNTRY

Ethel Donnellan - Davenport Downs

I spent all of my years in the outback. I was born in 1908 in what they used to call Hergott Springs. This was before the war, the Great War. When the war came they changed the name because Hergott Springs was German and there was trouble about it so it was changed it to Marree. They must have got a bushman to change it because Marree is an Aboriginal word. It means 'springs in the downs'.

My father's people were on a station there called Mulka. He had been there since he was five years old. His father had been a miner and he went up that way sinking wells. There was no fresh water. When Grandfather retired he left Mulka to his three sons. His fourth son went to the war and he married a southern girl and after the war he got one of those soldier settlement blocks. We used to call him 'Alphabetical Dick' because his name was John William Richard Lacy Coles Scobie.

And my father said Mulka wasn't big enough for three families so he took up the adjoining block named Ooroowilanie. Ooroowilanie meant 'a big lot of water running into a catchment', because there was a government dam there that they had put down for travelling stock. There was no other water on the road; just a government tank, fenced off, and with a post with 'W. White' on it. That was some relation of Dad's. My father's name was Alec Scobie, Alexander Frederick Scobie, and his father's name was Alec, too. My father married in his early thirties, in 1907 and I was born a year later.

Ooroowilanie was very pretty in those days. They had several big wells there, all open. You could fall down them. Dad built the house – him and his brothers – out of grass. Dad could do masonry but he didn't have the time at first. It must have been a good season the year they went to Ooroowilanie because that grass was eight to twelve feet high. It came from the lakes. The walls and the roof of the house were made of this cane-grass; tied into bundles. He made a hip roof with a good steep pitch, the roots at the top and the other end down. And never a speck of water got through. He made a big long room about twenty foot wide and sixty foot long, and he put double doors in that end in the hope that he would get enough money to buy a buggy to take Mum around. Mum's mother used to ride to the hounds in England in those rotten side saddles.

But as soon as he could Dad started to build a stone house. He dug the limestones out of the ground with a pick and shovel on his own - and cut them square with a tommyhawk. And he'd take the horses and go down the lake – it was a dry lake – and cut wood and hook it on with chains, and drag it up and chop it up. And he dug a big hole about six foot deep and he'd put kindling in that and then the wood and when it got right to the top he'd set light to it and put the limestone in and burn it. It would go to powder and he'd use that for mortar.

There was some clay-looking stuff around the place, and he'd put the limestone powder with it – I think it was two to one - and mix that with a shovel. When he built a room he'd dig a trench and put the squared limestones in and then he would put the mortar on top then another stone on top until he got the wall right up. And he made it straight with what you call a plumb-ball, a lump of lead he'd melted – on a string - to make it straight, straight as a die. He built four rooms, a dining room and a kitchen and two bedrooms. No bolts or anything. Things like bolts and nails were hard to come by. They had to come up from Adelaide on the train to Marree, and Marree was a hundred and fifty miles away from us and big sand hills to cross.

When I was born Dad said, 'Well, this is virgin country. It will have all sorts of bities and things that will kill a child. So when she's ready to walk we'll have to get a blackfella from the wild blacks to looks after her.' Mum said, 'No blackfella's looking after my baby! We'll get a girl from the siding.' She meant Marree. But Dad said, 'No. That's no good! They'd scream and run away if they saw a snake or anything. A blackfella would tell a little baby what was bad for her. I'll tell him not to touch her.' Mum used to put the poor old blacks down. She said, 'They're too dirty!' But Dad said, 'No they're not! You can go into the shop and buy nice things, a nice blanket and that sort of thing, and you can tell them they've got to wash their dogs before they take them into bed with them.'[1]So they got this old fellow, Kunki. And I learned to talk Kunki's talk quicker than Mum's. I still remember bits; 'murra' was 'hand' and 'mudla' was 'nose'. And so Kunki looked after me when I was little. He wasn't allowed to touch me but he had this whip handle about twenty inches long and he caught hold of it at one end and he poked it at me and I held the other end and he walked me around like that. I thought he was lovely. He was as black as pitch and he had a bone through his nose, in the soft part. They cut that and put the bone through when they are about fourteen, when they start getting whiskers. Kunki had big black whiskers. I wasn't frightened of him. Not a bit. He would come and we would go out on the sand and he would do all sorts of antics to make me laugh and he would show me things, plants and animals. He would point with this stick and he would say, 'Look-out long that fella. Him bitey-bitey fella.' It would be 'Look out long this' and 'Look out long that.' I learnt them

1 The century-old teasing; Alec Scobie's telling his young wife, she whose mother had 'ridden to hounds' in the Old Country, that the Aboriginals could be instructed to 'wash their dogs before they took them into bed with them' indicates that the Australian mastery of the laconic leg-pull was alive and well over a century ago. In my own years in the Northern Territory I was happy to have my baby daughter Elizabeth cared for by Old Alice, of the Wagait tribe, believing that though Alice smoked a crab-claw pipe and lacked several digits from both hands to 'shame' her errant husband, what she lacked in concepts of Western hygiene she more than made up for in vibrant good humour and all-encompassing love for her charge. Elizabeth spent much of her time being passed from arm to arm in the Women's Circles seated all day in the dust beneath the bloodwood trees but was always returned spotlessly clean, liberally anointed with Johnson's Baby powder and happier for the hours of contented love and laughter.

quickly. It was a great education. It is no good people saying the blacks haven't got any brains because they have.

But Kunki wasn't with me all the time. He used to go down to the Mission, the German – Lutheran – mission; not that I think the old Kaiser worried about his religion – but one end of Mulka, known to the Aboriginals as Nidnawandra Kurrakurr Carkina, was joined to the mission. The mission people used to depend a lot on Dad. He'd go down there and tell them what to do with their cattle. They had their own herd, but those Germans weren't stockmen, and they wouldn't employ anybody who hadn't been born in Germany. But the mission did a lot for the blacks. People would come in home and they would say about a certain one, 'He's a mission blackfella. He won't be any good.' But they would be. The mission blacks were good. The blacks weren't as bad as people said. They weren't immoral. The old gins, particularly, had good morals. The Aborigines are just like any other race. Some good and some bad. Every nation has got its rubbish.

In the beginning, when I was little, in a cot, my mother wouldn't have them in the house. She didn't like the smell of them. And they weren't serious enough. They would be laughing and giggling all the time. They would laugh about the mission fellows. They would say, 'That fella! Him mad! Him all day yabba yabba we gottem flea. We no gottem flea. We gottem louse! Dog, he gottem flea!' But as time went on, Mum got used to the idea of having them about the place. And they were clean enough, for those times.

Mum had a terrible dislike of people bringing up their children without education. She said it was wrong; bad for yourself, bad for the children and bad for the country. But they never had the money to send us away to school. She taught us herself at the start. But she wouldn't always tell us the things we wanted to know, if she thought it was something we shouldn't know. So we used to ask Dad.

When we were out riding I'd ask him, when we were right away from Mum. I'd say, 'Dad, what about this….?' Or 'Dad, what about that…?' 'Well' he would say, 'When your mother taught you to write, what did she teach you first?' I said, 'Strokes, like that. Slopey stokes. And you put a dot here and a dot at the bottom and you go out a bit there like that.' He would say, 'Well, what was that for?' I'd say 'That's the way you write. When you write you do it on a slope like that.' He would say, 'Oh, and what next?' I'd tell him, Well, the next thing we put a hook on it, and another hook at the bottom. A line with a hook.' He'd say, 'What then?' And I'd say, "When we put an 'o' and then we put a hook there like that, it makes an 'a'" He would say, 'What did you make that for?' I would tell him, 'That's so you can spell c-a-t.'

Then Dad would say, 'Well, now you're asking me questions, aren't you.' I'd say, 'Yes'. The he would say, 'Well, this is why I can't tell you. When you were born you were a tiny baby. You've seen tiny babies, haven't you?' I said, 'Yes. I did see one.' He said, 'Yes. Well, it grew, didn't it? And you grew, didn't you.' 'Yes,' I said, 'I grew.' 'Well', then when you grew your arms got longer and your legs got longer. Well, your brain is like that, you know. When it's little it doesn't know much and it gets bigger and bigger. Well, life is like that. As you get bigger you will learn these things you are asking me now, but now is too soon.' [2]

Dad could do beautiful plaiting. He started doing it before he was married. He became one of the most famous whip-makers in Australia. There is a special kind of knot named after him, the Scobie Hitch. I've got a trophy that he won at an exhibition. His whips were sent all over the world. The last whip I remember him making when he was very old was for Haile Selassie, the Emperor of Ethiopia. He wrote over for one. Dad's whip handles were carved - before he started plaiting he used to carve the handles first, with dingoes or sheep, those kinds of things. Dad taught me how to plait. I could do any leather-work. The men used to bring in things to me that needed mending; any repair work; I could do all that.

All my brothers became very good stockmen and cattlemen. There was poor old Monty; he had polio when he was little. He had a few operations on his leg. But he could always ride and he was a very good bushman. He went through the Murranji track up there, straight as a die through it and you don't see the sun for two days for the very thick scrub, they say. Yes, Monty was a good stockman and a very good plaiter, too. Some say his whips are the best. And there's also Don and Angus; they're very good. One of Donny's sons took a whip to America and when he cracked it the police came. They thought it was a gun going off in a murder.

Dad didn't start off with cattle. He started off with horses because they were a quicker return. When they were three years old you could break them in. Then he could sell them to buyers for remounts for India. The buyers used to come up to the stations. They'd go round and pick the horses up and walk them down to go on the boat. They never told us that they were going to the army or we would have cried if we thought they were going to the war.

Dad didn't employ stockmen. He didn't have the money. He had to do all his own work himself. When I was little, before the others came along, Mum used to go out and help him although she couldn't ride. There were thirteen kids in her family and she was the only one that couldn't ride. All the others could, both girls and boys. But Mum couldn't.

I was the first born in our family. The first was a girl and the last was a girl. The others, five of them, were all boys. Well, of course I learned to ride when I was about two. I could hold the reins and crack a whip and all the rest of it.

Mum had a lot of work to do with the seven of us. She used to do all her own washing. She had a thing like a broom handle with other bits of broom handle sticking out of it. And you twisted this thing in the water and it would go swish, swish, swish, swish. It was a sort of washing-machine. We had tubs, big old tubs with two handles. I think Grandma gave them to her.

When Dad got a bit of money he started to get a few cattle. There were people called French that had cattle and their country dried out, so they moved their

2 It is tempting to assume that the question Ethel had asked her father was, 'Dad, where do babies come from?' and that his preliminary discourse on the intricacies of forming letters was to give him time to think how best to answer the little girl's question; a charming insight into family relationships of over a hundred years ago. In the original interview Ethel exclaims at this point, 'He was a cunning old devil, he was!' tacitly acknowledging her father's tactful evasion.

cattle up along the road to feed them. The cattle were as poor as sticks. They were just staggering along. And these people gave us one cow because they couldn't shift it any further.

And she turned out to be a wonderful cow; a marvellous milker. Her milk would give a pound of butter. We had a couple of other cows and then Dad got a bull. Mum wouldn't do the milking. She was afraid of the horns and all that. So I used to help Dad do it. I would do the bailing up and he did the milking. And Dad would make a few more whips and as he got a bit of money together he'd get some more cattle, just a few at a time.

But Mum would make the bread. And I would stand on a kerosene case and knead it for her. Those kerosene cases, we used them for everything. We had settees and all made out of them. Everything we had had to be made out of something. The kerosene tins made good buckets. There was no way of getting the water up to the house from the dam. So Dad had a big yoke like a Chinaman's yoke and he'd have a bucket on each side and a chain on a hook. And he would fill them and carry them up to the house and pour them into the tank .He did that for a good many years. But the water was a bit muddy and to settle the mud we would put ashes in it to bring it clear. Not too much or it would make it hard. We would put just a bit in the top and you'd see the mud going down. We'd do it when we were going to bed and in the morning it would be all clear.

Oh, it was a hard lonely life for poor Mum. And then the time came when she couldn't teach us any more. Some of my cousins over on Mulka never had any schooling at all and then they got a Mr. Polkinghorne. I was seven at that time and Dad used to put me on the pommel of his horse and take me down to Mulka. Then Uncle Jim said I could stay there because he had a bigger family and more rooms. First he had just a little cottage but then he built a bigger house. So I used to stay for the five days and then Dad would come and get me.

There was New Well station that was on the edge of Mulka, and then there was Mulka –and then the Oooroowilanie block joined there. And the next block was Mungeranie. That was my uncle. He didn't believe in education; had a good one himself but never mind about anybody else.

When the war came, Mr. Polkinghorne that they had teaching there, left to go and enlist and go to the war. So then we had Mr. Stephens. He was a mongrel. He gave me the cane, six handed, for swearing, and I never swore. We weren't allowed to swear. We never swore at all. And that caning stiffened my hands. And my auntie sat me on a box out in the sun because it was so cold. And then Uncle Jim was coming home. He'd been up to some other settlers who were leaving and he had bought their furniture and a drag with twelve bullocks in it. And this smarty, Mr. Stephens goes out to help Uncle Jim, thinking he would get into trouble about me with him, because he would have. And he took the collar off Old Faith, the leading mare, and bent over to put it down, and Old Faith bit him on the behind. I clapped my hands and they all heard me.

And then Mum said, 'It's no use having men. We'll get an older married lady with a child of her own and she'll have some other interests. So then we got Mrs

Bridgeland, and her rotten boy. He taught us more things that we shouldn't know than she taught us that we should know. She only stayed a few months.

And Mum said, 'Well, we'll see the government, if they can give us a teacher.' So down she goes (presumably to Maree) and there was two men. There was Mr. Butterfield who was the governor (possibly the Shire Clerk) who looked after our part and there was Mr. Mosely; he was the Frome fellow. And she went to Butterfield. 'Oh!' he said. 'They won't go out to that god-forsaken place! No. You can't get a teacher there.' So she went to Mosely. This Butterfield and Mosely used to fight. They say old Butterfield even used to punch poor old Mr. Mosely. So Mum went to Mr. Mosely. She said, 'Mr. Mosely, Mr. Butterfield can't get us a teacher. Do you think......?' 'Oh!' says Mr. Mosely, 'I can get you a teacher! Only too pleased to!' Mum was cunning!

He said he had four to choose from and he said to Mum, 'Take your pick.' Mum said, 'I think I'll have that farmer's daughter. She sounds as though she could stand it out there.' So we brought her out. And she was good. Miss Elphick, her name was. And she stayed a full year.'

We had a lot of trouble with dingoes on Oooroowilanie. The place was overridden with them. I can remember seeing a pack of forty dogs. The government used to pay us seven shillings and sixpence a scalp for them. Grandfather had started out with sheep on Mulka but he had to change over to cattle for the dingoes.

Sand was always a bit of a problem. You'd get bad sand storms. You couldn't see your hand before your face. Terrible sand storms. It would blow up against fences and buildings; and up against the house. When the wind came from the south we'd have a sand hill at the back of the house. If it came from the north we'd have a sand hill at the front. But it didn't build against the walls of the house because Dad had built a lee and the sand stopped there. But at the old mission station at Killalpannie it would build up right up. It would come right in at the bedroom windows, because the silly old things, being German, they didn't know. But they had built a beautiful church, a Lutheran church, there.

I was twenty-one when I married my husband Frank; twenty-one in March and married in July. My husband had been educated in Adelaide. He was one of a family of thirteen. His grandfather came from Scotland, from Glascow and when his grandfather died his grandma took Frank and sent him to some Freemason's, and he grew up there. He was six when he went there and he grew up there until he was fifteen and his mother wanted him back. So they sent him back to Oodnadatta.

So then he did station work. He was a good stockman and ended up managing properties. He was managing when he was eighteen years old. Then the people bought another property that joined and he was managing them both. First he was on Dalhousie.[3] Then Mount Dare, south of Alice Springs.

3 The author has been to the ruins of Dalhousie homestead while retracing the southern section of the historic Overland Telegraph Line with friends Nic and Brenda Wilson in 1991. The stone-built chimney and tumbled walls stand in a sea of glittering stone that was once the floor of an ancient sea. You can only stare in disbelief at the 360 degree treeless horizon and marvel that it ever could ever have been possible for men to have brought livestock there and expected them to survive. The only source of water was a string of salt-encrusted mound-springs.

When I met Frank – he was really Frank William but he wouldn't have the William – he'd been out from Oodnadatta and there was a drought on. And all he had were two myalls and one yellafella and they had to shift these cattle. And when they had done shifting them he said, 'Now, they'll have to be shifted again in a fortnight.' And he came in to the owners and they told him, 'Muster the fats. We'll get the fats away while they are in condition.' So he mustered them with these two blackfellas and this yellafella and got them on to this water. And he thought they would do there for a while and then he'd shift them onto another water.

But when he went in to the owner – he didn't have much faith in this owner – the owner said, 'We want you to take the fats in and look after them.' He thought it couldn't be done; before he got there they would want shifting again and he only had the two blacks to help and they wouldn't want to do as he told them. But he thought, 'I'd better do as I'm told. It's not my place. He's paying me.' But when he went back out to the station the blackfellas told him, 'Oh, we haven't shifted them yet. They'll be alright.' He said, 'Oh, no they won't be! They'll be dead!' So he got the two blackfellas and the half-caste and they went out to where the cattle had been left. And most of them were dead alright. They were dead in the bog. And the only water that was there was where the cattle had been making tracks into the bog and it was just mud. There was nothing that they could drink. So he shot the ones that were bogged and he took the ones that could still move and started walking them on to this other water. And the four men, they were nearly perishing. They had stones in their mouths for the saliva. And it was perishing cold. And the two blackfellas just sat on their horses. They'd give up. And the yellafella, he just slid off his horse and laid under a tree. Frank had to get off his horse and threaten him and lift him or else he'd have died there. And the exertion strained Frank. But he got the yellafella on to his horse and into the station. By then Frank couldn't talk. His tongue was all swollen, and his lips and his mouth. He laid in his hut for four days and when he could talk, he talked alright. He went and told the boss what he could do with the job.

So he went into Oodnadatta and of course, he had no money. They never used to get much money those days. And someone offered him the job to take a mob of horses to Queensland, so he took it. And when he was on his way, old Mr. Pratt – he was a travelling manager for Sir Sydney Kidman – he come looking for a manager for Cowarie station that was next to my father's property, joining it. And Frank said he'd take it. He'd take anything. So that was how I come to meet him.

He was managing Cowarie when we got married in 1929, in Marree. But you go from the frying pan into the fire because in '29 we had a dreadful drought. I went straight out to the camp with him. We didn't have a honeymoon. The stock camp was the honeymoon. And straight to work. Mum didn't approve, but that was the sort of life I wanted. Then I did some droving. I'd go out and meet Frank with the cattle and help bring them down. There was nothing for the poor beggars to eat. We used to have to feed them along. It was my job to bring the lame ones up, steady, steady because Frank only had new chums for stockmen. He had a good head stockman, a half-caste from Bungalow in Alice Springs.

I think we started droving in 1930, it must have been, because Ray was born in 1931. But I didn't tell Frank I was pregnant. I was sneaky. I didn't say anything. I stayed on and brought the first mob of cattle over the plain after a flood. And the yellow-top was up to stirrup high and you couldn't see the ground for it. Frank had to go on ahead and pick the camp site and I was left with the cattle and this one fool boy. He was no good at all. He couldn't take a wing because then he would have no-one to talk to!

And when we got over the plain you could see the line of the trees where the channel was. And I knew as soon as the cattle saw that they'd split up in small mobs in and out the trees and we'd never see them again. Anything to get away from us and look for water. I thought, 'I'll have to turn them in but I don't want to have to gallop because I don't know what's under our feet for the yellow-top and if we fall it might be the end of the baby.' And the cattle were striding out, striding out and suddenly away they went. I thought, 'I'll have to chance it.' And the next thing I heard galloping, galloping behind me and it was Frank. He got to the lead and he stopped them.

Then I thought the baby might be starting to come so we took the short-cut through Dad's place and Frank said to me, 'Now you go on in to your mother at the homestead. You're going to be alright. You know the country. I have to see to the cattle.' So I went in on my own and Mum's eyes nearly popped out of her head when she saw me; 'Why didn't you say! Why didn't you tell us!' Oh! There was a to-do!

But my baby wasn't born at Ooroowilanie after all. Frank handed the cattle over to another fellow to send them then he jumped on the mail truck and came back and took me in his Chev Tourer- and Dad, he came too – into Marree and Ray was born there.

We shifted to Davenport in 1932 because Cowarie was droughted out. Davenport was another Kidman property and they shifted Frank up. We went up there in Frank's Chev Tourer. An unmade road and big sandhills. We'd have to back up a hundred yards or so and get a good pace up and then fly over; take your life in your hands, as it were. But we got there eventually. The house was terrible; just an old store. The main house had been burnt down. No electricity and a big old wood stove. The kitchen was a fair way from the house and I had to run backwards and forwards, and all the fly-wire broken and hanging down. But the travelling managers came up and they decided to build a kitchen on for me and put in some rooms and cement floors. Sir Sidney Kidman was a very good firm to work for. They did their best. There was a howling drought on and I understood. Having come from my father's property I knew you couldn't have things that you couldn't afford. I made curtains and made the place look decent. We got some furniture. At first all there was to sit on were some old squatters chairs with long legs.

It was difficult to get good stockmen because they couldn't afford to pay big wages with the drought on and no income. Sometimes I'd have to leave the kitchen, ride out and help with the stock work then come back and cook their tea.

One time Frank was away - see, Frank at that time, as well as managing Davenport, was also managing Palparara and Diamantina Lakes. Davenport was

3 000 square miles and with Palparara and Diamantina Lakes it was 8 000 square miles. It was a big thing. My brother, Angus Scobie, was there for many years running the camp. Frank had to do all the books and all the saddlery. When we first came there all the horses had sore backs. But Frank knew about saddlery. In those days you had to do whatever you had to do, like it or not. So this time Frank was away and some visitors were expected and I didn't have any meat for them. I had to go out to the bullock paddock and find a killer. But I couldn't kill a bullock. There was a man there doing some yard building and he shot it for me and I skinned it and cut it up and brought the meat back.

Davenport Downs homestead, the home of Frank and Ethel Donnellan for over forty years. Davenport Downs was a Sir Sidney Kidman property.

I made bread every second day. I could cook thirteen loaves at a time in the big stove. There were two ovens. I'd put the little single loaves in one oven and the big double loaves in the other. But before I could make the bread I'd have to cart the flour over from the store, a fifty pound bag, on my shoulder, because often we didn't have a cowboy. It was too isolated for them and they wouldn't stay. And if the flour had weevils in it you had to put it out in the sun to drive the weevils out, and you ate it just the same.

It was always difficult to get workers and stockmen because they didn't understand the conditions. They thought you could work cattle in the middle of the day, but you can't. We would sit down in the middle of the day and work the cattle in the cool of the day. City fellows just didn't understand. They liked to stick to their hours.

When the boys went away to school they went to Thornburgh in Charters Towers. We had a few pack-horse trips meeting the mail-truck at Brighton when the floods were up. Seventy five mile and quite a few creeks in between. We had to cross the Mayne. When the Mayne comes down its pretty big. It hits the Diamantina just there. We had to make a canvas boat to get across. You get the best camp-sheet you've got and spread it out. And you put a pack-saddle either end and you pull the camp-sheet up over the pack-saddles. You put all your gear in between, with a stick to keep it level and then you swim and pull it and somebody behind swims and pushes it. The boys had tin suit-cases so that the water wouldn't get in. We swam the horses across and the boys swam over to catch them and they jumped on the last horse and rode him catch the others. They were only little fellows. Then when we got to Brighton Downs they would take them into Winton in their car. They took the train from Winton to Charters Towers. And we had to get back to Davenport the same way as we come.

The homestead at Davenport was right on the outside channel of the Diamantina and after rain like that we'd get floods. In the big flood of 1950 it came right up into the house. And there'd be snakes everywhere. Up the windmill, in the house, dozens of snakes washed out of the river.

The pedal radio on which Ethel Donnellan called the Flying Doctor Base in Cloncurry when accidents occurred on the station.

At first on Davenport we didn't even have a wireless but after a few years they put one in for us; a pedal set. You had to pedal it. We were able to call Cloncurry then. Cloncurry had the first Flying Doctor Base. Our call sign was 8UV and Diamantina Lakes was 8XD. It made a marvellous difference and you got a fair bit of help over the air when something went wrong. You had a big medicine chest and everything was numbered and you were explained what it was. They would tell you what was in it and you learned something from them. And you could talk to the doctor. But the static was the problem. Sometimes you wouldn't be able to hear a blessed thing. There was one time at Oooroowilanie when I didn't now what to do. This chap was yarding cattle and his horse fell with him. It was just on dark, the sun had gone down and this chap broke his leg and the bone was sticking through, sticking out of the skin. They brought him straight over to the house to me, of course.

I got on to the Flying Doctor and I was calling and calling, but you couldn't hear for the static. Just crash! Crash! Crash! Then all of a sudden a voice came on and it said, 'Are you in trouble? Do you want help?' 'Yes!' I said, and I explained to the voice – the doctor I thought it was – and I explained what had happened. And he said, 'Where do you live?' I said, 'Half way between Birdsville and Marree.' He said, 'Well. Where's that?' And I got annoyed because I thought he was a useless doctor if he didn't know the places he was going to have to come to. He said, 'What country are you in? 'I said, 'Australia, of course!' He said, 'Well, you've called America!' America came though!

And he said, 'Tell me what you want. I might be able to help you.' So I told him. He said, 'You want to put ....' And he give me a funny name. I said, 'Oh! I don't know anything called that!' He said, 'Well, if you're in Australia you call it Friar's Balsam.' I said, 'I've done that. I've poured it over. But it is still bleeding.' He said, 'Yeah. It will drip for a while and then it will stop. It'll be alright. Don't worry. And now I'll get some more information for you.' But he faded out and I couldn't even thank him or anything. But I did what I could. The Friar's Balsam stopped the bleeding and in the small hours of the morning I finally got through to the doctor. He said, 'I'll be down at first light.' We didn't have much of a strip then. We had just cleared a bit away. But he came down at first light - just the little plane they had then - and took him away. I heard afterwards that he was alright.

And at Davenport we had a tragedy about a little baby. Old Tommy Green and his brothers, they didn't have much education; didn't have any. And Tommy had a fencing contract to do the boundary between Monkira and Davenport and he also had the mail run to Davenport. But he didn't have anything in the way of a tool box. All he had was a bar of soap and a box of matches and a knife. And if he got a hole in anything, the fuel tank, or anything, he'd sharpen a match and stick it in. And to do that sixty mile run it would take him, oh, goodness knows how many hours.

And their baby, he was five months old, took sick at their camp. And the poor woman she did what she could for it of course, but she had nothing to do it with. The manager of the place where they were fencing was away and his wife too, and they had the place locked up. So they come down to us and when they pulled up at the house, I thought, 'Well, that's a funny thing for them to do.' They used to always pull up over at the kitchen. So, I went out and I said, 'Look, the cook's in bed, but if you like to come in I'll get you something to eat or a cup of tea or something.' 'Oh, thanks,' Tommy said. I said, 'I'll take the baby.' And they give me the baby. And when they did a hand come up on my shoulder and he said, 'I hope you don't mind. It's dead.' 'Oh! No!' I said. 'I didn't know!'

The mother had a little girl about three and she'd already lost a previous baby so she must have been heart-broken. So I took them in and I said to the book-keeper's wife – she always knew everything before anyone else did - I said, 'Will you take Mrs Green into the bathroom and get her and the little girl a shower. I'll put the kettle on and then I'll attend to the baby.' The baby was, well, it had been 104 in the shade that day, and they'd left their camp at sun-up and it was twenty past nine at night, and he was just going a bit coloured in the tummy and those places. I put him in cold water, bathed him, sponged him with cold water. And I got the book-keeper to get - we used to get the dried fruit in nice pine boxes, 28lb boxes - and I told him to get one of these and I lined it with an old quilt and put the baby in it.

And he had one eye, oh, a beautiful blue eye it was – I can still see it – wide open, and I put a coin on it to close it. And then I half-filled our cement washing tub with water and put a drum in there and put the box on top of it and put a little copper over it to cover it so the ants and the flies couldn't get at it when the sun came up. Then we were all ready and Frank goes out digging a grave.

And while he was digging the grave, this girl, the mother, comes and she says to me, 'We want it buried as a Roman Catholic.' I said, 'Well, we're not Roman Catholics. We're Presbyterians. But I'll see what I can do.' So I looked around. We hadn't been at Davenport very long at this time but I found a prayer book, a little Roman Catholic prayer book. And I looked but it didn't have a burial service. The Presbyterian has the burial service. But the only thing I could find was a prayer that the priest reads to a dying person.

So I said to the girl, 'Look, do you want this? I know Frank won't mind reading it, though he's Presbyterian. We've only got one Roman Catholic here, the cook. I'll go and ask him; he might know something.' But the cook said, 'No, I don't know anything about religion. I used to run away down the creek when it was church time; when the priest come.'

So at the grave, Frank read the little prayer out, that's how we did it. But I noticed the cook was there, cleaned up, for all he'd said. So the little fellow is buried there with two other graves that were on Davenport when we come there. And later they put a headstone on it. But I'm not sure they put it on the right one.

And then young Maguire, he was buried there. The river, the Diamantina - an outside channel of the Diamantina; the house was built right on it - come down in a big flood, and my sister and her boyfriend, they all went in for a swim. And this young Maguire would go in too. And Jean said to him, 'You want to watch out.' But he dived in. And he didn't come up. They dived for him and dived for him but they couldn't get him. A few days later the cowboy was down where the fence of the night paddock went across the big hole there, and he found him, caught up. So young Maguire is buried on Davenport and another young dark fellow, too.

And Dad, well, it was a battle for him and Mum for many years on Ooroowilanie. Dad was thirty-two or thirty-three when he got it and he was seventy-five when he died. But he had sold it and retired by then; retired and gone to live in Marree. He was a Justice of the Peace there. They grabbed him straight away for the courthouse because they knew he understood the blacks. He knew the good ones from the bad ones and if there were any causing trouble Dad would sort it out. If there were any killings among them Dad would decide whether it was 'Accidental' and if he was doubtful he would send them down to Port Augusta to be properly tried.

An Officer and a Gentleman

Introduction

The phrase, 'An Officer and a Gentleman' might well have been coined for Rob Whelan. It comes as something of a surprise, then, to learn, on hearing this account of his life story, that Rob never went to any of Queensland's Great Public Schools, that in fact he had very little formal education, and that though he served four and a half years on active service in the Commandoes during World War Two he was never an officer. None the less, anyone meeting Rob for the first time immediately senses that they are shaking the firm hand of a man with every quality of leadership, from the quiet but authoritative calm of his voice, the relaxed assurance of his bearing, and the sense that his word on any matter is as good as a pledge of honour.

I was particularly struck, during the tape-recording sessions, by Rob's remarkable power of understatement. Although he spent months living as a guerilla fighter in the mountains of Timor with the Second Fourth Commando Company of two hundred and fifty which managed to immobilize two divisions of the Japanese army, killing over fifteen hundred of the enemy for the loss of forty of their own men, and possibly preventing an enemy landing in Australia's north, Rob never once resorts to dramatics in the telling. There are no 'blood and guts' in his account. Fired upon after a successful ambush by a Japanese pistol-gunner, Rob merely mentions how much faster it can make you dive for cover, even, with remarkable generosity of spirit, giving the pistol-gunner the accolade, 'courageous'. He admits volunteering to remain behind on Timor when the main force was evacuated Gallipoli-style, not for reasons of heroism but simply because his six best mates did, and that he would 'never be able to look them in the eye again if he didn't.' Larry Dalhunty, writing in the North Queensland Register in October 1999, remarks of the Timor Commandoes of which Rob and his 'mates' were part, 'The exploits of these men provide enough material for a dozen adventure movies. If they had been Americans they would have all been heroes.'

Rob and his charming wife Margaret now live at Brackley, their retirement property on the Lynd Highway north of Charters Towers. The gracious new homestead is like a centrefold from the pages of Home Beautiful, each room enhanced by enviable examples of Margaret's collection of Australian art. Brackley homestead seems built for hospitality, the wide front verandahs have insets of polished timber for comfortable seating between the supporting pillars. This archetictural detail seems to say, 'Come on in! You're welcome!' Inset into the tiled floor of the front entrance is the dark blue double diamond of Rob's wartime Commando Company, the Second/ Fourth Independent. In the distance, across the newly laid-out gardens, can be seen the bulk of coastal Mount Elliot, reduced to a mere whisper on the horizon, across the valley of the mighty Burdekin, explored over a century and a half ago by Joseph and William Hann, Rob's intrepid forefathers.

The late Eddie Hackman's bronze, 'The Stockman', is iconic of The Stockman's Hall of Fame, at Longreach, Western Queensland.

Chapter 6...

AN OFFICER AND A GENTLEMAN

Rob Whelan – Pastoralist And Soldier

Getting the wagon down Herveys Range was the hardest bit. The old bullock-track was narrow and there were steep pinches with a fair drop over the side. The brakes would never have held. But Dad had been around the bush all his life. He felled a tree, hitched it behind the wagon, and that steadied it for the descent. I was six years old at the time and my sister Bae was only three but we were both on horse-back helping push the cattle down. That's my earliest memory. This was in 1926 and we were moving to our new place, ten thousand acres, at Bluewater, north of Townsville.

My father's family had come from Ireland and had been all over the mining fields of the north. Dad had been a miner at Bendigo and he was always a sick man on account of this and not long after we got to Bluewater he died of miners' phthisis. So my three sisters, Elizabeth, always called Bae, June and Barbara, were sent up to Maryvale station, where Mum's parents were, to be brought up by Grandma Clarke. At ten I was the eldest so I stayed on at Bluewater to help Mum. In the 'thirties things were very difficult and those were also very dry years. Bluff Downs were shifting their cattle down to the coast and I did a bit of work for them; not getting much in the way of education except a bit of Correspondence.

A couple of years later Mum married Len Carrington who leased a place just outside Townsville, known as The Queen's Farm, because it was owned by the Queen's Hotel. It was on the south side of the river where the University is now. The lease payment was to keep the Queens's supplied with firewood.

I got on well with my step-father though he could be pretty fiery. He was a good man with an axe and I'd give him a hand cutting the firewood for the Queens. We had two draught mules and a four-wheeled wagonette. We'd fell the trees and saw the timber into lengths of about two foot six. (35cms).There was also a herd of dairy cows. Often we'd be milking by 2 o'clock in the morning, and then I'd ride my horse in to Mundingburra School. There was no bridge and I would cross the river through the sandy shallows where the stock route came through. The Aitkenvale area was all open country in those days; long grass and Chinee apple. There was a horse paddock at the school for the four or five kids that rode.

The Maryvale grandparents sent the three girls away to boarding school and I was offered the chance to go to All Souls. But I told them, No, I didn't want to go. Len, my step-father, told me, 'I tell you what I'll do. You can have the cows and milk them and you can have the money from that. So I did that. I used to save it up and put it in a little .22 bullet case. And at the end of six weeks I had six pounds. My step-father said to me, 'These old cows need a bit of feeding. You'd better give me that money.' So I was a bit disillusioned with dairy farming.

My Uncle Edgar Clarke, who was running Maryvale for his mother, said to me, 'Y'know, you're never going to retire on what you're earning now. You'd better come and work at Maryvale.' So I went up to the Towers on the train and then out on the old mail truck. Before that it had been a four-in-hand coach owned by a chap named Peter Nolan who'd run it for twenty seven years; just a buck-board with a seat across the front and a tarpaulin he'd rigged across the back. He used to overnight at Hillgrove station; change the horses and then carry on up to Clarke River.

We used to think going to Maryvale was wonderful when we were kids, although the old Grandfather and Grandmother were pretty strict; you couldn't go racing through the house, or come in without taking your hat off; and at meal times you sat up straight and used your knife and fork properly. They had Aboriginals working on the place; some of them born there. There was one family named Masso. The father was a South Sea Islander, a Kanaka. He was on the place until he died; a fine old man; one of nature's gentlemen. All the Masso family were very fine people.

But starting work on Maryvale wasn't any holiday. In the first couple of months I never had a day off. One day Uncle Edgar and I were taking some bulls out to one of the camps and he said to me, 'You haven't had a day off since you've been here, have you. We'll have to see you get a Sunday off, sometime.'

I worked on Maryvale until I was twenty-one and then went down to Townsville to enlist in the army. That was on the 27th November 1941. Old Dr Brienl, a gruff old German, examined me. He said, 'Get your clothes off. Right! Turn round! You want to join the army? I said, 'Well, I'm not looking to be any hero.' He said, 'Righto! Away you go!'

So I went down to Redbank, the big army training camp outside Brisbane. I'd been there about a fortnight when the Japs came into the war. We were on parade one day when an officer came out and called for volunteers to join a special unit. I was standing beside a fellow named Jimmy Martin. We said to one another, 'What about this?' So we went for the interview and they discovered I could ride and shoot and find my way around in the bush so we were accepted.

We were sent to Wilson's Promontory for training in unarmed combat, that sort of thing. Most of the blokes there were from the bush. We were the Fourth Independent Company. We trained and I have never been fitter in my life. One morning I said, 'I'm not going to do normal PT this morning. I'm going to the top of Mt Oberon!' which was about two thousand feet and three miles away. I got to the top in forty-two minutes and back to the camp in eighteen, which I thought was pretty good. But one of the others said, 'What are you talking about! There was a Pommy major here a bit back and he did it in thirty-two!' So I never talked about it much after that.

At the end of our training we were sent by train from Melbourne to Mount Isa. In those days of slow old steam trains they had to pull up every so often and replenish with water. We would use many of the old water tanks beside the line to get a bit of a clean-up. The tanks had a long canvas hose that we called 'the elephant's trunk' and we'd turn it on and all get under. You weren't supposed to be doing it. On one occasion the Officer of the Day said, 'Come on, you fellows! Back on board! Through the first window and in!' So, stark naked and dripping wet, I dived in through the nearest window, straight into the 2IC's lap! He gave one look! I said, 'Sorry, sir!' and bolted, grabbing my shorts around me.

From Mount Isa we went on by truck to Katherine. It was pretty hot and dry. They gave us a hot beer at Banka Banka and it tasted just as good as cold. The Japs had bombed Darwin and we passed the evacuees heading south at Elliot. The extent of the bombing wasn't known down south. It was kept hush-hush so as not to cause panic. We had six weeks in Katherine with very little to eat. A mate and I went bush and knocked off a bullock and we were up before the CO for being away from camp without permission. But two days later we were called back and told, 'Right! You fellows go out and see if you can find us a bit of beef!'

We were told that the Japs had already landed and the Fourth Independent Company was spread across the Top End from the Roper in the east to Auvergne on the Victoria River to report their movements. After some time we were pulled back to Adelaide River and then moved up to Darwin and told we were going to Timor. The damage resulting from the bombing raids on Darwin was pretty shocking. The Post Office had copped a direct hit, but we weren't allowed to wander around looking at things. We were camped near the wharf, which had been badly damaged, ready to embark for Timor. When we saw what the Japs had done we thought, 'Oh! Well! We'll shoot a bit straighter when we catch up with the bastards.'

The Second/ Second Independent Company had been in Dili on Timor when the Japs landed and they had withdrawn back into the hills. Our task was to reinforce them and then relieve them. We landed in the dark and then had to get inland as quick as we could. We each had a forty pound pack and whatever weapon we had. I was a Bren-gunner and you needed a fair bit of ammo. A Bren is a machine gun that fires 303 bullets; I had great respect for its ability. It's a beautiful weapon. The Bren gunner carries the gun; twenty-three pound, and your off-sider carries the ammo.

So we moved into the hills and dispersed in groups; a captain in charge and a lieutenant to each section. The Japs would have known we were there because the destroyer that had transported us across went aground on the rocks in the process, but the local people treated us wonderfully. We lived amongst them and were fed by them and they were our Intelligence. They hated the Japs because they had been badly treated by them.

Timor is something like a man's hat. It has a coastal plain all round like a brim and mountains in the middle. The Japs knew the Australians were in the mountains but they had become very wary of marching in to look for them. The Second Seconds had laid some very successful ambushes. A crack officer had been sent especially to get rid of them. He was known as the Singapore Tiger and he always wore white gloves when he went into action. The Second Seconds had very little trouble wiping his entire column out.

We knew they were constantly using the road from Manatutu to Baucou so five of us went down on to an open, bare ridge overlooking the road where it came up a bit of a rise, and laid an ambush. We were about a hundred and seventy yards up above the road, looking straight down. We got a utility with five Jap officers in it. We didn't want the utility to go again, either, so we put a couple of rounds into the engine.

About a fortnight later, twelve of us went back to the same spot, the theory being that they would never expect us to hit them in the same place twice. We got into position on the hillside overlooking the road, and along came seven trucks loaded with troops. The old burnt-out utility was still there. And as the leading truck came up, the fellows in the back were laughing and pointing to it. We were able to stop the first and the last trucks and did the ones in the middle a bit of no-good. Then we pulled out. But the second Bren gunner was a bit late moving. And a very courageous Jap pistol-gunner in the first truck - none of us saw him jump – came charging up the hill. And when 'Kit' Carson went to get up, this fellow was right on top of him. 'Kit' grabbed his Bren gun; it was red hot from firing - and ran, and this fellow took several shots at him. But he must have been shaking from running up the hilll because he missed him. So we tore down the hill and dived into a bit of a gully that was full of prickly pear, and you could hear these pistol bullets going 'Ssst! Ssst!' into the big fat prickly-pear leaves. It took half an hour to disappear back into the hills instead of the normal two. That's the power of a pistol-gun! It makes you move a lot quicker knowing it's behind you!

After five and a half months of this it was decided by Headquarters that we would have to be pulled out [1]. We were told we had to rendezvous on the east coast with a destroyer, the *Arunta*. So we started to move east. We had Timor ponies, loaded with gear; one loaded with new army boots. At one part of the track there was a fair drop over the side and this pony started to slip. Our C.O. Dan O'Connors somehow got himself up on the outside of the line and heaved it back. There was no way he was going to lose those boots!

One night when we were camped up in the hills above the low-lying country - well! - the fireflies! I've never seen a better display! Next morning; about half-past four or five, I heard the O.C. calling for volunteers to stay behind on the island. I said to one of my mates, 'Well, that poor bastard's got a strange sense of humour, hasn't he!' Ten minutes later there was Dan O'Connor in front of us asking who would stay. We had an Englishman with us, Lofty Hubbard. He said, 'We all volunteer, Sir! And my six best mates including Hayes, Hansen and this Hubbard put their hands up. I looked at them, and I thought, 'God! I'll probably never see them again, but if I did I'd never be able to look them in the face!' It wasn't anything

1 Callinan, Bernard J; Independent Company; The 2/2 and 2/4 Australian Independent companies in Portuguese Timor; p.xxvii; After 1942 air power was able to control the Japanese threat to Darwin. The presence of the Japanese on Timor was then no longer seen as a threat to the Allies. It was decided to withdraw the Australian Commandoes and let the enveloping movements of the later stages of the war isolate them and force their capitulation without further loss of life.'

to do with heroics. It was that you stuck by your mates. So I said, 'Aw! I'll be in it!' And Dan O'Connor said, 'Alright! We don't want a bloody auction!'

We got down on to the beach, where the destroyer was standing off shore under cover of dark. The sea was running high and one dinghy with a lot of the equipment turned over and lost the lot. A lot more was abandoned on the beach. The captain of the ship kept sending signals, 'Last boat! Can't wait!' Those that were strong swimmers swam out beyond the breakers to get picked up. The officer of the last lot of blokes to get off the beach still owes me a beer. He said, 'I'll buy you a drink when you get back to Australia.'

Rob Whelan, right, rescued by American submarine, on his return to Perth after months of service behind enemy lines in Timor.

So ten of us stayed. Actually, there were thirteen of us in all, because we were joined by three others who had been away on a patrol and hadn't made it back to the rendezvous in time. One of their mates had been killed [2] Our job was to get information about Jap movements and relay it back to Darwin. But once the main force had got away our first task was getting rid of all the equipment off the beach before daylight so the Japs wouldn't wake up to it that the unit had pulled out. As long as we had them thinking the force was still on the island it tied up numbers of their troops and kept them out of New Guinea. But all we had time to do was to throw the gear back into the scrub

Then we headed back into the forest and set up a bit of a camp. The idea was to lie low for a while before we began moving about. But one of the locals informed on us. I don't blame them because they were being shockingly mistreated by the Japs to get information out of them; and this fellow led them to our camp. So we had to get out of there in a bit of a hurry. We lost most of our equipment and the wireless was damaged. We could receive but not send. At the other end of the island were a few Z Force fellows and they were having a bad time too. They were a separate lot, trained to get information; not so much for fighting. They had a wireless and could transmit but not receive. We joined up with them and got a message out to Darwin. A couple of Hudsons came over and dropped us some more equipment including a wireless and the order that we were to be picked up by an American submarine and where the rendezvous would be.

We had a four day walk to the rendezvous point, including wading through swamps for hours on end. And right in the middle of this swamp we came across a little island and a hut where one of the Portuguese administrators was hiding out with a few Timorese. They had some native whiskey called bomba in a genuine

2 ibid; p.22; ' The volunteer party comprised Signallers Ellwod, Wynne and Key, Corporals Hayes and Richie, Lance-Corporals Hubbard and Whelan, and Privates Duncan, Fitness, Jacobsen, Phillips and Miller. A few days later the party from Ainaro, comprising Corporal Wilkins, Signaller Frazer and Private Finch joined them having, despite suffering badly from malaria and tropical ulcers, fought their way through Japanese lines. In one skirmish Howell had been killed. The role of the Force was to observe and report on Japanese activities.'

old White Horse whiskey bottle. A couple of swigs of that each and we were right! We didn't quite get up to JC's tricks but we made it to the rendezvous point on the beach. We rigged up a sheet to signal the sub that we were ready. But that was a long day, when we were on the beach, waiting. There was nowhere to run and we knew the Japs were behind us. We had tied up three thousand Japs looking for us, which was the main good to come out of the whole exercise.

The rubber dinghies that the Hudson had dropped were damaged; only one was any use. But Bill Hayes – he had been in a bank before the war; and he'd been a life-saver – paddled out in the dark in it to the submarine, the USS *Gudgeon.* Bill had grown a massive black bushy beard, and when he put his head up over the side of the sub, one of the Americans said, 'Hell! It's Father Neptune himself coming on board!' Anyhow; they got us all on board and we ran on the surface all that night then submerged the next day. The air was pretty thick with the extra men. Subs weren't so sophisticated in those days. But those Americans treated us pretty well. They gave us fresh clothes. They even gave up their own bunks for us. They fed us up; ice-cream and tinned chicken and coffee. And that made us sick because we hadn't eaten anything decent for months. What we were mainly craving was fresh bread and butter. It took eight days to get down to Fremantle[3] and we had a couple of weeks in hospital and then got two weeks' leave. Out of our own group we had lost six killed in Timor and forty in all from the Company but we had killed fifteen hundred of the enemy.

In New Guinea we lost our greatest number of men when our convoy was attacked somewhere between Milne Bay and Finchhafen. The LST behind the one I was in was hit by a torpedo bomber. We lost some thirty of the Second Fourth Company at one go. Once those LSTs come under fire they lock the water-tight doors so that even if they are holed the ship still has buoyancy. Our fellows were trapped in the accommodation quarters and drowned.

We went to Milne Bay; and fought most of the way to the top of Sattelburg - mostly mud and slush - and on to the Song River. From there we were sent over to Morotai. There was no jungle on the beach there. The Americans had blasted it out of existence. Then over to Tarakan and copped a lot of casualties there. It was on Tarakan in the mopping-up stages of things that the news came through that it was all over.

Once the second atomic bomb had been dropped it was very obvious that the end was near. I didn't shed any tears over the Yanks deciding to use the bomb. We knew what the Japs had been capable of in the places they had over-run. And anyone who doesn't think they wouldn't have done the same thing in Australia is talking 'what-the-bull-left-behind'. When the news came through that it was all over we had a bit of a celebration. We'd been preparing some home-brew; dried fruit and sugar in a four gallon drum of water then you leave it under your bed until it bubbles; and that's your beer. But some of them put it through a still. They'd rig up a long tube and wind it round a bit, and put some fuel in a pile of sand underneath and let that heat it up and what dripped out the end of the pipe was

3 Then a major submarine base for the Indian Ocean used by both the US and British navies.

clear white liquid – pure alchohol. It never interested me because you got no lift from it. There was no humour and talk like you get with a beer.

Then we came home in an LST to Brisbane. It felt pretty good to be heading up the Brisbane River. When we were tying up, one fellow from Western Australia, Frank O'Connor, saw all these wharfies on the wharf and he yelled out, 'What! You bastards here! I thought youse would still be on strike'. They had staged plenty while we were away.

For getting out of the army there was a point system; so many points for being married; so many for having a family; for length of service and so on. I had four and a half years service and I was selected to go to the Victory Parade in London. The Australian contingent consisted of two hundred and fifty all told; one hundred and fifty were army, and the rest made up of air-force, navy and women's services.

We were sent down to Watsonia outside Melbourne to get our drill polished up. We were issued with new uniforms, including ties, which we objected to. As far as we were concerned only officers wore ties, but we were told we had to have them. Then we marched through the streets of Melbourne. All our gear was on the *Shropshire*. But at the eleventh hour at the wharf one of our Military Medal holders, Bill Curtain who'd been our Medical Orderly all the way through, was told that his drill wasn't up to scratch and he couldn't go. So we said, 'Well, if Curtain doesn't go we don't go.' We were told, 'This is absolutely outrageous! You can't do this!' But we stood off for about an hour and a half and finally they said, 'Alright! Curtain can go! Now, get on board!'

In London we were encamped in Kensington Gardens and were visited by the two Princesses and also Churchill and then we marched through London. The Royal Family took the salute, and never have I heard anything like the roar of the crowd as we swung into Oxford Street. What it does to you when know you are representing your country! It is indescribable! And after the march, the crowds! If you had your arms up that was where they stayed! We were entertained at the Goldsmiths' Guildhall and Princess Elizabeth, the present Queen, came round and spoke to every one of us. I very much wanted to souvenir a teaspoon but I was sure if I did a well modulated Pommy voice would say, 'Will that Australian soldier with the teaspoon please return it!' So I didn't.

After coming back from England we were de-mobbed and I went back to Maryvale and ran the mustering camp for thirteen years. It was a big camp and they were shorthorn cattle so we just kept going; mustering, dipping and branding. Later on we introduced Devon bulls to get a little more hardiness into them. Bluff Downs was all shorthorn-Devon and Wandovale to the north was all Herefords. But with the British breeds you never stopped because of the ticks. The first two years after I came back from the war I got into town four times. You just couldn't get away.

At one stage, my step-father, Len Carrington was working for me in the Maryvale camp. Len knew how to work! He always had to be first up in the morning. If he knew you were getting up at four o'clock, it wouldn't be long after three when you would hear the old wax matches being struck for his first smoke of the day. On one occasion he said to me, 'What are we doing tomorrow?' I said, 'We're going to muster the top country up the river on Kangerong.' Kangerong was part of the back country. Later, in 1948, it was balloted off Maryvale. But on this occasion Len said, 'What time are y'getting up?' I said, 'We'd better get away by two because I want to be on the job by daylight.' So at one o'clock you hear Old Len's matches start scratching! But then with the introduction of the Brahman strain things started to get a bit easier.

Louisa Clarke Hann, aged 12 and her sister Elizabeth Caroline Hann, aged four, taken in Melbourne in 1872. Rob Whelan's forebears, Joseph and William Hann, had explored the north in the early 1860s and had taken up Maryvale Station and Bluff Downs.

The Maryvale brand was HN1. The original brand was HAN, one of the oldest registered brands in Queensland, but then when you had to have a numeral it became HN1. William Hann was my mother's grandfather. Originally the Hanns came out from England and settled in Victoria. But that was the period when pastoralists were moving out looking for new land, so William and his father Joseph came north in the 1860's. They explored this area and took up Maryvale and Bluff Downs.[4] They had partners who were the financiers; Klinginger and Bland, but they never came north out of Victoria. Daintree, the Surveyor General of Queensland, was also a partner. They stocked both places with sheep but because of problems with the Aborigines[5] and the spear-grass[6] they weren't profitable. Even when I was working on Maryvale as a young fellow, when we butchered a sheep there would sometimes be as many as a hundred spear-grass heads between the skin of the sheep and the carcass that would have worked their way in. And speargrass heads in the fleece would have lowered its market value. So William overlanded nineteen thousand sheep to the Victorian border to sell. He was on the road with them twenty-two months. Just a few days before the sale Bluff Downs was sold for two hundred and fifty pound, so William Hann bought Maryvale for the same price and came back and stocked it with cattle.

4 See Appendix B; Clarke, Harry; William Hann, Expedition of Exploration to the Endeavour River, 1872.

5 Because of the dingoes, the sheep had to be yarded at night by shepherds living in isolated huts ten to fifteen miles from the homestead. It was not easy to get men willing to take on the lonely task which was perceived as being dangerous because of the possibility of attacks by Aborigines. Rob has no recollection of any account of spearings on Maryvale. However it is very likely that the Aborigines speared sheep for food which they would have seen as a right upon their traditional hunting lands.

6 Speargrass. *heteropogan contortus*; the sharp seeds can penetrate the skin with sometimes fatal results.

Rob Whelan on Cindy Lou, his favourite mare, an excellent face-of-the camp horse.

Not long after this the government asked him to do an exploring trip into the peninsula. He went north through the back-country and was the first to discover gold at the Palmer River, but the government weren't interested. He had been sent out to look for pastoral lands. From there he went up into the Princess Charlotte Bay area and back through Cooktown to Maryvale. After that he settled down and built up a very good herd of cattle as well as draught horses. By this time he was married. In fact he'd been married since before coming north with his father. In those days couples seemed to accept that there would be long periods of separation; wives would be left somewhere for twelve months while the husband was away looking for land or buying and selling stock. But William's wife would have been left reasonably comfortable. He had built a decent sort of a homestead. There didn't seem to be any trouble with the blacks although some of the old slabs that came out of the original kitchen had loopholes in them. But there is a family story of a big corroboree that the blacks on Bluff Downs held on the red ridge opposite the homestead when William Hann's mother was there by herself. She wouldn't have been entirely on her own as in those days they normally had a couple of old Chinamen gardeners around the place.

Maryvale is about eighty miles north of Charters Towers on the Clarke River. It is basalt black-soil country; about two hundred and fifty square miles, with about fifty square miles of rough country. It is black soil plains and red-soil tablelands, timbered with bloodwood, ironbark and gum; open forest country. Hann's Creek on the Lynd Highway was always known to us as Big Sandy, but they changed the name when the Hann Highway from Hughenden to Mount Garnet was put through. Joseph Hann was drowned in the Burdekin River. He couldn't swim and he used to swim the rivers by holding on to his horse's tail. On this occasion his daughter was very ill and he was trying to get across the river to her but got swept away, somewhere on Burdekin Downs. His body was never recovered.

One of the Hann daughters, Elizabeth, married Charles Clarke and she had ten children on Maryvale; eleven if you count one still-born; but only five of them survived babyhood. They are all buried there. The eldest would have been about three and a half. Often the men would be away mustering for weeks at a time and wouldn't even know when these things happened. The women just had to manage on their own.

During the thirteen years I was head stockman on Maryvale the only times I ever got away into town were to the races. I liked to ride in the jumbos, the minimum weight for which was thirteen stone. I was only about ten stone so I had to carry a bit of lead to make weight. I used my grandfather's colours, pink and green, and re-registered them in my own name. I had a few horses on Maryvale and a fellow named Norman Whelan – no relation - to train them. One of our horses, Sepoy, won the trophy in 1952. Then I discovered I couldn't afford racing any longer and I gave it away.

Margaret and I were married in St. James Cathedral in Townsville in 1955. William Hann had given a thousand pounds towards the building of St. James in the early days. And Margaret's family, the Rollinsons, gave the mural and the front pews and the Bishop's chair. After Margaret and I were married we lived at Maryvale in a flat at the end of the big house for five years, all dining together when the gong went at six, nine, twelve, three and six, on the dot. We had various cooks over the years but cooks are a fairly temperamental lot and in between times Annie Masso would take over.

Then in 1960, we went half-shares with Margaret's brother, Jim Rollinson, in the purchase of Old Laura station and Lakefield in Cape York Peninsula. Old Laura was a bit run down but no more so than any other property up that way. The quality of the cattle wasn't too good but the peninsula is good breeding country.

To start out, we men went on ahead, leaving the two wives at home. They both had new little babies and our little girl Lydia was only just three. But after a couple of months the women jacked up on this. They told us if we didn't come and get them there would be trouble! So we did. On the way back up north we stopped at Laura and little Lydia said, 'Where's the ship! I can't see the ship!' Because all the way north we had been telling her 'Soon we will be at Laura township.' Laura township was just the one corrugated-iron pub, the police station and a corrugated-iron store, run by a chap named Laurie Lewis.

It was about another eighteen miles on to Old Laura homestead and well after dark when we arrived. Margaret got left in the car to feed the baby and when she stepped out into the dim light that was all we had been able to rig up, she must have wondered what she was coming to. Old Laura homestead was a bit on the primitive side; made from bush timber and the floor had been pit-sawn from Leichhardt pine. The facilities left a bit to be desired. The bathroom had a cement floor that had been undermined a bit and there were umpteen dozen toads under the floor. The two women weren't too keen on showering with the toads! There were no beds. We slept in swags at first. The rooms were covered with photos of nude women and race horses. But these came down pretty quickly once the women got to work.

Margaret is a very capable woman. She grew up on Nosnillor south-west of Charters Towers and as a girl she'd had to take over cooking for the men when her mother was sent down south to hospital. She was only about nine or ten at the time but she knew how to get on with a job and as well as the cooking she and her brothers all helped with the mustering and stock work.

The roads in the peninsula weren't up to much but Main Roads had started to grade a new road right down to Lakefield and there was bulldust that deep you could lose a vehicle in it. My father-in-law came up one time in his big Fairlane and we were going down the river to the Twelve Mile to fish. I said to him, 'Mr. Rollinson, you can't take the Fairlane down the river.' He said, 'I can take this car anywhere you that you can get that thing of yours.' So away we go; I'm in the Jeep and this Fairlane's following. All bulldust. And when he went to turn off the road down to the river, the wheels just shuddered and sat down. I went back and said to him, 'Well, if you want to come fishing, you'd better get in the Jeep with us.' He didn't say another word about Fairlanes after that. He was a fine man but he didn't understand that Peninsula bulldust.

That little Jeep, a left hand drive, could go anywhere. One time I was taking Margaret and the two children out to have a look around the place, no roads, straight across country, and we came to this steep little gully. Nowhere to cross but there was an old railway trestle bridge from the gold-mining days. I said, 'We'll give this a go'. So we got on to the bridge and started bumping across, sleeper by sleeper. Jimmy would have been about two and he was grizzling a bit and saying, 'I don't like it. It's scary'. I said, 'Daddy wouldn't take you anywhere that was dangerous'. We were about halfway across when one of the sleepers gave way and down she goes on the chassis. Margaret got out and took the children across on the sleepers. I managed to get the jack under the axle and then I hopped back in and revved it enough to jump it over the gap and get to the other side. Then we all got back in and away we went home, the long way round.

Laura township is famous for having the railway bridge that was never used. They were going to build the railway line across to a mining town called Ebbagowlah so they built the bridge at Laura, a trestle bridge, a fair sort of a construction. But the gold cut out so the actual line was never built. The only time the bridge was ever used was when an engine ran across to test it. The last rail-motor ran while we were at Old Laura and we all went in to see it leave. It was quite an occasion.

Laura Races. The finishing post seems to be the forty-four gallon drum beneath the fence on which the children are perched. Three judges are in position and several by-standers have field-glasses up, so perhaps a race is underway. Behind the new shelter shed an older, traditional bough-shelter can be seen.

Old Laura homestead, Cape York Peninsula; from a pencil drawing by noted North Queensland artist John Newman, in the private collection of Rob and Margaret Whelan.

The airstrip on Old Laura came right to the front of the house. You just walked out of the house and down to the garden fence and that was the strip. We had a weekly mail service. One time young Jim had a bad ear infection. He was running a temperature so we got on to the Flying Doctor. He said, 'He needs to come down. We'll send the aerial ambulance.' Margaret went down to Cairns with him and was away about a week or ten days. The only other medical emergency was when my favourite horse, Filibuster – the best horse I ever rode - bucked with me directly under the gate-cap of the yard gate. It got me right across the back of the neck. I bounced it three times before I'd had enough and thought, 'I'd better get off before he does me some damage,' and jumped. My neck wasn't broken but the doctor told me I'd better not go jumping off any five-rail fences for a while. I've walked a bit stiffly ever since.

Margaret never seemed to be worried by living in such an isolated place. She comes from pioneering stock and knows how to cope. She is always prepared to do whatever has to be done. At our Golden Wedding celebration recently someone said to me, 'How the hell did a lovely lady like Margaret put up with you for fifty years!' For company when I was away, which was more often than not, she had two very well trained house girls who had been taught by Mrs. Wallace of Butcher's Hill station[7]. She also belonged to the CWA of the Air, a branch that had been formed by Thelma Atkinson of Wairuna station. Margaret was the branch

7 Mother-in-law of Lennie Wallace, author of *'The Battlers of Butchers Hill'* et al

correspondent for the Peninsula. One Sunday afternoon they were having their meeting on the two-way and suddenly she looked up and there was a brown snake that had come up over the window-sill and was heading across my desk in her direction. They'd come in like that to find somewhere cool out of the heat. She raced out to the kitchen to stoke up the fire for boiling water. Meanwhile the other CWA ladies are calling, 'Come in, Old Laura station! Come in!' They had no idea what was happening. Margaret wasn't about to go back into the office to tell them! Eventually she got the water boiling and took a saucepanful and threw it over the snake where it had settled itself on the concrete. That sent it skedadalling. That was the way they dealt with snakes on Nosnillor when she was a girl. They didn't use the shotgun inside the house so as not to blow hole in the ceiling.

Things always seemed to crop up when Jim and I were away. One of the old Aboriginal stockmen, Charlie Want-eye had a pack of kids but he got into the habit of trying to sneak into the house-girls' room. In the middle of the night Margaret would hear this squealing, 'Missus! Missus! Halpim'me!' but she had enough sense to keep out of it. She didn't want to get a knock on the head too. She told Charlie to pack his swag and sleep somewhere else until I got back.

Another time when I was away with the cattle, one of the water pipes was leaking. We were right on the river but we had a bore and the water was very hard. Margaret got up the windmill to try to fix it and got stuck. Luckily Wally Thompson, the A.I.M.[8] padre turned up. He called out, 'What are you doing up there?' Then he stayed on for a couple of days and sorted the water problem out. Those Inland Mission padres were good men and most of them could turn their hands to any kind of job. They were always welcome.

We had just under three thousand square miles on Old Laura and Lakefield, in four separate leases; a lot of very good country; a fair issue of scrub along the rivers and a lot of good kunai grass on the bottom end, but with some rough country in with it. The eastern side was pretty-well rubbish. Jim Rollinson and I took a ranger from the Lands Department out once who insisted on seeing the eastern country. We ended up with not much hood left on his Land Rover and a couple of tyres staked. The next day he went on down to our neighbour's, Stan Watkin's place, Kalpower. He said to Stan, 'I've been told from Head Office to have a look up around that Brown's Creek area.' Stan told him, 'Well, I don't know why. It's much the same sort of country as you were looking at on Old Laura yesterday.' The Land's Department fellow said, 'Hell! In that case, no way! I don't want to see it! I've had enough of that country for one lifetime!'

Most of that area is Lakeland National Park now and just being wasted, breeding feral cattle and other pests. A lot is good grazing country that could be used. If you are going to have national parks they should be managed just as people on properties are expected to manage their land.

We had six years on Old Laura station and Jim Rollinson and I tried to do a lot of improvements but you couldn't get any finance from the banks. So when we got an opportunity to sell to Sir William Gunn and an American consortium we

8 Australian Inland Mission

decided to take it and go into partnership on Trelawney station, eighty-four miles west of Clermont.

We were on Trelawney for thirty years. We put in a lot of improvements, mostly fencing to make the place easier to run. The kids grew up there, and went to school from there; Jim and Timothy to All Souls from the time they were quite young and Lydia to Blackheath and then down to Tara. Once again Margaret had to cope when I became very involved with the Belyando Shire Council and the Graziers' Association. The ground around the homestead was very hard and stony but she carted loads of soil and manure and established a vegetable garden inside an old water tank that had had its day. On one occasion when the two boys were little they had a bit of an argument with an axe. Jimmy's little finger was cut off and the one next to it left hanging. Margaret dosed him with pethedin from the Flying Doctor kit and raced him into Clermont hospital. She had thirteen gates to open and shut on the way. I was away at the time with two of the Appletons shifting a mob of bullocks. They operated on that hand for six hours.

We had a run of bad years; an eight-year drought. One year when we needed good, soaking rain we got just the one vicious little storm that filled all the little gilgais that are right through that brigalow country. Afterwards, every one of them had an old cow bogged in it. There was no way of getting them out. Once you would have had a handy old horse that was up to the job, but those days are gone. I just had to shoot them.

Then our son Timothy had a bad accident off his motor-bike. He and Jim had turned a mob of cattle out and were heading home when a dingo ran out on to the track in front of them. Tim said, 'I'll have this fellow!' and took off after him. When he was almost on this dog it shot off into the bush and Tim followed it and hit an ant-bed. The bike went up in the air and came down on top of him. Jim raced in home. As soon as Margaret saw him coming she knew something was wrong. They phoned the ambulance and in the meantime Jim gave him pain-killer shots from the Flying Doctor kit. The ambulance took him in but it was a slow drive. They stopped every fifteen minutes to administer to him and he was evacuated by Air Ambulance to Rocky. I went down with him. We didn't get there until after dark. He was in Intensive Care several days; punctured lung; broken arm; broken ribs; badly smashed up. We thought we would lose him.

I was Chairman of the Works Committee of the Belyando Shire Council at the time and we were in the middle of a committee meeting when someone came in and told me there had been a serious accident and I was wanted. I told the Shire Chairman, 'You take over! I'm off!' That was the end of my involvement with Local Authority. I never went back. I'd been on the Council for fourteen and a half years.

We were on Trelawney for the thirty years. Margaret loved the place. We always regard Trelawney as having been our home.

'Brackley', Rob and Margaret Whelan's retirement property north of Charters Towers.

Charlie Rayment

INTRODUCTION

When I first met Charlie Rayment at the 2002'Year of the Outback' celebrations in Charters Towers, I knew I was in the presence of an almost legendary figure. Charlie Rayment has been, in his lifetime; a radar operator in the Royal Australian Navy, a horse breaker, a head stockman, a drover, Team Catcher of the Australian Champion Bronco Branding team, and, as the result of years of tremendously hard work, with the backing of his devoted wife Pauline, a successful pastoralist.

In September 2004, to record something of Charlie's life we drove to Eildon Park, eighty miles south of Winton. Driving in from the main road past the airstrip we were intrigued by the long white hummocks edging the waterhole on which the homestead stands. 'Oh, Yes,' Charlie told us over corned beef and baked pumpkin dinner, 'There's a good depth of water in that creek. Forty feet. During one Dry I pumped the last of the water out into a holding pit and then excavated the length of the creek. Done the same for other waterholes on the place.'

Now a vigorous eighty, Charlie is still mustering, yarding, branding, fencing and doing the multitude of jobs it takes to keep a property running. He has the enthusiasm of youth and a boy's sense of wonder in the unusual or the astonishing. He tells you he was 'down the well the other day' – it is sixty feet deep – as the noon sun shone directly down the shaft; 'The light was amazing!' We got to share something of this phenomenon, when, detaching the mirror from the bathroom wall, Charlie showed us the star-burst effect of midday brilliance in the old well. Then, at each of the watering points we saw cattle so sleek they scarcely moved off the track as the vehicle approached. From the wall of one turkey-nest you could have run a ruler around the 360 degree horizon of mulga interspersed with spinifex and flats of silvery Mitchel grass. 'Sometimes you can't see the feed,' Charlie says, 'But the cattle are fat. In this flood-out country we get a variety of herbage. There's always feed of some sort except in very bad years. As long as you've got water you're right.'

Of pioneer stock, with a keen sense of the importance of pioneer history, Charlie recounts tales of the overland wagon journeys made by previous generations of his family which are of epic proportions, involving distances that even by today's air-conditioned four- wheel drive vehicles are formidable.

Listening to Charlie's account of great drovers and of droving trips down the inland rivers of a half a century ago I knew with certainty that Charlie Rayment was the very embodiment of the men Banjo Paterson immortalized as having 'gone a-droving down the Cooper' and who knew the 'pleasures that the townsfolk never know.' I felt privileged to have met him.

Chapter 7...

WHERE THE INLAND RIVERS FLOW

CHARLIE RAYMENT – DROVER AND PASTORALIST

It was the Depression years and things were tough. Even tougher out at Windorah. So my father went fencing and dam-sinking and from an early age I was his horse-tailer. For schooling, I had to teach myself on Correspondence lessons. They'd come in a big brown envelope. I had to work them out for myself. I had a pile of these envelopes stacked up. It took me a good few years to get through one year.

Charlie Rayment left the stock -camp to join the navy as soon as he turned seventeen, remembering his years of service as the 'best thing he ever did'.

But those old Correspondence School teachers, the patience of them! You couldn't make any excuses, like, you 'didn't have any ink', because they would send you some out in a powder that you had to mix with water. But they would write little letters of praise to you in your book or give you a purple merit stamp for good work. So I struggled along with it. Later, during the war, those teachers used to regularly send parcels and letters to all of us who had been pupils of the Correspondence School.

By the time I was fifteen I was working in the stock camp on Brighton Downs. Then war broke out. The manager, Laurie Luke, joined the Eighth Divvie and he

Charlie served on HMAS *Australia*, 'the pride of the Australian fleet.'

ended up on the Burma Railway. The head stockman joined the air force and was killed over Germany. The ringers joined the Ninth Divvie and ended up in Tobruk. The navy would take you at seventeen so I joined the navy; the most sensible move I ever made in my life. After being in the stock camp the discipline didn't worry me. You were mates with everybody in your own mess deck. You all had to pull together. We were proud to be on the pride of the Australian fleet, H.M.A.S. *Australia*.

I was put on a training course for radar, which was new at the time. Only the *Australia* and the *Shropshire* had it. Even the officers were skeptical about it. We had an air-warning system called the 281 and we worked out with our officers how to report incoming aircraft and the technical terms and signals we would use to communicate with the bridge. My mates and I got pretty good at it. It ended up that the *Australia* was better at handling radar than the Yanks, so whenever we were with them, the *Australia* was the flagship of the task force. We were the fighter-direction ship and they relied on our radar. With hindsight it is amazing the responsibility that was put on us. We were only just kids of eighteen.

Heading up towards the Philippines the Captain, Captain Emile Dechaineux, must have thought we needed tutoring up with a bit with religion. So we're having this service on the quarter deck and everyone's dozing off, listening to padre saying his bit, and all of a sudden Jap planes come over and the alarm sounded. Our fellows are all pretty toey by this time and they were like a mob of cattle rushing! They were galloping! The officers had a manhole on the quarter deck and the old surgeon, "Guts" Flattery, he had a big fat belly on him, he gets stuck in this manhole, looking up at the action!

And then towards Manilla, the Japs started broadcasting Tokyo Rose propaganda. They told us they were going to sink us. There was only the *Shropshire* and the *Australia* that had three funnels and we were flying an admiral's flag as well. Tokyo Rose told us we'd be easy to pick out. But we'd laugh it off.

We were in battle dress; khaki shirts that had our name in block letters on the back. And the navigating officer, a commander, his name was Rayment too, and this day he said to me, 'Rayment! Where do you come from?' And I told him, 'From out Western Queensland, Sir.' He said, 'I think we've got relations out there somewhere. I'll have a yarn to you sometime. We're probably related.' In those days the lower deck never talked to the officers. That was the discipline. That must have been the day we were heading towards Layte because he got killed the next day! Killed on the bridge. So I never found out what connection there might have been.

Leyte was the first big landing in the Philippines; 20th October, 1944. The *Australia* and the other fighting ships went in ahead of the troop ships to start the bombardment. It was just breaking daylight and whichever way you looked there were ships in line, battle ships, cruisers, destroyers, troop carriers and everything that floats. There would have been four hundred ships. And just on sun-up we copped our first suicide plane. It hit the bridge. Captain Dechaineux[1] was killed,

1 Captain Dechaineux's name appears near the head of the list of naval personnel killed in action on the walls of the National War Memorial in Canberra. No rank is given; simply E. Dechaineux.

and the navigator and all the personnel on the bridge plus about thirty ratings. Two mates of mine were killed, seventeen year olds that joined when I did, and two killed in the radar hut. The damage control parties and the sick berth attendants were grabbing all the dead ones off the bridge and getting them down on to the B deck.

The radar shack was directly beneath the bridge and all our aerials were knocked out so we were ordered to start sewing these poor beggars up in their hammocks. We had to put a lead ballast in with them so they would sink. Then they slid them down over the side on a board. We were under attack all the time so we had to be smart about it. It was an awful business. A couple of Yank ships came over to us and they yelled, 'You guys put your fires out and we'll keep the bastards away!'

When it was over, the Australia was sent back to the New Hebrides for repairs. Then it was back again to the Philippines for the next big landing at Lingayen Gulf. We got a new Captain and navigator and new ratings. Two Australian Tribal Class destroyers, the *Arunta* and the *Warramunga* were with us. All the way through the Pacific campaign the *Australia*, the *Shropshire* and our two destroyers were combined with the Yank cruisers and destroyers to form Task Force 74. As the Australia carried the senior officer we were the flagship of the group.

Men of HMAS Australia marching in London.

As soon as we got north of Manilla the Japs started suicide attacks again. We averaged one a day. Wiped out all our gun crews, all the ack-ack, all the four inch and the pom poms, the Oerlikons and the Bofors. In the end they were using stokers and sick-berth attendants for reloading the guns. The pom-poms blew one kamakaze out of the air just before it hit us but it dropped a torpedo that put a hole fourteen by seven in our waterline. Another kamakaze went straight into a diesel tank full of fuel but because there weren't any fumes we didn't catch fire. Which was lucky because we were floating in a sea of diesel. Another suicide plane ended up down the funnel. Not the wings; just the fuselage. All the ammunition dropped into the boiler. They kept exploding in the heat and blowing holes in the funnel casing. If any of us was ordered along the main deck we'd run like hell. The Australia was the most knocked-about ship still floating at Lingayen.

After that we were sent back to Sydney for repairs. When we were coming into the harbour we had a Jap plane hanging out of one funnel, another funnel hanging over the side; bullet holes in the casings. The ship was a mess. We had the flag at half-mast for the seventy-four killed and the hundred and thirty-three wounded. A ship generally flies a paying-off pennant coming into its home port. The length of pennant depends upon the length of service. The *Australia* had never been out of commission since the beginning of the war so our pennant was a terrific length.

The pennant was so long that when they hoisted it, the tip of it was trailing in the water behind us. It was a very still day and there wasn't enough breeze to lift it. It was a Sunday and the harbour was full of yachts. When they saw us they started coming out to welcome us. But we weren't in a welcoming frame of mind. We'd lost too many men; too many mates. So there wasn't much yakaiing going on. But the officer of the watch, when he saw the pennant trailing in the water, grabbed one of the ratings and told him to get down to the sickbay and get a dozen condoms. They blew them up and attached them to the end of this pennant. And just like big balloons, the condoms lifted the pennant clear of the water. So the *Australia* steamed up the harbour through all these Sunday yachts, with her paying-off pennant held up by condoms.

The *Australia* was so badly out of alignment that we had to be sent to England for a refit, via America. While we were in England we were given shore leave and my mate Bluey Smith, and I - we were only bits of kids - we thought we'd go up to Edinburgh. We met a couple of nice girls at a dance and they invited us home. And their family made us very welcome. The father had been in the Black Watch with the Australians in France in the First World War and the mother had been engaged to an Australian that got killed in Flanders. It was my twentieth birthday, and this lady said, 'Oh! Then I'll make you a clouty dumpling!' Well, I didn't think much of that for an idea. The only dumplings I knew were the greasy things the cook in the stock camp chucked into the meat bucket. So I was a bit cagey about it. But it turned out that a clouty dumpling was a great big pudding boiled in a cloth, like a Christmas pudding. They were lovely people.

When we went over to England we headed east, via America, and when we came home we were still heading east coming back around Africa and across the Indian Ocean. So we'd been right round the world.

By that time the war was just about over. We were all due for discharge but they wanted me to stay on and do more training in radar. I had it in mind to stick with the navy for a few more years. I enjoyed the life. But I got a telegram from Laurie Luke who used to be manager on Brighton Downs before we all joined up, saying he was going back droving and wanted a horse tailer. So I got my discharge and come back out west to go droving with Laurie Luke.

Laurie had had a bad time on the Burma railway. He was a chap that always preferred the cold weather. Even in Clermont in winter time he would only have a shirt on and I'd be shivering. The Japs started picking the fittest of them from the railway camps to send to Japan for a labour force. Laurie knew he couldn't survive another summer in the jungle so he made out he was a good deal fitter than he was and he was picked. He was put on the *Roteo Maru* and just up the coast they were sunk by subs. A Dutch submarine picked up a lot of the survivors and brought them back to Brisbane. But Laurie got picked up by a Jap destroyer that off-loaded them on to a Jap transport. Then the transport got sunk! But, coincidences that happen! Before Laurie joined up he was manager on Brighton Downs. And there was an Eighth Divvie mate of his from Roma in another camp up the line that he'd been trying to get in contact with but they'd never met up. So he gets sunk twice and he's in the middle of the China Sea in a bit of a ship's boat and he sees this other fellow swimming and hanging on to a plank. So he pulled him into the boat. And it was this mate of his from Roma!

Laurie survived Japan. He got discharged before me and started getting a droving plant together. That's when I got the telegram from him. I had horses of my own that I owned since I was a kid. And my Old Chap was fire-ploughing just outside of Winton, and he helped us out with another dozen clumpers and pack-horses. A coloured fellow, old Johnnie Williams, a mate of Laurie's, had a droving plant in Longreach. So between us we had the makings of a plant. As soon as I got my discharge I joined them at the old Forty Mile pub out from Elderslie, and we headed for Marion Downs to take the Marion bullocks down to Quilpie.

It was a very dry year so we short cut through those sand-hills, battling to get through. We hit the Diamantina at Monkira, crossed over through Currawilla, came in through Windorah and Eromanga and trucked at Quilpie; an eleven weeks trip. I was fetching the plant back by myself on my own and I had my twenty-first birthday at Windorah. From then on I was droving with Laurie until '47. Droving suited me.

The Inland Rivers country is my home. My grandfather, Charles Ebeneza Rayment, was an officer on a sailing ship that got wrecked in the Great Australian Bight. He swam ashore and was wandering about in the desert, nearly perishing, when he stumbled into a tank-sinking camp. He must have decided he'd had a neckful of this salt-water business so he stayed ashore and married a Scotch-Irish girl, Julia Ann Smith.

Then they headed up through the Centre into the Channel country. It wasn't that long after Burke and Wills made a mess of things, and my grandfather was a Pom, but his wife was a bush girl and she had two brothers, so it must have been their bushmanship that got them through. They built that big old yard at Flaggie on Warbreccan, halfway between Stonehenge and Jundah. At that time Jundah was only a bough shed with a constable and a mob of black police. They had a baby girl, Susan. She died and is buried just over the river from Stonehenge. The grave has got a rail around it with a little plaque; 'Susan; Infant Daughter of Charles and Julia Rayment; died 1882'.

From there they went across to Isisford and had an orchard, drawing water from the waterhole with a horse-whim. My father was one of the first kids in the Isisford School. My grandfather had a store and a hawker's van. And when prospectors were chasing opal on the opal fields at Jundah, the old grandfather used to grub-stake them with picks and shovels on credit. When they all went broke he went broke. But for years and years after, these old miners, as they got a little bit of money, would send him back what they owed him.[2] Then his health broke down

2 See also 'Boyhood at Koorboora' in the author's 'Barefoot Through the Bindies; Growing Up in North Queensland in the Early 1900s', in which Edward Cummings, commenting upon how bush store-keepers often made it possible for miners to survive by giving them credit 'when they were out of luck' , remembers one who returned after many years, saying, 'I went away owing you twenty pounds. I got on my feet and here it is.'

and the family, his wife and the girls and the youngest boy, went down overland from Isisford to Rockhampton in a couple of buggies and a spring-cart. My father was driving one of the buggies. He was fourteen.

I've been through those Boguntangan and Gogango ranges. It's hard country; rough going. It would have been an epic sort of journey for a woman and girls and a sick husband. He died not long after they got to Rockhampton but Grandmother lived a good many more years and the girls all married in Rockhampton.

My father came back out to the west where his brother Bert - they called him BJ-had teams out of Longreach. He used to cart down Currawilla way. BJ was twenty-one. They had two teams; BJ drove the big team with twenty horses and my father followed on behind. His wagon was smaller; only fourteen horses pulling his.

They were what you call overall wagons; the tray up above the wheels, with two smaller wheels in front that turn the turn-table, and the bigger wheels behind. You'd have your shafters in the shafts and the other horses three abreast. They never drove them in reins. They guided them by voice. They'd have a near-side leader that was an intelligent horse. They would call to him 'Over!' or 'Back!' to swing them. Those old teamsters were very smart with their horses. They'd often have a blue heeler nipping the off-side horses to keep any slack ones pulling that he couldn't reach with the whip. The driver of the team rode a quiet horse, or sometimes he walked. They'd have a few spare horses in case some of them went lame and a few spare saddle horses. They never hobbled them at night like you do with droving horses. They'd put big Condamine bells on them that you could hear up to four miles on a cold morning. But they never seemed to go far from the wagon.

This must have been about November of 1905 and Currawilla, down in that Corner Country, must have been late ordering their supplies and so their goods still had to be taken down. That year, 1905, was a very dry year and everyone's horses were poor but BJ took the contract. They loaded up in Longreach, threw on a bit of horse-feed to help along a bit and started off down the Thomson. At Stonehenge they turned west to Warbreccan. All the waters were drying at Farrer's Creek but they went on down past Connemara. Connemara Hole was dry so they had to push on to Muttee. They got a bit of very poor water there. The horses were getting knocked up and they only had enough left to pull the one wagon. So they left one wagon at Corrakie Creek and went on down towards Currawilla with just the main rations. The next water was at Dudley but they couldn't drink it. It was full of dead cattle. So they had to keep travelling. There wasn't any grass anywhere. The first good water they struck was at Booka Hole. The cattle there were close to perishing and they strung along behind the wagon. They must have thought the dust of the wagon was their mates up ahead in the lead. Then Engine Hole on Palparara was dry. The next water wasn't until they got to Currawilla. By then the horses were too poor to go back and get the second wagon.

A black boy told them there had been a storm out west near Wallami Bore. So they took their horses out there for a bit of green picking. They'd been there a week and down come the rain. That was the big flood of 1906 that they still talk about.

They put in the rainy period out there and the grass come away but the sandflies and mosquitoes were that bad that the kangaroos were just standing blind.

When the rain cleared they went back up to Corrakie and picked up the other wagon. It had gone underwater in the flood but they got it down to Currawilla. Then another big deluge of rain come down. They bought some draught horses from the station to replace the ones that'd died but a lot of them couldn't work. Birdsville disease showed up in them. They'd go in the loins with it and die.

When the cooler months came they headed off up Windorah way and picked up a load of wool from South Galway and continued on up the Thomson back to Longreach. They'd been gone the best part of half the year. It's no wonder Henry Lawson says those old teamsters didn't do much in the way in the way of talking. They had a lot on their minds. There can't have been much profit in that trip.[3]

I've always loved working with horses but for droving I preferred pack-horses because I grew up with them. With pack-horses you can go places that you can't take a buggy or a truck. You can choose your route, say, through the sand-hills on Cluny, and once you hit the Diamantina there are good hard clay-pans, good walking, close to the main channel, and you can stay closer in. There is a sort of etiquette among drovers. The pack-horse men would keep a good way off from the road and leave the feed along the road for the buggy men. With pack-horses you could get right in among the channels. It was also a little bit harder for the stock-inspector fellers to keep tabs on you in there, too!

In the slack between droving trips Laurie Luke and I would put in the time brumby shooting. Over two years, on Marion and Herbert, we shot over two thousand. We'd use a few of our fittest horses while the others were spelling. We'd camp on the Sylvester. The station provided us with 303s and bullets. Ammo was easy to come by. The army fellows coming back from Darwin'd sell it to you by the box!

The back of Marion Downs is all open country. The brumby mobs were hard to get close to. Very touchy. Coming in for water the bucks'd have their heads up looking for trouble. We found we couldn't shoot them at the waters. One time, we were at a water-hole on the Sylvester, lying low on the side the mob usually came in on. But this day they came in from round the other side. The wind was in the right quarter for where we were; but it was a long walk round the hole and they would have got our scent. So we stripped off and waded across, holding our rifles over our heads with the water lapping our necks. When we got across we started shooting. We shot a fair few and then the wounded ones had to be followed out and finished off. We always tried to clean up the whole mob so there were no survivors. Then we had to cut off the tails, to keep the tally. In the excitement we ended up about a mile out from the waterhole. And we're barefoot! It was November and the middle of summer and in those stony ridges the ground was blistering hot. We'd try to keep to the cattle pads to dodge the stones, but it was murder! Well, my feet! Ever after that, if ever we had to wade or swim any waterholes, I made sure kept my boots on!

3 ' He'll sometimes pause, as a thing of form, in front of a settler's door/ And ask for a drink, or remark, 'It's warm.'/ Or say 'There are signs of a thunderstorm.'/ But he seldom utters more.' (Henry Lawson; The Teams)

Then we found the easiest way to clean up a mob was to go out just on sundown where they were feeding. The sun would be a glowing red ball and we would get it behind us and if the wind was right we could almost walk right up to them. They wouldn't look into that blinding sun. When we started shooting they couldn't tell where it was coming from. Often they would circle and come right back over the top of us. Shooting out of the sun we could almost clean the whole mob up. You get the hang of it after a while.

It was a way of filling in time before the mustering started before the wet season. The money was good. We'd get two and sixpence a head for the first five hundred and five shillings a head for the second five hundred. As well as that, once they'd counted them, we could keep the tails and that was worth a quid or two. Down south they used it for stuffing upholstery and car seats. By the time we got to over two thousand we were on fairly good money and we were shooting more every day because we'd learnt the game and the country.

Right at the finish we were shooting with revolvers. We'd hold them back out from water for a good while and in that type of country, on the Sylvester, we knew they would gallop back into the hills when they were disturbed. We had two fairly fast horses but mine was the fastest and I was the lightest. I'd have a Luger on one side and a 38 revolver on the other. We'd wait out a while and let the mob come in and get a big drink. Now these were rogues, the survivors from all the other mobs, grouped together. We'd wait until they had a big bellyful of water and then Laurie would slip up and down them as fast as he could and jam them. By the time they got back out to me they'd be strung out in a line. The buck would have taken the lead. The young ones would be behind him. The old mares strung out behind. Their wind was gone by this time and I could slip in and start from the tail-end stragglers and shoot every one up the line; a spinal shot. They would drop instantly and my mate coming along behind would finish them off. We were always very particular about not leaving any wounded ones.

You might think as a horseman that I would have had a few qualms about shooting brumbies. But you just have to put any qualms out of your mind. They are a pest, like rabbits and foxes. They eat the country out. Even though horses were our life, both Laurie and me, and there've been times when I've nearly cried putting a horse of mine with a broken leg down, I did not get sentimental over brumbies.

There was only one time at a waterhole on the back of Marion where we used to camp, where we'd see this old fella coming in for a drink, that I felt a bit sorry. We didn't shoot this fella because, I don't know, he was a loner, and we thought maybe we could break him in. He'd come in steady, steady and he had a tail dragging down on the ground. Finally we saw the testicles he had on him and we realized he was a buck and he'd have to go. So we shot him. Well, he was all grey round the muzzle, grey all through his hide and his teeth were right down to his gums. That's the only old brumby buck I've seen. They usually die young from stress or fighting among themselves. But we felt awfully sorry for that old fella. He'd dodged all the brumby runners and brumby shooters all those years. He was a real survivor; the only one I felt really sorry about. But you get immune to it after a while if it is what you have to do. They are such a menace. Even when Laurie and I had shot over two thousand there seemed to be just as many left as when we started.

Laurie got offered the management of Coorabulka and that country was where I wanted to stay. But Old Bob Brookes had bought Croydon station out from St. Lawrence and he talked Laurie into going down there to manage it. So I tagged along too, though I wasn't that keen. That coast country was strange to both of us. It was different. The ringers were different. Out west it's dry. Down there it rains. The scrub's so thick a dingo pup can't howl in it. The Isaacs and the Connors head up out from Mackay and those mongrel cyclones hit the coast. There are 'gators there, and it's sour country! Out west you can't see the feed but your horses are fat. Down there you've got feed three foot high and your horses are poor!

And they had Hereford cattle there. Rotten things! They've got sharp horns. And if you don't drag the blighters out by the nose and dip them the ticks'll get 'em! And they don't thank you, either! Out where we came from it was all horse work. We never had yards; all the branding was open bronchoing; all the drafting done in an open camp. You never yarded bullocks. You watched your bullocks at night. Down there the only time you used your horses was for mustering. All the rest was done in yards on foot. And old time ringers never used to like getting off their horses and walking about in their boots. But, I stuck it out for a couple of years.

Jack Clanchy at Bedourie wired Laurie that he wanted his mustering done and Laurie recommended me, so I headed out west with a plant of half-broken horses. I had a bloke named Les Cochrane with me. 1950 was a very wet year. It wouldn't stop raining. We were breaking-in these young horses along the way, packing them and riding them. We headed out past Clermont and crossed the Belyando. It was in flood so we made a canvas boat out of pack-saddles.

We went out through Aramac and crossed the Thomson at Camoola. Had to swim it, too. All the rivers were up. We short-cut across the downs to Winton and camped on Yarraman Creek. It rained three inches in one night. Johnnie Frazer joined us there. He was a good ringer. He could ride most anything. We picked up a couple of other fellows too; Merv Kerr and Allan Burrow. So then we had a camp of men and away we went heading for Boulia. We pulled up there in the channels and I went up to Cazna and bought another ten or twelve horses, most of them clumpers. Gave them a very rough breaking-in. We continued on down southward towards Marion Downs. Camped through the boundary the first night and swam the river and camped at the Four Mile. We managed to get the packs on the unbroken horses and did a bit of bagging and handling of them. Next day we went on down to Bedourie and met up with Jack Clanchy and started mustering and branding on his place, Kameran Downs. I like that country. Once I got back out there, there was no way they'd ever get me down on the coast again.

We started mustering and branding out on the Mulligan; three weeks and we got a mob of bullocks together, about nine-fifty in the mob. Three hundred fat cows; the rest, big bullocks. 1950 was a very good year. The clover was thick between the sand-hills. The cattle were fat. Once we got the mob together we started them in for Quilpie. Got in past Windorah and a few buyers started looking at them. We got into the Cooper Channels. To cross the Cooper at the new bridge we cut them out, about a hundred at a time and put the horses in the lead and got them over in little mobs, and continued over Dead Man's Channel on towards Quilpie.

Then Jack Clanchy's buyers turned up and they bought the cattle. So instead of us going on to Quilpie we had to turn and head for Yaraka because the buyers wanted the cattle to go up to Rockhampton. We followed up the Cooper on the eastern side until we came to where the Barcoo junctions in. Then we followed the Barcoo towards Yaraka. The last twelve miles was all thick gidgea. Well, we strung those cattle along the road a couple of mile. There wasn't much motor traffic in those days. We were drafting out the fat cows when it started pelting down. We trucked the bullocks in pouring rain.We had a good delivery; our full number. That was my first trip in charge of a big mob. All of us were about twenty-five years of age. In the Year 2000 they had a Fiftieth Anniversary at Windorah of the bridge over the Cooper being opened. That mob of ours was the first lot of cattle that ever crossed it.

After this we went contract mustering for branders out on the Mulligan, right out in the desert, getting thirty bob a head for everything we could brand. It was getting towards the end of the year and we intended to head into Bedourie for Christmas. I started the camp on their way and told them to camp at Bindiyacca bore that night while I took a ride down the Mulligan towards Klidgewarra to look around. I told them I'd catch up with them. I was riding a pretty mare of Jack Clanchy's that he'd got from Clermont when I ran into a mob of brumbies. There were a couple of nice-looking geldings among them, which is uncommon as the stallion generally kicks them out of the mob, but these were following along. I thought, 'I'll get rid of this lot but I'll have those two geldings.'

So I got up beside this mob with a 38 revolver and managed to get most of them. I'd run them a good few miles when suddenly I realized I had no idea where I was. I'd crossed the Mulligan without realizing it and lost my bearings. So I let these geldings go and did a circle or two and had a bit of a spell and a bit of a think about things. Finally I picked up where I'd shot these brumbies a few hours before and from there on I was right. Next thing I spotted these two geldings again, but now they had a young buck with them. He looked as though it was out of a branded mare. I liked the look of him. So I hunted these two geldings and this colt ahead of me for twelve or fifteen mile till I got back to Bindiyakka bore where I'd told the camp to wait. The brumby buck ran along quite nicely with his mates.

It was just on sundown when I run them into the mob at the bore, maybe thirty or forty horses altogether. I thought, 'I've got to get a rope on this young buck and get some hobbles on him or he'll sneak off during the night.' So I got a rope and got up a tree and the other fellows pushed the mob underneath. I dropped the rope on this colt, choked him down, got the hobbles on him, put a halter on him and tied him up to the tree, snorting and kicking. Merv Kerr started bagging him down a bit and talking to him.

The weather wasn't looking too good so Merv and Les had rigged up the fly. But there were only two trees and Merv had tied this colt to one of them. I was last into camp that night and they were all in their swags and the only spot left for me was right next to this tree with the brumby colt tied to it. During the night when we were all sound asleep there was one hell of a crash and next thing this colt is down on top of my swag and me in it. He'd got his hind leg through the hobble strap and he was trussed up like a chook. I wriggled out from underneath him, saying a few unkind words. But I untangled him and booted him back around the other side of the tree.

So next morning we're heading into Bedourie and the others wanted to know what we were going to do with this colt. I was still crabby from the night's episode so I said, 'Merv can ride the bastard!' We got a saddle on him and Merv jumps up on him and a couple of roots later we shoulder him into the middle of the horses and away we go. He settled down and went along quite well. It took us four days to get to Bedourie and by that time we had him pretty quiet. Then it was Christmas and after a bit of a blow in Bedourie we jumped on the mail-truck and went up to Boulia for the New Year races.

After this we had a few months spell before we started mustering the bullocks again. By then it's getting on into the cooler months. We ran the horses in and the little horse had grown a bit and freshened up. With a bit of work he turned into a handy sort of a stock horse and he was part of the plant ever after. At one stage we were even using him for a night-horse. I've broken in a good few horses and all I can say is there are many ways of breaking-in. It depends on where you are at the time and how badly you want the horse.

I was there on Davenport once to attend a muster and to break in a few horses. Ray Donnellan had been reared on Davenport and ended up running the camp there. His father had managed the place for thirty years so he knew it pretty well. A big Yellafella was working there, Lou Bonning. 'The Black Cat' we called him; a decent fellow, Lou. He was breaking-in a clumper mare. 'Little Dumpling', he called her. He had the broncho gear on her, getting her used to it. The broncho saddle was a bit of a relic; an old-type military saddle. The seat consisted of two sections of leather that left the ironwork at the front and where it came to the back of the saddle there was a split in the leather and then it narrowed in. And this morning Lou was in a big pair of blue overalls. And in the process of breaking-in, the stitching of the fork of these overalls of his had given way. So when he got on this mare with these overalls on, his testicles must have worked down through the split. And when Little Dumpling started dropping her head and rooting, his testicles must have worked back into the v-part where the leather of the saddle come together. We couldn't see any of this, of course. But Lou was turning white by the second and getting fairly agitated-looking. The dust finally settled and the mare stopped. Lou was still there but a bit shaky-looking. Ray Donnellan thought he'd better cheer him up a bit. He said, 'Geez, Lou! You put up a good ride on that mare!' When Lou could get his breath back he said, 'Yeah, Little Mate! You'd ride well too if your rocks was caught in the leather of this stupid bloody saddle you got me on!'

Jack Clanchy was a Georgina fellow. He managed Coorabulka for many years before he took on Kameron Downs. At one time he had been in partnership with a chap named Bob Laughton but they split up. Bob Laughton bought a place named Brackenborough. There were a couple of thousand head of cattle involved in the break-up and I ended up buying some of them.

I had a place of my own named Kurran. I'd had it since I was fifteen working on Brighton as a stockman. My father was there with his teams and he happened to hear there was a bit of vacant country going over between Connemara and Davonport. There was six hundred square miles thrown up and nobody took it up. The Old Chap took it up in my name from the Lands Office in Jundah. It wasn't surveyed so we didn't have to pay survey fees. All we had to pay was the first year's rent; two and six a mile.

So Dad and I go over to have a look at this Kurran. That was its survey name. We were hopelessly lost the whole time. Finally, when we got our bearings we're halfway down to Palparara! But when finally we did get a look at the place, he said, 'It's no good to us!' But he couldn't throw it up because it was in my name. I was only fifteen at the time but you could hold an open pastoral lease. And I was hanging on to it! Then when I joined the navy, the whole time I was on active service I never paid rent on it because I wasn't getting an income from it and they added that length of time on to the lease.

So while I was droving and mustering at Brighton and Marion and Herbert and Brackenborough, every so often I would wander over to Kurran and have a bit more of a look over the place. I knew I needed a bit more experience before I moved on to it.

Kurran is between the Diamantina and the headwaters of Farrar's Creek. It's about six hundred square mile. Very rough country. All hills. And very light-on for rainfall; averages a couple of inches a year. No fences, so clean-skin cattle to battle with. Very little water. A few rock-holes at the start, but they'd all go dry. The cattle would go down on to the stations. They'd wander along the creeks and gullies towards the river. The Diamantina was only forty miles away and it could be in flood from its headwaters. Forty miles is nothing to cattle. Most of the year I would be attending at musters on these big company places.[4] I didn't mind that. Gradually I got a few dams down on Kurran. It was hard stony ridge country where water runs off easy so I would put high banks between a couple of hills and they turned out to be a pretty big success. The main thing about blocking off a creek or gully is you've got to make sure you've got a good by-wash.[5] If you get a downpour, you don't want the water spilling over your wall and scouring it out. A decent by-wash will hold any extra water that comes down and that saves your wall.

It was sweet country. A good mixture of grasses; a lot of light feed; a terrific variety of young tender grasses. You get button grass and Flinders grass in most country and if you get a bit of winter rain you get a lot of herbage that reacts along the creeks. And saltbush.

I met my wife, Pauline, when she was nursing at St. Helen's, on the south side of the river in Brisbane. I knew from the start that Pauline was the right girl for me. We were married at the coldest church in Brisbane, a little church from the 1860s up on the hill at Grovely. Talk about freeze! I nearly froze to death! The minister was doing his bit, and every time I looked sideways there were these big old gravestones right outside the window! I shiver every time I think of it! Pauline

4 Being present at musters on neighbouring properties in order to reclaim ones own cattle.

5 Provision for water to back up into adjacent gullies or low areas to form additional catchment.

had a bride's dress on and I had a suit and tie. That wasn't making me feel any better, either!

We come on straight away out to Kurran. I'd bought a three ton truck down in Brisbane and a little ten foot aluminium caravan and hooked it on behind. There wasn't much of a road into Kurran, just a bit of a track. And pretty rough when we got there. Just a bit of a shed. I made the double bed; a three-b'two frame with legs bolted on, and I bored half inch holes all the way round. Then I killed a bullock and cut the hide into strands about three quarters of an inch wide, and weaved it back and forwards all the way round. I think I might have used two hides seeing it was for the double bed. Pauline painted the frame pink. It made a pretty good bed. There was always a fair bit of spring in it. It didn't need a mattress. You could just unroll your swag on it and roll it up again easy in the morning. That was forty-five years ago and that greenhide bed has still got the spring in it. They've got it in the Waltzing Matilda Centre in Winton now, tied up on the wall.

We had fifteen years on Kurran. Three of the boys were born while we were there. Pauline taught them on Correspondence. She was on her own a lot of the time. Any discipline the kids needed she was the one. As the kids got up a bit they'd give me a hand. I was away a lot trying to build the place up. Pauline had it pretty tough when you come to think about it.

I started looking around for a place a bit closer in to extend Kurran a bit; a bit easier country. That fifteen-year drought, you don't forget those things. It had to be somewhere to the east of us, somewhere up the Diamantina. We knew Eildon Park was being run by the estate of the Johnson family. I had been through it in 1947 when I was droving and I took a plant of horses up the Mayne to Longreach. So I'd been through the bottom end of it. We knew it was a derelict place that all the stock had been taken off; not much in the way of waterholes and a lot of those used to go dry; the yards were in a mess; everything was in a mess. But you can only get into what you can afford to get in to. And you've got to build it up yourself with hard work. So we bought the place.

We moved the stock across in two trips, walking two mobs of five hundred cattle from Kurran to Eildon, watching them of a night. The boys were only little but they helped. There was no stock route. We come through Connemara. We'd always ask permission and let them know. Tonkaro let us go through and we've stayed friends with those people over the years. Each of those trips took three weeks. It took the cattle a while to settle down when we got them here. There were no fences in those days. We started patching up the old fences on Eildon straight away. The place was pretty run down. We got a couple of dams put down. We had to get an income coming in so we concentrated on the fencing and the waters. Nothing new. Just patching up all the old stuff.

It wasn't for a few years that we started on the house and built on to it. It was in such a mess when we first got here that we camped over the creek. We carted out all that was left of the furniture and burnt it. One old couch that the old fella had camped on stank of vomit. We burnt the lot. There were old derelict gardens and chook-yards out the back; a pig sty, but the pigs, a white breed, had escaped and were running wild. But, funny things, pigs. One kept hanging around and he got that way he thought he was a horse. He'd camp with the horses out in the paddock. He'd want to go mustering with us but then he would knock up and take a day to recuperate.

Eildon Park Homestead, eighty miles south of Winton. Charlie says, 'It was a wonderful old place the way it was designed. You could open all the doors and windows and the breeze would come straight through.'

But Pauline always managed and made the best of things. It was a wonderful old place the way it was designed. Upstairs you could open all the doors and windows and the breeze would come straight through. The lounge room was rusty old corrugated iron and a dirt floor. In the kitchen the floor was just a few flaggy stones and a bit of ant-bed. So we jacked the house up as high as we could and cemented underneath. We had to completely re-stump it; the white ants had eaten the posts. Actually the house was holding the stumps up. They were bolted to the beams and just swinging underneath. Everything was off level. None of the doors upstairs would shut. When you walked upstairs the whole place shook. We built the bathroom and the toilet out the back up on stumps for the floods, so we'd at least have a bathroom clear of the floodwaters.

When we first came here there were no septic toilets, only the old pit type. There'd been a fairly big flood a year or so before and the throne from one of these old toilets was stuck up in the fork of a high gum-tree on the other side of the crossing. So we knew we'd be in for a few floods.

We've had some funny episodes with floods here. It's only about twelve miles to the top of Paddy's Creek but all that area up the top is hard stony country and it runs off fast. When it comes down it floods from the cattle yards half way across through the horse paddock. It comes four foot through the house downstairs. And the funniest thing was, the first time we got flooded, this lad I had working for me had all his gear, his boots and saddlery, in the corner of the dining room. I come down in the middle of the night with a torch, and there was a current coming in the front door and going out the back, and there's one of Davy's boots heading out the back door with a mouse sitting up on top of it.

The water only lasts twenty-four hours and then it's gone, except you've got to sweep the mud out before the water goes off it. Another time, we had a big poinciana tree out the front; one of those that drop those long black beans. And I wasn't quite aware of how much of a storm had hit up the top of the creek. The water was up to the gate and I didn't think it would come any higher. I had my rocking chair there in the kitchen and I thought, 'I won't go up to bed. I'll just doze in the rocking chair and keep an eye on things.' And round about midnight I woke up, and the next thing I know I'm up to my knees in water. So I raced out to get over to the shed where there were a couple of motor-bikes and other gear to push up, and in the dark, these beans from the poinciana, they curl around your legs like black snakes.

We don't lose any stock in the floods. They swim to higher ground. But it is surprising how many drowned kangaroos come down in a flood. They are creatures that can't handle the mud. As they hop they get bogged. And when they get caught in the channels, that's it.

We had a lad, Norm Forster, working here once and he had a couple of blue dogs. He had them tied in the shed. And the flood came up and up. I went over in the dark and one of these dogs was sitting up on a twelve gallon drum until the drum got washed away from beneath him. I unhooked them both off the chain. One fellow hit the current and away he went. I thought, 'Well, that's it. He's a goner, poor fella!' Well, when the flood went down we found him sitting up in the fork of a tree down the creek a couple of miles. He'd been howling for a day and a half.

The floods make it quite interesting really. This is the Diamantina catchment area. All the water goes down to Lake Eyre. Our creek joins the Mayne and then it flows west into the Diamantina at the old Mayne pub. The Thompson watershed is north of here of here on Suvla. It's handy if you know all your watersheds. You don't get lost then.

At first there was just the one little windmill out the back of the house pumping up the water from the creek to a little overhead tank full of holes. But that tank wasn't high enough to give us any pressure inside the house, so we got on to Merv Sales, the plumber in Winton – Merv can fix anything – and he set a new fibreglass tank in, a lot higher.

A waterhole on Eildon Park. Charlie Rayment has deepened all the waterholes by scooping them out during the Dry. He would rather have good waterholes than bores.

Bronco Branding Champions, Longreach Hall of Fame, 1991. Charlie Rayment and Bruce Rayment, catchers Ann Blacket (later Mrs. Bruce Rayment), Shane Mills and Mike Elliot. Charlie's team has won Queensland State and National Bronco Branding Championships, and, on Charlie's eightieth birthday, the Camooweal 2005 Drovers' Camp Championship.

There were a couple of Yugoslavs, Joe Jurak and his mate Branco - but I used to call him Broncho - that were out this way scratching round for opal. They weren't making much of a fist of things so I got them on to digging this well. There'd been a bore there so we knew there was water sixty feet down. The idea was that if we put down a well with a few drives we'd have more storage for water.

At the time I had a little old chap named Beano Thomson working for me as cook. He used to be in the stock camp when I was droving. Well Beano used to beat up a jugful of powdered milk every morning to see us through, and he'd put it in the fridge. But this Broncho, he used to come across at about eleven o'clock and barge in and open the fridge and grab the jug - he'd never ask! – and he'd drink the lot! It used to annoy Beano. At the time my kids were hand-rearing a little foal on mare's milk supplement called Denkavite. So I suggested to Beano that he mix up a jug of this Denkavite and put it in the fridge.

So the next day Broncho comes in, sweat pouring off him, opens the fridge, grabs the jug and drinks half of it. Then he stops and looks thoughtful and he says, 'Different taste!' 'Yair,' says Beano, 'Different brand.' So Broncho goes, 'Aw!' and puts his face in the jug and drinks the rest of it. So for the next week or ten days we fattened old Bronco up on this Denkavite. He got sleek and shiny! Beano was scared stiff he would wake up to it and do his block! But in the end both Broncho and Joe got a serious thirst and off they went into town. We didn't ever see them again so the boys and I finished off the well. I was down that well the other day. It must have been right on midday. Just for a moment the sun shone directly

A bronco branding team in action. The sport has become increasingly popular.

down and the whole shaft lit up with this amazing light. Like a starburst! It was a wonderful experience.

Over the years I have deepened every water-hole on Eildon. During the Dry when the water level was right down I'd scoop out a holding pit to one side of the waterhole and pump out into it. Then we'd move into the bed of the creek with the blade and excavate down. Some of them are forty feet. We'd always hit a bed of white clay called kaolin. That's the white hummocks you see when you come in off the main road. Nearly every creek on the place has been deepened like that. We might not get the rainfall here but we never run out of water. I would rather have dams and waterholes than depend on a bore. A bore can fail. A good depth of water in your waterholes will see you through.

I've always had a working dog or two, a red dog or a blue. But in this country the distances are too long, and the ground and the prickles are too hard on their feet so you can't use dogs moving cattle very much. You can use them for yarding-up. Over on Kurran where we had a lot of scrubbers we'd use dogs for pulling bulls down. But we have a problem keeping dogs on Eildon because there are sheep places adjoining us and they get a bit careless throwing 1080 when they're aerial baiting for dingoes.

I don't have a problem with dingoes. I like dingoes. In my book they do as much good as harm. In a good season when the cattle are strong you don't lose many calves to dingoes. But in a drought, cows will park their calves with the one old cow and leave her behind to look after six or eight little calves while they walk the long distances in to water. Well, one old cow can't do much if a dingo comes wanting a feed. So when a dingo kills a little calf in a drought that saves the mother because then she hasn't got to feed it. A cow without a calf draining her energy has got a better chance of surviving. In a lot of cases you'd lose both the cow and the calf. None of us likes to ride around shooting perishing calves. So if the dingoes get a few it sort've helps to balance things out. It's the law of the wild; survival. And I don't mind listening to dingoes of a night. I like to hear a few bush sounds, a scrub bull singing out or the dingoes or the odd curlew.

I've always believed that it's good for boys to get out and work a bit. Some of them are staying on too long at school these days. I'd get them out here at fourteen or fifteen and they'd get the discipline of holding down a job and saving a bit of money for a few years. Kidman used to get kids looking for a job in Adelaide and he'd send them up parcel-post to his different stations and some of them worked their way up through the stock camp to become head stockmen and managers.

So from time to time we'd take a couple of boys on. We've had a few beauties! There was Gary, he'd run away from every detention centre in Brisbane. He couldn't tell the truth if he tried, but he picked up stock work and turned out really good at it. And another tough little beggar was Jason. He would have been quite good as far as work was concerned but he was from Ipswich and all his family had been in the mines and they'd learned to work the compensation racket.

At the time I had a bloke named Frank Crowley sinking a dam, so I had this Jason off-siding for him. And if the silly young coot doesn't decide to lop off the top of his finger and get on compo! So Frank Crowley throws him into the truck and runs him into Pauline. She stops the bleeding and bandages him up. But Frank Crowley was very suspicious and he went back and tracked him up and he found the little log where this Jason had had a couple of goes and the end of his finger was still there. Pauline had him propped up in bed with his hand held high and the bleeding had stopped. But this other kid, this Gary, gets to him and tells him, 'Hey! You're not going to get compo that way!' So he lets his hand hang down and gets it bleeding again. So, righto, we chucked him in the car and run him into town. Then I got on to Gordon Tynesmith, the copper at Stonehenge, and showed him the little log this Jason had used as a chopping block with the cuts on it, and the end of his finger. And it all comes out! After that we heard no more about compo! I got rid of him after that.

We have put in an airstrip here across the creek but we've never had to use it in an emergency. Pauline has always patched us up. Any accidents we've had we've always relied on ourselves. Pauline is a good nurse. She's very kind. Even with me! It's only eighty miles to town and if someone's really hurt you just pick them up and toss them in the car and race them into town.

It has always been Pauline that kept everything together even when things were rough and that gave me a free rein to go out and get on with my work. She kept the house and everything nice and she did a wonderful job with the kids, making their clothes and teaching them their Correspondence. We tried to get governesses; even got a demountable for a school and quarters, but it didn't work out. It was a bit isolated for them. Girls prefer those big company places. In the end we bought a house in Winton so the kids could go to school and then they went to Blackheath and Thornburgh in Charters Towers. When Alan got to be School Captain I said to him, 'You must have been pretty cunning to

For Charlie's Eightieth birthday in September 2005, the family gathered for a reunion at a rock-hole on Kurran.

keep a clean crime sheet for seven years! I know how difficult it was in the navy!' All the kids have turned out well. Bruce has taken over Kurran and has another place, Boolbie, and Alan is taking over Eildon Park. Don has a contract fencing business at Boulia; Laurie is a musician in Sydney and Beth is a lecturer at Tafe in Townsville.

We're proud of the lot of them and of the grandchildren. And, now, a first great-grand-child!

Pauline has always stuck by me. It needs to be two of you to keep a family going. And Pauline and me, we've made it now for forty-odd years. That's not too bad. She has been a wonderful wife and a wonderful mother to the kids. I wouldn't have been able to do it without her.

Pauline Rayment

Introduction

Pauline Rayment is one of those women of whom one automatically thinks, 'What a lovely lady!' – softly spoken, feminine, thoughtful, a wonderful mother, a devoted wife.

Pauline has a remarkable sense of the history of the Outback she has grown to love. In the backyard of the family home in Winton she has established a collection of Australiana comparable with many a town museum's. It includes an item familiar to many a grateful outback mother, a meat-safe cot. Into one of these you could pop your baby or toddler, close the lid and be assured it was safe from flies, centipedes, snakes and any other crawling or flying nasties. If you stood the legs of this practical but unlovely-looking piece of furniture in tins of water, you knew your baby was also safe from ants.

Aware of the significance of her husband Charlie's life-story, Pauline has amassed an archive of back-ground material, an invaluable resource. She herself writes short-stories and poetry.

While I was interviewing Charlie I became aware that his wife was keeping a very low profile in the background, providing us with cups of tea in Shelley tea cups and with delicious home-made scones and tea-cake. I said to her, as the recording of Charlie's story progressed, 'All of this could not have happened without a woman in the background. I would like to hear your story too.' But, by then we had run out of time for any further interviewing. As we said good-bye Pauline promised she would make a tape-recording and send it.

When the tape later arrived at my home in Sussex I was spell-bound as I listened to Pauline's account of her early years on Kurran, first as a bride, then as a young mother. This story, in Pauline's own words, conveys the overwhelming sense of loneliness, the heat , the isolation, all faced by her with undiminished love for the man she had fallen in love with as a young nurse in far away Brisbane. George Essex Evans could have written his memorable lines especially of her;

'They left the vine-wreathed cottage, and the mansion on the hill;
The houses of the busy streets, where life is never still,
The pleasures of the city, and the friends they cherished best,
For love they faced the wilderness, the women of the west.'

Chapter 8...

FACING THE WILDERNESS

PAULINE RAYMENT

There was a time when the outback was a mythical world to me. At school I had read Mrs. Aeneas Gunn's, 'We of the Never Never', recited Dorothea McKellar's 'My Country', and had enthusiastically sung Waltzing Matilda. Albert Namitjira's paintings were becoming popular and many people had a framed print of one in their homes. I saw a documentary about the mail-run on the Birdsville Track; I read about Flynn of the Inland; I'd heard of the Royal Flying Doctor. An awareness of somewhere called The Outback was nudging itself into my consciousness. But, like Outer Mongolia or Tibet, I never thought I would ever go there.

Then I met Charlie. He was the friend of a friend. My friend was ill in the hospital where I nursed. She rang her bell for attention and when I went into her room to answer it, I saw that she had a visitor, tall, dark, and ruggedly good-looking. With a smile, he stood to shake hands and in that moment I knew that I had met my future.

Our courtship was brief as Charlie had to return to his property, Kurran, a rough, unimproved block which he had held since before joining the navy. I learned that apart from his years in the navy, Charlie had spent all his life as a stockman and a drover. He also told me that his family had been pioneers of the Inland Rivers country, settling there just a few years after the ill-fated Burke and Wills expedition of 1860.

When Charlie returned to Kurran, my life became a period of waiting for letters from him. They were precious and few and far between. There was no mail-run to Kurran. Charlie had to leave his mail-bag at the nearest property, Connemara, about fifty miles away, depending on whether he could get away to drive across. From there it was taken on to Winton once a week. But, in the Wet, of course, mail sometimes didn't get through for many weeks. When I did receive a letter from Charlie I would read it over and over again, and then carry it around in my uniform pocket, or in my purse, wherever I went, to make him seem closer.

But then at last it was time to start making wedding plans. Charlie and I were married in the lovely old Anglican Church of St. Matthew at Grovely, Brisbane, with all my family and friends around us. My family was a happy one; my father and mother, my sisters and my one brother, had always been close. But in the outback where I was going there would not even be a telephone to keep us in touch.

I could only tell everyone that they would be able to reach me by letter but that there was no way of telling when it would get through.

After a honeymoon of cool mountains and golden beaches, Charlie and I began to prepare for the journey west. Charlie bought a three-ton Morris truck and a small aluminium caravan. Then, my heart churning with apprehension and excitement, it was time to say good-bye to my family, and to head off a thousand miles into the unknown with my new husband.

We drove for days, passing small towns, camping and continuing on. We had problems towing the caravan. We also had a dog and some bantam chooks to be looked after. Finally, we reached Longreach. We stocked up on food supplies, bought a Crown wood stove, a copper for boiling the clothes and tin tubs to bath in. Then, early one morning we set off across open downs country on the last couple of hundred miles towards what was to be my new home.

The dirt road to the south-west ran parallel to the Thomson River. After about three hours we reached the township of Stonehenge, population about thirty. There was a little store, a Police Station and a Post Office. Mrs. Iris Buntine had been in charge of the Post Office for thirty years. Many years later she would become Queenslander of the Year. The people were very friendly. There were lots of goats wandering about. Later I got to own some of them myself and learned to milk them.

We crossed the Thomson and headed west for another ninety miles. Late that afternoon Charlie told me that we had crossed our boundary and would soon be home. There was no fence. Only a line of trees along a dry creek bed marked the start of Kurran country in the Diamantina watershed.

Charlie had never embellished the truth of what I could expect at Kurran. He had never tried to make it seem more attractive than it was. He had given me the facts; vast distances; no house; no laid-on water; no electricity; no phone; no amenities of any kind and no neighbours within fifty miles. Because I knew there was no house, I had made 'gunyah-dresses', not 'house-dresses' for my trousseau. All I knew was that there was a hut and a spinifex shelter.

I had a sketchy mental image of what to expect, but the memory of the moment it came into view is imprinted on my mind as though with a hot iron; the setting sun, the red hills dotted with grey-green spinifex; some horse yards, and a hut, crouching against the hillside. All it needed were the blood-curdling whoopings of Red Indians on the warpath to complete the picture. But it was not a Hollywood movie. It was the Outback. I had arrived. I was excited. It was all so awesome. And this was my home; my new home. Charlie switched off the truck engine and the silence hit me. I was to get to know it so well. I had entered the crucible of experiences that meant I would never again be the same person I had been when I left Brisbane as a bride.

That first night we backed our small caravan alongside the front of the hut. The back of the hut fitted into the side of the hill. In the back wall was a low doorway, blocked with a sheet of corrugated-iron on a frame that you could lift in and out if you wanted to close it. This was to get to the open-fire place out the back where an assortment of camp ovens and billies sat waiting for me. I had to bend over to get in and out of the doorway, not because I'm very tall but because it was a small doorway; five foot four inches, because of the hill at the back. Sheets of iron covered the south end of the hut and wire netting was stretched around the open sides to keep out the wild life; kangaroos, dingoes, scrub-bulls, crows and camels.

The other two walls were of corrugated-iron and bush timber. The dirt floor was covered with swags, saddles, fuel-drums and stores and other droving-plant equipment in great quantity. I stood there, mesmerized, looking into the dark interior, my eyes searching for something familiar and homely. But there was nothing; no stove; no fridge; no toilet; nothing of any comfort. But, after it got dark, Charlie and I decided we could work things out next morning and that as long as we had each other, things would be alright, so we went to bed. The bed was made of plaited green-hide on a timber frame. Charlie had made it himself.

On our first morning I thought I would look around before I began the settling-in process. I wandered around the hill and there were no tracks, or any sign that any human being had ever been there before me. I might have been the first female to ever walk on this particular patch of earth. Certainly there was no other woman walking about on it at that moment but me. As I walked I picked a bunch of yellow and purple flowers and when I got back to the hut, put them into a jar, covered the top of a fuel drum with a tea towel and arranged my bush bouquet in the centre. Closing my eyes, I blessed my home in the wilderness with a prayer.

So I got through that first day and it was followed by many, many more. Life took on a reality that changed me for ever. Having to be alone and having to cope while Charlie was away was the hardest. At first I would shed tears and beg him, 'Please! Don't leave me!' But he told me, 'This is how it has to be. There is work to be done and I've got to go!' We loved each other but this was the reality of our situation. He would have to be away mustering or working out on the property. He didn't like women in his camp and besides, he needed someone to be at the hut to look after things there and to check the waters and feed the horses and chooks and dogs.

So I had to learn to be alone. And that is 'alone' as in no other human being visible; no-one to talk to; no-one to come if you called or screamed. No telephone; no radio transceiver; no electricity to light the dark nights. Anything you did was within the circle of the kerosene lantern or the candle. And no other sound except the dingoes howling at night and the crows in the day. Nothing! And no-one! For days and weeks.

I would climb the hill at the back of the hut and look around at the immensity. And I would throw my voice out into this space around me and imagine, 'Can you hear me, Charlie? Can anyone hear me?' But, of course, no-one could. There was no-one. As far as the eye could see were ironstone ridges and red hills. And mulga and gidgea. And I knew that beyond where that ended there was more of the same. And I knew that there was no human figure anywhere in all that vast horizon. So I would climb down the hill, get a fire going, and make a cup of tea. And, oh! The soothing joy of a cup of tea! It soothes anguish, both mental and physical.

Spelling

Sailors don't like very rough weather. ✓

The stream followed a corse (course) through a quit (quiet) valley. ✓

Your corrections should be written out Beth.

Section of a Primary Correspondence School spelling lesson; Beth Rayment, 1982. Pauline drove fifty miles to Davenport Downs to collect the mail-bag with the children's lessons off the mail-truck.

But these times of being alone developed different dimensions when the children arrived. I had the children to talk to and by then I had a Traegar transceiver[1]and contact with the Flying Doctor Base and my neighbours Ethel and Frank Donnellan, on Davenport Downs. They were just wonderful. They were fifty miles away but just hearing their voices! But the transceiver would only work if I had a charged-up battery. And atmospheric interference could blot out the signals.

With the children there was always the concern that if they were ill what could I do. The Flying Doctor plane wouldn't have been able to land because we didn't have a strip. There was no-where suitable. I would have to get to the nearest strip, or set out the two hundred and fifty-miles to the hospital in Winton.

And then I would think, 'What if I die!' So, very early, from an early age, I taught the children where they could get water. And I made sure there were always dry biscuits that they would be able to reach. And I told them, 'If anything ever happens to Mummy you must stay inside the hut.' By this time there was a bit of a wire fence around it. So I taught them, 'Stay inside the fence and wait. And Daddy will come back one day and get you.' But of course, it could have been weeks. So, in my heart, my fear was always; the children! The children!

I used to have to go to Brisbane to have the babies because the doctor said I needed specialist attention. Also my mother and sisters could help to care for the older ones. So that was wonderful, to be with family and friends for a while. But I

1 Low-powered, portable, pedal-powered radio transceiver invented by Adelaide electrical engineer, Alfred Traeger, and integral to the development of the Royal Flying Doctor Service which began in 1928 from Cloncurry, N.W. Queensland.

had changed. I was used to myself, and I had learned to keep to myself. The noise and the bustle were alien. I longed for my little bush home and the contentment of baking the bread and watching those glorious sunsets and the peace and tranquility. And I always missed Charlie.

He could never be with me when I had to go so far away for so long. We had five children, and only once was he able to manage to be there for the birth; for our third son. He could never be away from Kurran for very long. In those days the father just waited outside until they were summoned into the room. But I was so happy to have my husband there at visiting time, and that for once Charlie could have the pleasure of holding a newborn son in his arms. The others he had to wait to see until I took them back out west. They would be over a month old by then. And when Charlie was at Kurran by himself, there was no contact, no phone. So there was always this blankness; this someone who you couldn't contact. Well, you just got on with things.

But when our only daughter, Beth – she was the last baby - was born Charlie was camped out down at the southern end of the property. Laurie was away at boarding school. I had Allan down in Brisbane with me. We rang Stonehenge exchange and asked old Mrs. Buntine to try to get through to a friend at Tonkoro, Kevin Whaley, to ask where Charlie might be. And Kevin drove over and found Charlie asleep in his swag and woke him up and told him, 'Wake up, Mate! You've got a daughter!'

As the children got to school age, well, that was another thing to be faced. I gave them lessons from the Correspondence School in Brisbane. The lessons would be on the mail truck and we had to set off to collect them. I'd load the children on board the truck and off we'd go, over quite a rough road, to return the mail-bag with their lessons and pick up the next consignment. But they loved their lessons and I loved teaching them.

By then we had the wood-burning stove inside and I did all the cooking; the bread and cakes. Just improvising if we ran out of anything. We didn't have butter, of course. I'd use rendered down fat from when we killed. We got our supplies probably two or three times a year. We tried hard to keep any perishables as long as we could; potatoes and onions and pumpkins. Charlie built a spinifex shed, all open, with wire racks – old shearers stretchers – hung from the rafters for the air to circulate and that way we would keep them as long we could.

We butchered our own meat. When I first had to help Charlie with this job I was quite upset as I had to take the pieces of meat from him and put them into the correct hessian bags, corned meat here, steak here, and so on. The flesh was warm and quivering and blood was everywhere. That was another of my reality moments. We'd rub coarse salt into the corned-meat pieces and put them into the double hessian bags and hang them up from the rafters in the spinifex shed. Then at night we'd put it out on stretchers to air it, to get rid of some of the moisture that seeped out. Then, first thing in the morning, before the sun and the flies, we'd bag it again, going through it to throw out any pieces that were starting to go off in the heat. The dogs and the chooks would eat that. Nothing was wasted.

At first we had no refrigeration, keeping what we could in the safe with wet bags over it, constantly wetting the bags. I kept the babies cool the same way; in a cot with wet sheets over it. Later we got an old kero fridge which smoked in the heat and terrifed me. About this time there was a fire on one of the big stations and the family were burnt to death, and they put it down to the kerosene fridge. It was said that kerosene fridges were the cause of many a fire. I kept old towels wet and wrung out, thrown over the top of this fridge to try to keep it working; just to keep a bit of fresh meat and the milk from the goats. But definitely you just could not keep butter. Our eldest son, Laurie, was born in January, the hottest month, and he could never have candles on his birthday cake to blow out. We would put them on, of course, but they would melt and topple over before we had finished singing Happy Birthday!

A meat-safe cot, a god-send to many outback mothers, in Pauline Rayment's collection of Australiana.

At first the hut had just the dirt floors which I used to keep watered to keep the dust down. Then Charlie cemented the floor. Oh, I appreciated that! Every improvement that was done was a thrill. Then he added a section that gave us three more rooms. I felt I had a mansion! It had such a beautiful view; the hills and the dam with the water sparkling and the windmill turning. I taught the children to swim in the dam and they had great fun.

I carried water in kerosene tins made into buckets with a piece of wire for a handle, to boil the clothes in the copper outside, and hung them to dry on a wire clothes line kept up with a forky stick. They didn't take long to dry!

I missed my mother and sisters when I went back to Kurran with each new baby; not having anyone to call upon. But I realized that, as a Christian, my faith was growing. I'd been a Sunday School teacher, and I began to realize that God's church was this great country, this wonderful creation. Over the years my mother and sisters came out to Kurran to see this place that used to swallow me up. They liked it but they didn't understand my love of it. But of course, it was the man that I loved, and for that reason my love for the land was growing. Charlie and the children were the pivot of my life.

I always yearned for masses of flowers, but it was too hot to grow them. I would just hunt around and find what I could. A typical bunch would be sprigs of gidgea or gumleaf or yellow or purple blossoms from the shrubs that grew in amongst the mulga. When the children were tiny they used to bring me little posies that they would make and I would be thrilled and put them into a jar of water.

From the time they were very young, Laurie, Don and Bruce, learned to help Charlie with the stock work. They contributed to the running of Kurran from a very early age. I would be pulling riding boots off some very sound-asleep little boys of a night-time. Charlie did at times have some men to help, but mostly it was a family concern. Especially, a few years later, when there was a nose-dive in cattle prices and everyone in the cattle industry was having a very hard time. We were all working extra hard then. The children and I would go up and help in the yards. It was a tough time. But it was the way of life. We all pulled together. The only time we had other men in was when we had contractors in to get new dams put down. That was very exciting for the boys, seeing the big equipment.

I always tried to make Sunday different when I could. I'd give the children Sunday School lessons, and make cakes with pink icing for smoko, as a treat, to keep Sunday a bit special as God's day. Sometimes you could pick up hymns or a service on the radio.

The children listened to the ABC programmes for children; the Argonauts Club, the reading of The Muddleheaded Wombat by Ruth Park, and on Saturday nights, from 4LG Longreach, the Ranch Club, with all the Slim Dusty songs, Click Go the Shears, and Trumby. They loved all of those. So that was our entertainment. But, every September, when it was possible, we would go to the Birdsville and Bedourie races. We would join up with our friends at Davenport, Ethel and Frank Donnellan, and travel together for the long hot trip. We would take our little aluminium caravan, hooked on behind. Ethel was a wonderful woman! She was my mentor into the ways of bush life.

There was a ladies' session over the transceiver – a 'galah' session - and for weeks before the races we would be planning and sewing for the Flying Doctor's stall, planning what to cook, how many loaves of bread we'd need for sandwiches, how many cakes and biscuits we'd need. And we would be poring through the mail order catalogues from the big city stores, David Jones', McWhirter's and McDonald and East's, choosing dresses and hats and gloves. I did all the children's sewing on a little Singer sewing machine with a wheel turned by hand. You turned the wheel with your right hand and pushed the fabric through with the left. But you got very skilful at it.

Then in December we would go to the Bedourie Christmas Tree, with a Santa Claus and a fancy-dress party for the children. These events were a chance for the children to mix with other children and for the adults to have a good yarn. You got to see the folk who were just a voice over the transceiver for the rest of the year. You would see a face and then you could put it to the voice. And I began to realize that there were other people in this vast outback, and that all of them were ready to come to the aid of the others. All of us were linked. It was the Spirit of the Outback that they talk about. It was palpable.

There came a time when we purchased another property called Eildon Park, about eighty miles south-west of Winton, not far from the famous dinosaur tracks at Lark Quarry. We were then only about eighty miles from a doctor and a hospital and other amenities, and our nearest neighbour was only twenty miles away instead of fifty. Two more children, Allan and Beth were born.

The boarding-school years were now upon us and the horrible, horrible feeling of leaving your children behind. You miss the children. The children miss you. But you get through it, with a few dramas and tears. But at Eildon Park we had a weekly mail service right to the door so we were able to get regular letters from them.

Eventually the older boys began to be more involved in the running of the place. In 1987 we purchased another property called Boolbi, on the Boulia road, eighty miles west of Winton, in partnership with our son Bruce. And it is Bruce who now owns Boolbi and Kurran. Allan owns Eildon Park and Charlie and I look after it for him. Don has a contract business, Laurie is a musician in Sydney and Beth is a lecturer at TAFE in Townsville, happily married, with twins. So the family continues to grow. There is even one little great-grand-daughter!

Charlie and I wouldn't live anywhere else but here in the Outback. There is always a fire going in the kitchen with a billy on the boil ready to make a cup of tea for anyone that calls in. It means so much to us to be living here. I came to the Outback as a stranger, really. It was only love for Charlie that brought me here. But now I am no longer a stranger. I know I belong.

Bill Petrie

Bill Petrie

Introduction

Most Queenslanders will be aware of the significance of the name Petrie in the history of early Queensland. In and around Brisbane, Petrie is a familiar name; Petrie Terrace in the city, Petrie Bight in the Brisbane River, Petrie the suburb, Petrie the prosperous district to the north. Andrew Petrie, Bill Petrie's great-great grandfather was one of the earliest Queensland settlers, arriving as newly appointed Superintendent of Works when Brisbane was still a penal colony where convicts in leg-irons shuffled the muddy streets.

So I was immensely delighted when Bill Petrie, whom I met at the border township of Camooweal where he and his wife Ina run a tourist facility, agreed to be part of this project of recording the life-stories of some of the current generation of Queenslanders. Long an admirer of 'Reminiscences of Early Queensland' by Tom Petrie, Bill's forebear, the lively account of boyhood in early Brisbane, it seemed Bill's story would be a link with that vigorous early colonial period. Bill proved to be an excellent raconteur with confidence in the worthwhileness of recording his own 'reminiscences' of a period of Queensland history which is now is its turn fast disappearing.

In compiling the tape-recordings which went into making this story, Bill had a relaxed, conversational style, and his account of his boyhood at Petrie, to Brisbane's north, are in much the same vein as his remarkable predecessor's. We can almost hear the swish of the cane in the two-teacher school and be silent witnesses at the almost daily fights in the play-ground occasioned by the tauntings of 'Youse think yer Jesus Christ, doncha! Just because yer name's Petrie!'

Bill also showed himself to be a master of the Australian art of understatement. A serious fall from a horse was, 'a bit of a fall'; a fall in which he could well have broken his back was 'a fair bit of a fall'. Bitten twice by a Down's tiger he thinks, 'I'd better do something about this,' and wades into the bore-drain to wash the venom off, his voice so laconic that in the writing of the story an exclamation mark was not necessary.

As well as working on properties all over Queensland from Coorabulka in the Channel Country to Wandovale in the Gulf, Bill managed three of the Northern Territory's best known stations, Cattle Creek, Nutwood Downs and Hodgson River. Bill remembers that his father, Rollo Petrie, was 'a great diary keeper and a bit of an historian' and that he 'should have written a book.' Bill says he would like to write one himself. Bill is a large man with a large enjoyment of life's challenges and possibilities. With his remarkable powers of observation, his lifetime of experiences to draw upon and his huge sense of humour I think he should. We would all want to read it.

At a time when horses were still an accepted mode of transport, children were put on horses at an early age.

Aged about two, Bill looks calmly self-assured.

Chapter 9...

REMINISCENCES OF AN OUTBACK LIFE

Bill Petrie – Station Manager and Pilot

The first Petrie to come out to Australia was Andrew Petrie on the *Stirling Castle*, landing in Sydney in 1831. He had a number of sons, among them, Tom Petrie who wrote 'Reminiscences of Early Queensland'. One of Tom's sons was Walter Petrie, my grandfather, and one of Walter's sons was Rollo Petrie, my father. Old Andrew Petrie built a home for his family on the Brisbane River which is how Petrie Bight how it got its name.[1]

Old Andrew was a builder, an architect and a town planner. He built a lot of early Brisbane, including the old General Hospital. Not long ago when they were doing renovations on it they found a beam with his name on it. He also built the first big Post Office in Brisbane. He had a lumber yard and was a bit of an explorer. He sailed up along the coast to the north and reported on the timber on Frazer Island and discovered the Mary River [2].

Andrew's son Tom grew up among the Aborigines of Moreton Bay and spoke about six of their dialects. He also got on very well with the convicts and got into trouble for sneaking them in tobacco and various things. Old Andrew Petrie and his wife were very strict Scottish Presbyterians and didn't let him get away with much so he got plenty of floggings.

When he was quite a young fellow Tom Petrie took up a piece of Whiteside station up in the Pine Rivers area. In those days that was pretty hostile Aboriginal territory. No-one could get on with the blacks except Tom because he could speak their languages. For this reason he was much in demand as a guide for anyone who wanted to have a look around the country. Dalalpi, the head-man of that North Pine area took Tom under his wing and showed him a good place to build a

1 Constance Campbell Petrie, Reminiscences of Early Queensland, UQP, 1992; 'The Petrie family came to Queensland on the *James Watt*, the first steamer to enter what are now Queensland waters. ...They came as far as Dunwich in the *James Watt* then finished the journey in the pilot boat manned by convicts. Kangaroo Point, Newfarm and South Brisbane were then under cultivation but the rest was all bush, so thick around Petrie's Bight that one of the workmen building a house was speared.

2 Ibid, 'In 1862 my father started from North Pine in a ship's longboat with about ten blacks, a few having their wives with them, to go to Mooloolah and Maroochy to look for cedar timber. After landing and refreshing themselves they went up the river some miles, turning at last up a creek which they named Petrie's Creek, my father being the first white man there.'

homestead. So Tom built a lovely old home and called it Marumba, meaning 'Good Place'. He ran cattle there and bred horses for the Indian army.

So my young brother Jim and I and our sister Jan grew up at North Pine. But in 1910 when Tom Petrie died, the railway had changed the name of the siding from North Pine to Petrie. The locals didn't take too kindly to the name being changed. Jim and I always got it rough at school about it. We had to fight every day because our name. They used to say, 'Youse think you're Jesus Christ, doncha! Just because yer name's Petrie!'

The head master at the school was a cranky old fellow, Arthur Hansen. He had been gassed in World War One. After the Japs came into the war all the young, able fellows had been called up, so they had to staff the schools with whoever they could get. I used to feel sorry for old Arthur and I would get him drinks of water when he had a bad turn. I had a sneaking sort of respect for him. But that didn't prevent me getting eighteen 'cuts' straight off, one day. It's an example of how when you are a kid your parents are always right. It was a two-teacher school. A young lady took the Babies up to about Prep Four and after that you got to Grade One and into Mr. Hansen's room. It felt like being in the condemned cell. One time my class was out on the verandah draped around the railing doing a reading lesson. One of the words was 'castle'. My mother and father always pronounced it as 'carsel'. The monitor – it was a girl! – reckoned I said 'carsel' instead of 'cas-el'. She sent me in. She said, 'Go in!' Being told to 'Go in' was the same as getting the death sentence. You'd go in to Mr. Hansen and tell him whatever it was you were supposed to have done and he would give you a belting. He said, 'What did you do!' I told him. He said, 'Read it to me!' I called it 'car-sel' again. He gave me six cuts. He said, 'Now! What is it?' I said 'carsel'. He gave me another six cuts and said, 'What is it!' I said, 'carsel'. He gave me a third lot of six cuts. He said, 'NOW! What is it!' I said, 'carsel'. He said, 'Ah! Get out of here!' By that time it didn't matter. My hands were that numb!

I've never had any fear of snakes or poisonous things even when I was very little. I used to play under the house with a pet red-back spider. I thought it was pretty and I'd slide under and see it every day. Mum said, 'What have you got under there?' When I told her it was my special red spider she got the long-handled broom. There were a lot of snakes around the place and it used to frighten the life out of her that I liked them and would try to pick them up.

This was wartime so there were Bren gun carriers and troop trains on the railway, day and night. And all night long the air-force would be doing training flights. On moonlight nights they would do simulated engine failures over the river along our bottom paddock. So all our toys were toy aeroplanes or toy tanks or machine guns and Bren guns that we made ourselves out of bits of wood.

I was an expert in making gings, which is what we called shanghais. We used to get a green forked stick and bend the stick and tie it back on to a cotton reel and put it in the oven. It would dry and set so that the fork was wine-glass shaped; which didn't make it any better but it seemed better to us. And you cut rubber bands out of bike tubes for ammo and for the long sling straps you'd cut the long seam out of the tube. For the pouch you would use the tongue of one of your

Dad's old boots. We used to carry two of these things; a ging and a bum-stinger. The police-sergeant at Petrie was down on them and when he caught us we would shove the good one down our shirt and we'd leave the bum-stinger hanging out of our pocket. We would hand over the bum-stinger and put on a down-in-the-mouth face about losing our ging. But all the time the good one would be down our shirt. We were pretty good shots with these things. Poor old Blue Mountain parrots! I am ashamed to remember what we did to them!

At about eight I started to use Dad's Stiz .22, a German make, single shot, self-cocking. I was pretty handy with it. It was deadly accurate, a beautiful thing. Dad was terribly strict when it came to handling firearms. He drilled it into us; you weren't allowed so much as to point a toy gun at one another. We grew up with a healthy respect for firearms.

Loading the pack-horses, Marion Down, 1940s. It is interesting to compare the labour-intensive work involved in droving with pack-horses compared with today's motorized transport.

You spend a lot of your time as kids trying to kill yourself. My cousin Jim McGuire and I were down the bottom paddock once. We'd get these snail shells and screw them on to the bark of a gum-tree to take shots at. Then we'd check to see how we went. And one time I'd had a shot at this shell and hit it and I'd gone up to screw another one on. I was just turning round to walk back when a bullet whizzed past, going through my shirt. Jim had a rifle with a hair trigger and where we'd been leaning our rifles against this stump he had bumped his and it had gone off. If I had told Dad about that! Well!

One morning going to school we witnessed two Spitfires in a mid-air crash. It started as a Spitfire and Lockhead Lightning dog-fight. Then the Lockhead pulled out. They used to do what they called a salute before they pulled away. They would roll and make a bit of a pass. Then another Spitfire came and engaged the first one in another dog-fight. He went to make a pass but he clipped the first one's wing. Their tails locked and they both went into a spin. There were army camps on both sides of the river and one of them actually pulled out of the spin and tried to take the river on, to avoid crashing into the camps, but too late. He hit the water and smashed to pieces. It was a horrible thing to see.

I only went to Grade Seven. I wouldn't sit for Scholarship. My father wanted me to do a trade; to be a draftsman with Walkers Ltd in Maryborough, the shipbuilding and engineering works, but I flatly refused. I wanted to get out and smell the branding irons. Then in 1946 we shifted out to Marion Downs. Things were still pretty rough after the war. Petrol was still rationed. I finished up in the stock-camp on ten shillings a week just before I turned eleven. I thought, 'This is the life I wanted!' and there was no chance of getting me back to school after that. I did a bit of Correspondence, but, no, it wasn't for me.

Dick McCullough was head stockman. He kicked my arse and drove me head first on to the tucker table because I went to put jam on a bit of brownie. I got up and I tried to fight him. Then he gave me a belting! He said, 'We've got six weeks' tucker and it's going to last six weeks! You don't put jam on your brownie!' But he was a good horseman! That man could ride!

I had my eleventh birthday in the camp. The cook was a fellow named Frank Cavanagh, well-known in the Gulf. He told me he would make me a birthday cake. He made this damper in a little drover's oven and put it in the ashes. Then he got interested in the cutting-out and forgot about it. When he came back it was burnt to a cinder. He showed it to me. He said, 'There you are, Bill! There's your birthday cake!'

Marion Downs was a beautiful place. I loved it. It had such a variety of country on it; a bit of downs, a lot of stone, timber, creeks. The original homestead was made of stone and pise; ant-bed and straw. It was a very old place. The old store on Marion was an incredible place for Jim and me because of the smells; ammunition and rifles all over the place and black powder, and dehydrated potato, and horse-feed and dry stores, and old saddles and harness; a dirt floor. Rats everywhere, of course. There were four thousand square miles on Marion with probably around fifteen, sixteen thousand head of cattle; shorthorn only. They used to get most of their bulls from Weebollabolla in New South Wales.

You could ride all over Marion and not see any grass but the cattle were all sleek. In fact Marion Downs held the record at Bowen meat-works for 6000 head of cattle off grass in one year, average dressed weight 934 lbs. The secret of that country is that it is Channel country, with a lot of herbage along the channels; a lot of Flinders and Mitchell grass. The closer you get to the coast the less nutritional value there is in the Mitchell and Flinders, but out in the Channel country it is very sweet. In the Wet those rivers, the Georgina and the Diamantina come down and they flood right out and afterwards you can muster up and down the channels and you get cattle just rolling in fat. In those days there were no fences so it was all open country; all broncho branding; watching cattle at night. You would cut out what you were looking for, say, six hundred fats and you would organize for a drover to come and he would take delivery of them and you would give him one or two nights' watch until they settled down. Then away he would take them into Winton or Quilpie or wherever.

It was on Marion that I saw the Min Min light for the first time. There was a big water-hole about sixteen miles long, called Carrapitchie; brackish water, full of yellow-belly. There was only one place where you could cross, a sort of natural causeway. And we were camped there one night expecting a drover called Jack Gurdler to come along but he hadn't turned up. And in the middle of the night they saw this light going down the other side of the water-hole. They assumed that this Girdler had stopped and got out of his vehicle and got a carbide light going to go looking for fire wood. But there was no wood at Carrapitchie. It was right out in the middle of the desert country. But the horses all took off and their bells started up. I'd been on early watch. They came and woke me up. They said, 'Here! You'd better come and have a look at this!' They'd figured if it wasn't Gurdler it could only be one thing and that was the Min Min light.

Later that year it came up to the homestead at Marion three nights in a row. My brother Jim and I fired some shots at it and it just sort've stopped and retreated back up the Bedourie road where it had came from. No tracks next morning. And once on Wongera Waterhole, three nights in a row it came across Diddibu plain at the speed of a jet, but no noise, following the contours of the ground, below tree-top level, over very rough ground covered with blue bush and salt bush and lignum, where the gilgais drained into the Wongera. No vehicle could cross it. Scientists from all over the world have tried to explain what the Min Min is. Some say it is a form of gas. It can move very fast or at the speed of a man walking. But the one thing I noticed about it was that it didn't shine; didn't throw any beam like a car light would. I saw the Min Min nine times altogether, all on Marion except once, and that was on Coorabulka[3].

I had my first fair bit of a fall off a horse on Marion Downs off a big bay called Jenkins – he'd been broken-in by a Yellafella named Jenkins from up Boulia way. He fell with me. I was on dinner- camp watch and a bullock trotted off the other side of the mob. And this Jenkins, you couldn't hold him. Or I couldn't. He put his foot down a hole and turned over on top of me. They thought my back was broken. It was hurting a fair bit. They carried me back to camp and they only thing they could do was that they had a mincer mounted up on the tree of a pack-saddle and they put coolabah leaves through the mincer and filled a shirt sleeve with this pulp and wrapped it round my back.

Dad got a contract building a trucking yard at the Narrows waterhole on Marion Downs.

Marion was the first property in Queensland to use trucks to shift cattle. They got six Leyland Hippos out from England and used them to truck the fats from Marion to Dajarra. Marion Downs was the bullock depot for the North Australia Pastoral company's places in the Territory; Alexandra, Soudan and Gallipoli. They would walk the stores down from them and we also had about six thousand stores of our own on Marion. Other N.A.P.Co places were Monkira and Glenormiston.

3 Neuroscientist, Professor Jack Pettigrew, of the University of Queensland claims the Min Min lights are an inverted mirage of light sources hundreds of miles away, caused by a temperature inversion when cold dense air is trapped near the ground beneath a layer of warmer air, which causes light near the ground to be refracted so that it travels in a curved path around the globe. A similar phenomenon is the Fata Morgana in which landforms beyond the horizon appear to float above it. It would be interesting to know if sightings of the Min Min occurred in the pre-European settlement era when there would have been no light sources at a distance to cause them. Sightings of the Min Min occur most frequently in the Channel Country, and may appear as stationary or travelling at speed and are reported at any time of the year.

It took Dad a long time to build that yard at the Narrows. He travelled for a thousand miles to get the timber; up the Georgina and up the Burke; there's a lot of coolabah up there. Those yards were all timber. The big posts were coolabah, all cut with the cross-cut saw, axes and adzes and drilled with a double-action brace and bit. When I was twelve years old I bored thirty-six miles of fence posts on Marion Downs; that's two holes to a post; thirty-six miles of it.

Dad had some funny old fellows as off-siders. There was one old chap, Bill Jones, an old kangaroo-shooter. He had a big walrus moustache and always rode a bicycle. Like most of those old fellows, he had his own secret dingo lure. He used to mix strychnine and treacle and boot tacks. He'd put this on a pad where he thought a dog would come trotting along and he'd kick a bit of dust over it. Old Bill's theory was that the dog would come trotting along the track, tread in the treacle, get a tack in his foot, lick the treacle, get the strychnine and die!

Old Bill was a bit of a death adder but he taught Jim and me how to get three dog scalps out of every dingo. A scalp was worth fifteen bob in those days. Old Bill was a bloody artist at it. He'd cut down behind the dog's front leg to the pad and that was the nose. Then he'd cut two ears around the shin; then round the ribs and down the back leg, which would curl up and look just like a tail. He would pack this in with a lot of putrid stuff that the burners in town had to examine – the burners were supposed to examine them and count them before they paid you; often it was the policeman or the local JP. But they'd look at this stuff and say, 'How many you got there, Bill?' and he'd tell them. They'd be satisfied and they'd pay out. Bill also used to do pig snouts – they were worth about two shillings each in those days – out of dried apricots. He mix them up with rotten liver and stuff like that to make them stink to high heaven. They would pay him the two bob, alright! Years later, I heard that the poor old fellow did three months in Longreach gaol for faking fifty dingo scalps out of a chestnut brumby foal's hide.

Another hard case Dad had working for him one time was known as the Fox. Everything he said he would add 'said the fox' on the end of it; 'Good morning, said the fox'. 'I'll get some wood, said the fox', and so on. But a harmless old bloke. His skin would crack after a while and he would go up to Boulia and get on the grog. The windmill on the town bore in Boulia never used to function and when the Fox had a skinful he always used to reckon he could fix it. After one of these sessions we thought he was about due back at the camp so we'd go out to the road to meet him. We'd say to the mailman. 'Have you seen anything of the bloody Fox?' He'd say, 'Nah. He hasn't been around for a while.' But they found him alright. At the bottom of the town windmill. He'd climbed up and fallen and broken his leg and died there. Poor old Fox.

I've been bitten twice by snakes. Coorabulka was full of them. I got bitten twice there and once on Laglan. A downs tiger, the first one. It was on Coorabulka at Number Seven bore-drain, in the lignum. My job was to go along the bore-drain with a pitch-fork and clear out all the roly-poly bushes that would have got into it. This downs tiger got up and took a strike at me. I took my hat off and tried to rattle him a bit but I didn't quite judge his length and he got me. I thought, 'Gees! Mongrel thing!' and tried to kick at him and with that he got me again. I thought,

'I'd better do something about this.' so I waded into the bore-drain – hot water, not far from the bore – and washed my leg and that was all I did, really. I had no ill effects at all.

Bill Petrie on the station stallion, Senor Manfredo, 'Jackie', at Oakvale Station, 1958.

I worked on Coorabulka for three years and then went down working for Jack Clanchy on Kameran Downs at Bedourie. It got very dry and there was a rat plague on. We were trying to feed horses but all you were doing was feeding rats. So I went kangaroo shooting and horse breaking. I did a fair bit of brumby shooting on Bimba, an out-station of Byganna on the Belyando. Bimba was owned originally by a fellow called Harry Bushell. He used to breed draught horses for the sugar-cane farms on the coast. He had Bimba organized like a wagon wheel. The homestead was in the middle and the fences radiated out like the spokes of a wheel so that he could muster on his own. And he would walk these horses right across to the coast. But this Harry Bushell was found dead at the bottom of a windmill. He must have been up the mill working up on it and fallen. He was found by a fellow called Hughie Murphy who was out that way doing a bit of trapping. The draught horses he'd had in the yard were dead and he was dead and all rotted away.

The word was that this Bushell used to come back with plenty of money after selling his horses on the coast and bury it. Dad said to me once when we were out there brumby shooting, 'I reckon if I was going to bury money I would bury it under the galley fire.' So we hurled ourselves on to this old galley fire with shovels. We dug down about four foot and we found a tin, an old empty biscuit tin. But that was all we did find.

Dad and I learned two things about brumbies when we were there. The first thing was that it is virtually impossible to spot-light brumbies at night. They will come over the top of you. And the second thing was that they are very hard to skin. The best method is to use another horse to pull the skin back but we only had the old truck. The skins were used for railway seats and razor strops and machinery belts and things like that. But by the time you skinned the carcass and folded them and wired them together a certain way, and got them to the railhead it turned out to be a lot of very hard work. They were all run-out, inbred Clydesdale things with long tails and big manes.

I then went droving with Charlie Rayment. Charlie used to say how he once did sixty mile a day with his horse-plant for thirty days straight when he wanted to get back out west from the coast. His horses got very leg-weary. Which I know, because Charlie's horses damned near killed me twice.

There was a big yellow bay, an ugly-natured thing. We were at Terrabo waterhole, cutting-out, and Charlie told me to take his horse and ride to the yards and bring this yellow bay back. He said, 'Go in and catch that yellow bay and saddle him. Put a neck bag on him and bring him out here.' So I go in and catch this fellow and went to saddle him. That cranked him right up! Then I undid the hobbles and swung up on him. All hell broke loose! I got hung up in both irons and he gave me a fair sort of a massaging around the back of the head.

Old Smithie, the cook in the camp, came shuffling out to me. He thought I was killed. But I wasn't, or not quite. He said to me, 'You want to tell old Charlie to ride his own bloody horses, Boy! There's no bastard should have to ride that mongrel thing!' I went back out to the camp a bit subdued.

Another time, on the stock route near Winton, there was a trough; and those western cattle aren't used to drinking out of troughs. You have to flood the trough and then when they smell the wet dirt they will scent water and come in to it and start drinking. Every drover does this and consequently, when the mud dries, it's all packed solid cattle-tracks like concrete. Charlie had disappeared and there were some bush cattle coming in behind us. I was on this horse called Tadpole, one of those that had done this sixty mile a day trip with Charlie, and when we got in there this Tadpole goes to jump across a gilgai with these hard cattle-tracks. When we hit the other side he just crumpled up. We got a fair sort of a fall out of it. He knocked the point of his shoulder off and his eye out. I landed down on my shoulder and did my collar bone and pushed it right across my neck. I got up before the horse and got him up and I was hobbling round and round when Charlie rode up and said, 'What happened!' I said, 'This useless thing fell!' Charlie said, 'No bloody wonder, eh! The way you've been pushing him!' That was all the sympathy I got. I only did the one trip with Charlie. After that I took off on my own.

I started breaking-in horses for four quid a head. I'd keep them four days and charge them four quid a day to work them after that. I worked on Bladensberg out of Winton, then Monkira, then was head stockman on Marion for three years, then up to the Inside country, to Laglan, out from Clermont, owned by Fred Appleton, Wandovale up in the Gulf, Kameran Downs, Oakvale, Laglan, Yakkamunda near Colinsville and Meteor out of Springsure. There was a story about Meteor. Meteor Creek and Skeleton Creek headed up in the Carnarvons, wild bushranger sort of country. The two fellows who owned Meteor were murdered by a gang of cattle duffers; Doyle, Dahlke and the Kenniff brothers. A couple of them were hanged for it.

It was while I was on Meteor that I met and married Ina. She was the youngest hospital matron in Queensland at the time, and a good-looker. She was at the hospital in Springsure and I went in to make a blood donation. I always say that it was while I was in a weakened state that I proposed. We were married at the Presbyterian Church in Rocky and not long after that we headed up to the Territory to manage for Vestey's.

I managed Cattle Creek on Wave Hill where their bull-breeding project was in operation. Then we moved to another Vestey's concern, Nutwood Downs. We then gave Vestey's away and moved to Hodgson River which was owned in conjunction with Elsey by a Chinese concern, E.W.C. Wong.

Ina and I have five children, Karen and Heather, Helen, Tom and Mhari. They were all on Correspondence. We had a governess, Jenny Roberts, a lovely girl who became like a daughter to us. She'd been a book-keeper and an ace on computers but she loved the outdoor life on Hodgson Downs. Ina did the nursing on the station. If any of the blacks were sick they would say, 'More better you git longa Missus! Him fix you good.'

There were 250 blacks on Hodgson; and two yella-fellas, old Dan Farrer and his wife, very good people'[4]. The rest were full bloods. They were all good blacks there. No alcohol. If a ringer went into Mataranka I would tell him, 'Get a skinful if you like while you're in there. But don't bring any alcohol past the boundary gate of this place.'

We had a fellow there called Harry Selmes, a real old bushman; a real old recluse and a great shot. He'd been brumby shooting on Wave Hill for Vestey's for many years. He used to shoot for hair - for the value of the manes and tails; and he got 2/6 or about fifty cents in today's money for a pair of ears. He'd bring the ears in and we'd count them and pay him and he would send the hair away to M.E. Humphries in Brisbane to be used for stuffing upholstery for quality cars and furniture. So a few years later when we were on Nutwood, he got in touch with me and asked was there any shooting there. I told him, 'Well, there's a hell of a lot of damned donkeys here if you want to have a go at them.' So Harry started shooting on Nutwood and he shot fifteen hundred donkeys just in the homestead section.

Then when we were on Hodgson Downs, Harry sprung me again. I told him, 'There are brumbies and donkeys here on Hodgson. If you want to have a go at them for the hair, you can.' So he came. He had everything set up nicely in a long-wheel-base Land Rover, a bunk and all. He was totally independent. He carried fuel and boxes of cartridges and cases of tinned stuff. Every so often he might come in to the station then we wouldn't see him again for ages. He turned up when he turned up. Then we didn't see him for a very long while. We asked around if anyone had seen anything of him. Someone told us they thought he might have gone up Katherine way.

Then one year when the blacks were walking about after the Wet they came in and told me, 'There's a motor-car in that creek out that Roper Valley road.' So I went out and had a look. I found the Land Rover in an open forest area. There were the remains of a body in it. And it was poor bloody Harry. The vehicle was completely burnt out, except for some reason the tyres hadn't burnt. Of the body there were just a few teeth and some bits and pieces of bone left. And there was a brand new billy-can hanging in a tree nearby. I didn't touch anything. I went back to Hodgson and got on to the police at Roper Bar.

4 Mentioned in the author's Red Dust Rising (CQU Press) as having known the site of the historic Durack's camp on the Wilton River on Urapunga Station.

The policeman and I went through the gear. And in the billy-can there would have been about eight hundred dollars. Harry must have deliberately left it there. Colin Pope from the C.I.B. in Darwin came down. But it looked as though Harry had set the thing up himself. Ina remembered that the last time he had been in at the station he had a big lump on his leg. She had told him, 'Harry, you had better get that seen to.' But he had said, 'Nah! She'll be right!' and she couldn't talk him into it. It must have been giving him a lot of pain and he must have decided it was cancer. Those old bushmen are fiercely independent. They can't stand the thought of being taken away to hospital. So he'd put an end to things in his own way. Eventually they took the remains back up to Darwin and identified them through DNA. So that was poor old Harry. He was a decent sort of old bloke. I felt very bad about it for a long time. Poor old fellow, dying out there on his own like that.

One year on Hodgson, our young Tom got very sick. Fortunately the army were doing a big exercise in the area with helicopters and we managed to get one of them to get him away to hospital. Then, just before Christmas 1974, little Heather got bad with appendicitis. We were going to take her up to Darwin but at the last moment something made us change our minds. We thought, no, the doctors down in Brisbane will be better. So we headed south. We got there in thirty-six hours straight and got Heather into hospital just as her appendix ruptured as they started operating. And it was just as well we had decided to give Darwin a miss. That was the Christmas that Darwin got wiped out in Cyclone Tracy.

I started getting worried about having a young family in such an isolated place. In the Wet you couldn't use any sort of a vehicle. I decided I was going to look into learning to fly. So I went up to Darwin and started flying lessons and got my commercial pilot's licence.

Then I started looking around for an aircraft. I was talking to Dean von Einem, up at Bachelor. He said, 'What sort of aircraft are you looking for? Do you want me to keep my eye open?' I said, 'Yeah.' And not long after, he got back to me. He said, 'I've got a Cessna 180 up here. It belonged to Eddie Hackman[5].' So I went up and saw Eddie and we did the deal. I got it for four and a half thousand dollars, but I had to spend quite a lot more on it to get it going.' So that's how I started flying.

The Cessna 180 is a 'tail-dragger' – with a rear wheel – very prone to ground looping. With the rear wheel the centre of gravity is behind the main wheels. When you put the brakes on it is liable to turn round on itself. They reckon there are two kinds of Cessna pilots; those who have tail-looped and those who are going to. But the 180 is a beautiful aeroplane; the kings of aeroplanes! And Cessna 180 pilots are the elite of pilots. We don't even drink with the other sort. I have also flown a Cherokee 140 and a Cherokee Warrior. But the Cherokee is a tame little aeroplane. They are so underpowered you open the cowling to look at the engine and you're thinking, 'Where the hell is it!'

We used helicopters a fair bit for mustering on Hodgson. Peter Underhill was the pilot. We had drums of fuel in various places, one of them being on the main air-strip which was about three mile from the house. And one day we put down

5 Eddie Hackman, noted sculptor of horses and horsemen, for example, the bronze, 'The Drover' at Newcastle Waters and 'The Stockman' at the Stockmen's Hall of Fame, Longreach.

there to refuel and while he's doing this I just happened to walk around back of the tail-rotor and I see this oil oozing out of the studs. I drew Peter's attention to it. He said, 'Oh, Christ! That's no good!' So we got on the radio-telephone to Carl Timms at Rotor Services in Darwin and he flew out with a mechanic in a Cessna 172. He pulled the tail-rotor gearbox off and in it there were bits of ground-up metal you could have filled a tobacco tin with. He said, 'Well, you wouldn't have got far with that lot!' Peter said the only thing he had noticed was a bit of a vibration when turning. So we were a bit lucky.

We had a girl out from Scotland once, working as book-keeper. She was a lovely girl, a geologist. She was absolutely in wonderment about this cattle-station life. We were helicopter mustering at the time. The pilot was a well-known bloke from Clermont and we knew him well and liked him. And this girl talked him into taking her round. He said, 'Alright, then!' and way they went. And after a while we thought they'd been away a fair while so Jessica hopped on the quad bike and went out looking for them. She found them, alright; both dead. They'd clipped a tree and gone in. And the usual thing with helicopters; both necks broken. The chopper had gone over on top of them.

We left Hodgson and I started aerial mustering for Ashley Daly on Mount Leonard at Beetoota. But not using my own plane. Using his. I used to fly people round looking at properties and I'd take sky-divers up. By this time we'd bought a ten acre block down at Pialba and I used to fly people over to Frazer Island and land on the beach. They'd take a few photographs and hop back in and I'd take them down to photograph the *Cherry Venture*[6], just skimming along over the waves.

The hairiest take-off I ever did was one time when I said to my father, 'Do you want to go out to Indian Head on Frazer Island and throw a line in off the beach?' It was tailor time, and tailor time is westerly wind time. So out we go and we land on the beach. There were a lot of people there fishing; hundreds of them. So I motor this thing up into the dry sand and we walk a fair way to where the fishing is. Dad gets a couple. Then, later, when we get back, the tide's changed and it's coming in. I think, 'Oh! Shit!' We get in and I pull the tail round as best I can and I bore the engine up. And with a prop that turns clockwise, from behind it, you get the wash clockwise on your left, which steers you to port. That's your prop-wash. Also with gyroscopic force when you lift or change direction it will operate at ninety degrees. So that wants to twist me to the left as well. The wind is under my left wing and she is almost lifting and I'm thinking 'I'm having a bit of a job to get this damned thing up.' The starboard wheel is almost in the top of the waves. And I can't get enough way up to get sufficient rudder to steer. And this westerly wind is coming over the sand dunes. Dad's not saying anything. I'm thinking to myself, 'Well, it's now or bloody never' and I bore the engine, and here's all these blokes fishing and looking up at me, and I'm thinking, 'I'm gonna get a bloody fish-hook in my windscreen any minute now.' And I bore over the top of their heads right along the beach and at last I get the thing up. And once I get it off the beach I slew it round

6 A 1600 ton cargo ship en route from Auckland to Brisbane which went aground in heavy seas in 1973 on Cooloola Beach on Queensland's Sunshine Coast. The crew of twenty-four was winched to safety through heavy surf by breeches buoy. The rusting hulk has become a popular tourist attraction.

into the wind and then everything is OK. We're up and heading for home. Dad's gone quiet. He's just sitting.

After a while he says, 'That was a bit close, wasn't it.' I say, 'Yeah. A bit.'

Hector Moody

Hector Moody with his sister Edna, 1920.

INTRODUCTION

When you drive into historic Square Post station at Mingela, west of Townsville, a plume of dust as fine as talcum powder rises behind your vehicle. A mile from the low-set brick homestead a mob of weaners stands stoically waiting to be fed, yielding no more than a pace or two of ground when you get out of your vehicle to photograph them. They are hungry. Drought has had this part of the north in thrall for too long. Even the encircling mountains look faded.

Despite heat and dust a cheerful welcome awaited us from Hector Moody and his wife Margaret and daughter Jean. But first we had to negotiate the garden gate where a keen-eyed Blue Heeler tensed himself, eager for the first ankle to set foot on the pathway. A lover of Blue Heelers from way back, I asked, across the magenta of the bougainvillea hedge, 'What's his name?' 'His name is Bastard Nuisance,' replied Hector in no uncertain terms. 'Someone picked him up along the road near Tully and dropped him off here. Now we can't get rid of him!' Under courteous escort by Hector we trooped along the path to the latticed smoko-verandah. Several family members and friends had dropped in to share the occasion. The recording session around the generously large table began to take on quite a festive atmosphere as smoko turned into what could have been Christmas Lunch. Hector is much esteemed as Father of the Family.

Afterwards I walked with daughter Jean to look at the remains of the old homestead, a high-set gracious building with internal staircase, high arched passageways and leaded bow-windows on to wide verandahs. 'Careful as you go,' warned Jean, 'It's not very safe. White-ants got into the timber and the carpenter told Dad it would be cheaper to build a new place than to repair this one.' The intricate fret-workings of termites could be seen in the high ceilings, their schematic tracery criss-crossing the polished silky-oak with dire purpose. 'During the war they used to have dances here,' Jean said. 'I often found coins or medals or buttons in the dirt when I was little.' The melancholy of long-departed laughter and music seemed to pervade the once gracious home, now used only for storage.

Hector then joined us for a walk a little further along the road to where his little grand-son Ben lies buried. Ben was killed when out shifting cattle with his father at Wall's Creek, the fattening property on the basalt wall north of Charters Towers.

The men were back-burning dry grass. The little boy's horse reared and threw him. He never recovered consciousness. Now, in a beautifully maintained miniature park, emerald green with lawns, crotons and palms despite the drought, he rests beneath a headstone on which are inscribed his name, 'Ben' the dates of his birth and death, 1986 -1991 and the historic station brand, Y9M. Hector would like to dedicate this story to Ben's memory.

R.I.P.
Benjamin David Moody.
Aged 6

Chapter 10...

MORE DREAMS THAN DINNERS

HECTOR MOODY - PASTORALIST

There is a well. I am sitting on the top of it, knowing that Dad is down below trying to find water. Dad takes the blasting charges down the well with the shortest possible fuses to save money, and Mother and I are here to help him up out of the well once they are lit. He has a lad to wind him up in a bucket, but when the fuse is lit and Dad is half way up, this lad takes fright and flees for shelter. Mother and I are on our own winding him up the shaft before the blast goes off. Mother is terrified. I am three years old.

That is my earliest memory. I was born in 1918 so it would have been in the early 'twenties; 1921. Dad had won this grazing selection, resumed off a big property called Dotswood, in North Queensland. He named it Waratah. On that block he sank five wells, mostly on his own. Mum was a town girl and couldn't even wind a bucket of dirt. So, later, when I was six or seven, I would be down the well helping. Dad was making a bit of a drive into the wall of the well so it would hold more water. My job was to hook the buckets of dirt for him to wind from up top, then hide myself back in the drive in case anything fell out of the bucket and hit me on the head.

Dad's grand-father came out from England as a child with his parents on the ship *Parsee*.[1] When he grew up he married and settled in Drayton on the Darling Downs. Later, with his young family and two other families, the Bamfords and the Wellingtons, Grandfather travelled overland by drays and wagons to his brother's place, south of Clermont. His next move was to manage Bosworth station on the Burdekin. My father was still just a young boy and he and his brothers used to spend a lot of their time with the station Aborigines, from whom they learned bush lore and how to track.

From Bosworth Grandfather moved on to Charters Towers. He broke-in horses and was a horse dealer and ran a few cattle. His brand, Y9M, is still used by my son Graham on our property Square Post, at Mingela.

As a young man Dad got around a fair bit; mining in Tasmania and then Bendigo, where he broke his thigh in a mining accident. He went to China with a boatload of horses. Horses breeding at that time was an important industry in the North, particularly cavalry remount types. Next he went to the Boer War in the cavalry.

1 Listed among the passengers when the *Parsee* arrived in January 1853 was John Moody, aged 26. He was later to settle in Drayton on the Darling Downs.

Afterwards he used to say that he was very sympathetic with the Boers. They were settlers just like his family in Queensland.

My mother, Ida Bussey, was one of a large family from Gympie. Her mother had died when she was in her teens and between doing her share of the housework and part-time Sunday School teaching, she had led a sheltered life. Her father was a book-keeper so she was a town girl, not used to bush life.

In 1914 Dad put in for one of the blocks being resumed by ballot off the big state owned property in the north, Dotswood, and won a block. Once he and Mum were married they set out to overland his cattle, about seventy head, to the new place. He and Mum owned two riding mares, Flirt and Octoroon. I learned to ride on Octoroon. At the time Dad had just enough money to buy twenty-one sheets of iron to put up a bit of a homestead and some wire to fence his share of the boundary. His only other assets were a vision and a big heart.

He built a homestead of two rooms of bush timber with iron roof and exterior walls of bark, with interior walls of bags sewn together and painted on each side with whitewash, a mixture of lime and cement and egg-white. They burnt limestone from the Fanning area to get the lime. No ceiling and an ant-bed floor. Ant-bed was just that – ant-beds crushed and watered to the consistency of cement, levelled and left to dry. A skillion kitchen at the back and a room for my sister Edna and myself. My brother Kevin was just a baby. Later he added a front verandah. Mum must have been very lonely a lot of the time as Dad was away from home a lot, fencing the boundary and paddocks and building the stockyards.

We kids were happy and we always thought Mum was happy too, but she was a town girl and she never adapted to bush life and must have fretted herself sick. She ended up with ulcers. Too much dry corned beef. Dad milked cows and grew a vegetable garden but these things were seasonal. I remember getting butter in tins. One time the dingoes killed all the fowls. They used to roost in a whitewood tree and lay their eggs in the hay-shed; until we found the nests. Then they would move somewhere else.

Dad was always poor, in the sense that he never had any money. But in another sense he was rich. He did not expect too much out of life and he was never discontented but he had more dreams than dinners. He was mostly cheerful though he had his silent moods. He must have often wondered how he was going to get through. He always maintained that it was better to work for yourself for a pound than for another man for two. He never owned more than four hundred head of cattle. His one ambition was to brand a hundred calves in one year. But he never did. Waratah was bitter country, very drought-affected. After rain it would fatten cattle well but some years we didn't get the rains. He had one bad season after another for many years. There was also a fair amount of poison bush on it. Most of the cattle were shorthorns or Devon. Later on, Herefords were crossed with the shorthorns and that was a step forward.

We could go six months and not see a stranger, so when anyone came to our place it was a big event. Mother gave us our schooling but she had only gone to Grade Four herself so it can't have been easy for her. There were no Correspondence School lessons in those days. Instead, an Itinerant Teacher called a couple of times

The abandoned homestead at Square Post station, Mingela. White-ants have infested the timbers.

Dances for American servicemen camped nearby were held on its wide verandahs during World War Two.

a year and would leave lessons and a few books for us to read. His name was Mr. Killeen, but we thought he should have been called Mr. Clean because he was always washing his hands. He travelled by pack-horse in the Wet and by wagonette once the Dry came.

Edna I joined the Golden Rules Club, the children's section in the North Queensland Register. Mail day, once a week, was a big occasion. We looked forward to seeing if we had had one of our letters published. We also liked to look for sections by 'Ben Bowyang', 'Bob Bloodwood' and 'Sundowner' and 'Along the Line' by a chap named Chisholm. Inigo Jones was the weather forecaster. Well-known names always in the paper were the Jardines, the Skuthorpes, J.S. Love who bought horses for the Indian Army, and Gladys Moncrief, the famous singer who grew up in Townsville. Dad would talk to us about all of these. I always loved poetry and kept an exercise-book full of my favourites from the time I was twelve; A Bush Christening; The Man from Ironbark; Lost; The Man from Snowy River; Lost; How the Chestnut Horse Came Home. Mostly Banjo Patterson. There's none better.

In winter it used to get so cold that we could put out a plate of water and have ice in the morning. Of course, we ate it, cold and all as it was. The water in the pipes would be frozen, and you could get an inch of ice off the horse troughs to play with. Edna and I made a cubby house and by the time it was up the borers had eaten through the uprights so I learned early in life that Moreton Bay ash is good for nothing as a building timber.

Dad had another block off Dotswood called Grasshopper,

Weaners on Square Post station waiting to be fed during 2004 drought.

named after a very bad plague of grasshoppers that went through. Once when I was about nine, Dad and I were shifting a mob of cattle up the Fanning River on to Grasshopper and we saw a young plain turkey. Dad slowly circled it, as he remembered being taught by the Aborigines as a lad on Bosworth, until he was close enough to cut its head off with his whip[2]. That night we had Johnny cakes cooked in the coals and boiled turkey for tea. Being young everything was marvellous to me.

We would get a six months supply of groceries. Lighting kerosene would come in two-gallon tins, two tins in a well-made pine case. Dad would then make these kerosene cases into furniture. Once he made a gramophone cabinet. And, in a drought, they were used as feed-boxes for the cows with a little pollard or linseed meal in them. The kerosene tins were cut open and made into useful buckets with a bit of fencing-wire for a handle.

We also got jam by the case, Jones' IXL brand, made in Tasmania. Mum and Dad made their own soap of boiled-down fat and caustic soda. It was awful stuff. Our water was so hard it wouldn't lather. We were told not to use it on our faces. It was good enough for dirty feet. And if we were sick there was awful castor oil in blue bottles.

At Christmas time we would use a kerosene-tin bucket to make a brew of horehound. Bottle seals had not been invented. The corks were tied down with string. Christmas and birthdays were always treated as special occasions. The food you had then you would not see the likes of until next Christmas. We made a lot of our own toys and got immense pleasure from them.

It was a memorable day when Reg Ramsay with his wagon and team of horses delivered a wind-mill and the makings of a five thousand gallon tank. Many years later, that same wagon would be used in the making of the film, 'The Irishman'. Up till then Dad had to wind all the water for his cattle out of wells with a windlass and bucket, which must have been very hard on him because he suffered with rheumatics. Once he got the windmill and tank erected it saved him a lot of bailing. He could not afford an auxiliary engine so when there was no wind he used a horse-powered whim.

My parents thought boys should be well-educated so at the age of nine I was sent down to Townsville to my aunt and uncle and family. It was the beginning of sad days for me. I never left home without tears. Dad would take me in the buggy to Mingela to catch the train. Mingela was called Ravenswood Junction in those days. It was a full day's drive in the buggy, starting early before sunrise. Sometimes, when the horses were poor, we would break the journey at Fanning, which was owned by Murray Prior, after he sold Bulliwallah to J.W. King. Mr. Butler was the manager.

When Edna and I were little we never made trouble for one another, but when I went to live with my cousins to go to school, I came up against problems I had

2 A similar bushman's ploy which the author has seen practised on Chatsworth station, south of Cloncurry, is, on sighting an emu, to keep very still but to hold up a handkerchief and flick it around overhead. Emus are so compulsively inquisitive that they can't resist circling closer to investigate. This is all very well if it is simply a photograph that is required of them, but in previous times Aboriginal hunters would wave a ball of grass in the same way to lure the luckless bird within range of a spear.

not experienced. I even started wetting the bed which I had never done before. I was a year older than the other children in my class at Railway Estate School, but because I was small for my age it wasn't noticed. At first I was way behind with my lessons but it wasn't long before I was up around the top four of a class of forty.

I learned to ride an adult's push-bike with my leg through the bar. In a school of four hundred children there was only one boy with a child's bike. Children just accepted what was given to them. In those days there were lemonade bottles with a glass stopper in the neck. We used to break the bottle and use the glass stopper for a marble. When Skuthorpe's buck-jumping show came to town we got in under the bottom of the tent and saw young Lance Skuthorpe ride. His sister Violet also sat a horse very prettily. We had the Warwick Rodeo in the Townsville Show Grounds. It must have been one of the first open air rodeos in North Queensland. They erected three posts out in the middle of the ring and the horses were snigged out and saddled. The riders mounted and were then turned loose. Two famous buck-jumpers of the time were Knickerbockerbuckeroo and Ginger Meggs. Cecil Pearce introduced bull-dogging as an event.

Twice a year I went home to Mingela on the train. I was so small that Aunty would put a ticket around my neck and ask the guard to see I got off the train at Mingela. Dad met me with the buggy. We stopped over at Fanning on the way home and Mr. Butler once gave me a photo of a racehorse he owned called Grandchester, but the white-ants ate it. Years later I worked on Bulliwallah and owned some descendants of that same Grandchester myself.

About that time Dad swapped Waratah for ninety square mile of country off Dotswood at Herveys Range and named it Glen Haven. The cattle on Grasshopper were mustered and shifted down. At Waratah they had been well and truly droughted-out. When Dad and Mum left, they were flat out to get enough water to give the horses a final drink. A lot of cattle had died with lantana. Lantana grows all through that country. You seem to mainly lose cattle that are very hungry. They lose their hair and then die. By then Dad was then down to about seventy head, the same number he had started with eighteen years before.

They moved into a section of the old Eureka Hotel left after a newer section of it had been shifted down to Townsville for a residence. The Eureka was built in the early days as a watering-hole for the teamsters on the wagon track up through Thornton's Gap on the old Georgetown Road. That was the only supply route to all the stations over the range and to the mining fields at Croydon and the Etheridge. Those teams took in everything; roofing-iron, fencing wire, rations, cases of kerosene, mining machinery, salt to preserve meat and rum. Everything! The ascent up the range was about eleven hundred feet in one mile. At times there could be up to twenty teams waiting at the foot of the range. They would hitch two teams to one wagon to get up the gradient and to take an empty wagon back down they would hitch a tree on behind as a brake. The pub was built in the early days right on the boundary between Charters Towers and Townsville to dodge having to get a liquor licence.

Dad built a new verandah to cover the scar on the north side of the building where the section had been removed and we moved in. We pulled up the old lino.

I loved the smell of all the old newspapers underneath; the Queenslander, in a pink cover, and all the cartoons of Billy Hughes, the Prime Minister, showing him as an old stinker-goat, a 'billy', always kissing babies. The Eureka became our peaceful home for many years. The main frame of the house is just as solid today as it was all those years ago; built mainly of stringy bark on low stumps set into the ground, all bearers adzed from nine inch diameter trees. The floor joists were adzed from split timber and floor boards from sawn hoop pine from the hills nearby. All the studs were adzed to about six by six and the walls of adzed slabs, dressed so smooth that there are no splinters and so true that a knife won't fit between the edges of the slabs and the studs. To me this old building typifies the spirit of purpose of the men and women who pioneered the north a hundred years ago.[3]

When we lived at the Eureka, relatives and friends would come up from Townsville and farmers and their families would come over and to the tune of an old accordion, they would dance until early morning. Other properties in the area were Tabletop, where we used to visit the Fryer family, and Coppermine, where Frank Eccles and his mate Mat Brennan were. Dad's brother Jim had Myrtlebank, not far away, but Dad and Jim were at loggerheads over something so we saw very little of them, though I remember a Christmas when Grandfather Moody was there and Aunty Dorrie sang 'In the Valley of the Moon' beautifully. There were raisins in a plate of brandy which was set alight and we children had to grab for them. People had brought a lot of these old ways over from England with them.

There was an old carpet snake that lived in the rafters. He was an old fool of a thing because sometimes he would go to shift himself to get more comfortable and over-reach himself and lose his balance. On one occasion Aunty Gladys had come up from Townsville for a visit. She was laughing that she had come to see for herself if the stories about the hardships of bush-pioneering were true. She didn't believe it was such a bad life! The next moment the old carpet snake fell out of the rafters on top of her. That settled the argument about living in the bush.

This was the early 'thirties and the whole country was in the grip of the Great Depression. The State Government was trying to establish a tobacco growing industry on Herveys Range. They started to put in a single lane road up the mountains. The labour force was recruited from the dole queues. The days of work that a man got were related to the number of his dependants. Work camps were set up at the foot of the range and at Deadman's Gully, half way up. No facilites; just open air cooking-galleys and rough showers and pit latrines.

The Great Depression was a terrible time for ordinary people. If a man was on the dole he had his ration card marked in the last town he was in. He could not collect rations again in the same town. So men and boys too, had to 'jump the rattler'- scramble on board the train when it slowed down on a gradient - to get to the next town. If they were caught they landed up in Stuart Creek gaol. Men going north would pass men going south. They always thought conditions would be

3 The Eureka Hotel on Herveys Range, built in the mid 1860s, is one of the best-preserved slab buildings in Queensland. Long a private residence, it now Heritage Listed and has recently been restored to begin a new life as the Heritage Inn which welcomes visitors for light meals and refreshments in the tranquil bush setting of this unique historic building.

better elsewhere. When they were heading home for Christmas they would always start six weeks early to allow for time in gaol for 'jumping the rattler'.

A bush school was erected, a provisional school built by the parents, on the Fryer's property, Tabletop. Mum and Dad took me away from Railway Estate School in Townsville and I went home to start at the new school. But that was my Scholarship year, with the Scholarship exam at the end of it. If you didn't pass that it was the end of your education. But I soon realized I was learning nothing at the new school. All the classes were in one room together and the teacher was only young and didn't have much idea. After wasting four valuable months and learning nothing I told my parents that I wanted to go back to Railway Estate School. By this time my class there had got way ahead of me. But when the time came, out of a class of forty, I was one of the only four to pass the Scholarship exam.

In these hard times, to try to get a bit of money coming in, Dad, along with a lot of other people on Herveys Range, started growing tobacco. There were about twenty farms within a two mile radius of our place and another ten or so further out at Keelbottom. But, the poor Herveys Range tobacco farmers! They got no help from the government. The advice they were given was useless. In their ignorance, the government advised people to grow tobacco on inferior sand-ridge country to get a lemon-coloured leaf which would be best quality. But it had no body in it. Then they advised them to use fertilizer. Well! Most of the farmers were so hard up they had had no money to buy fertilizer. Most of them walked off their blocks with the backside out of their pants.

The biggest property in the area was Dotswood owned by the Queensland State Government. Dad was friendly with Joe Reel, the manager there. After the first buggy he had, Dad had got a two-horse buckboard. Joe Reel arranged for the Dotswood blacksmith to put springs under it. We were over there once when an Indian hawker arrived with a horse-drawn van; an exciting event for everyone. Dotswood employed a cook, housemaid, laundress, gardener, cowboy, or rouse-about, a book-keeper, blacksmith, butcher, hangers-on and plenty of stockmen. Jupiter Mossman, the Aboriginal who discovered gold at Charters Towers was the butcher. But as Dotswood was state-owned, the manager never knew what the day's work would be until 8 a.m. when he got a phone-call from Brisbane.

One of the Dotswood stockmen was a fellow named Jim Kenniff, brother of Patrick Kenniff, who had been hung for the murder of a policeman. Jim had spent time in gaol for cattle-duffing and thieving horses down around Carnarvon. Jim didn't do much around the place on Dotswood. He told Dad he was getting his own back on the government for the time he had spent in gaol. Later on, as a young chap, I met Jim again when I was working on Blue Range. He was an irascible old bugger. He had everyone on Blue Range buffaloed.

Although I was one of the bright pupils at primary school, once I got to secondary school at Townsville Technical College, I was among the top kids from all the schools and I was just plain ordinary. There was a school uniform but a lot of the kids, including myself, were too poor to be able to afford it. My parents had decided that bush life was not for me and made me do a commercial course. Except for book keeping and business methods I reckoned everything else would not help my future. I wanted the bush life. If I had taken an Industrial course I might have been more interested.

King's Regiment, Hector Moody's favourite stallion, bought from Fred King of Bulliwallah.

After leaving school I got a job in town but out of a wage of eighteen shillings and ninepence a week I was paying eighteen shillings a week for my board. In those days once a boy turned eighteen he got the sack and a younger one was taken on. Well, for me it was good-bye to that job and good-bye to Townsville. I went home to Herveys Range to do a bit of droving with Dad, droving Blue Range cattle. I was generally the cook. As well, my job was to keep the droving plant in repair, counter-lining and repairing saddles, and learning to make pack-saddles and pack-bags. I found I enjoyed the work and learned all I could from Matt Walters, the saddler on Blue Range. Everything on Blue Range was new to me. I made up my mind to learn all I could from everyone.

I saw Arthur Garbutt castrating calves, taking one stone and then the other, and cutting both cords together. I had never seen it done like that before but I have done thousands that way since. I was taught by an expert, Romeo Boyd, an Aboriginal, how to handle a camp-horse. He would have been as good a man on the Upper Burdekin as ever sat a horse. Pat McEwan, on Wandovale, showed me how to mount a horse without putting my toe into his ribs. A small thing but I never forgot.

Then I worked on Lyndhurst. I had my own horse and saddle and swag. The men there were as good as any you would get. I have never seen better. But I don't know why they stayed. Lyndhurst was mean with the tucker and we worked daylight to dark, ten days a week, with a day off very occasionally. There were no tents and we rolled our swags out under the stars. The Lyndhurst horses were a nasty lot. They hated us and we hated them back. I have shot better horses. On Lyndhurst I rode more buck-jumpers than anything else. Well, bad tempered buck-jumpers weren't for me and I had the romantic notion of doing a long droving trip. I also figured that if I was working seven days a week as a ringer for three pounds fifty a week, I could go droving and get five pounds a week.

So I got a job with a drover named Jack Morrison who I met at Dajarra. At Camooweal we picked up Jack's son, Henry, and a cook and a Murri horsetailer. We were crossing the Barkly Tableland through Camooweal to a place named Morestone to pick up a mob when we cut out of bread. But there was some dry yeast in the saddle-packs, Malto Peptone, so I tried some and made a batch of beautiful bread.

We picked up twelve hundred steers and headed down the Georgina. This was just about the time buffalo fly was coming down into Queensland. At Camooweal we were told to burn motor-tyres and let the smoke drift over the cattle. If that shifted the fly we could continue down the Georgina. Well, it wasn't a success so we had to head back down the Gregory.

In those days, men from out that country wouldn't come too far east, so when we got to the Gregory and were heading towards Gunpowder Creek the horse-tailer left. I took on his job. Then, after the Leichhardt, heading towards Julia Creek, the cook left. Old Jack remembered my success with the bread-making so I was nominated cook as well. By the time we got to Gilliat, winter was on us and the buffalo fly had left. We could dip and cross the line.

But by this time we all had Barcoo Rot. At Julia Creek I bought some Uncle Toby's rolled oats and that cleaned it up. To break the monotony of just corned beef and damper I bought every type of sauce and pickle I could see in the store. We tried the lot but we all came back to Holbrook's Worcestershire.

Crossing that open downs country we had to pack wood to get a fire to boil the billy and then it was rotten bore-water. It was so windy you had to put your saddle and saddle-cloth on at the same time, or the wind would blow the cloth off before you got your saddle on. And the wind, blowing on your reins, would have enough strength in it to turn your horse. I used to make a fire-break with the pack-saddles and bags, to get on with the cooking but Jack thought they might get burned, so I had to stop doing it. I was glad to get into the desert country and see a bit of timber again.

Jack was a panicky old fellow. He wouldn't camp on a fence in case the cattle rushed. Sometimes Harry had to help water the cattle as by this stage there were only two men with the twelve hundred head of cattle. So I would be left to pack thirteen horses. That's where my principle of economy of movement paid off. If I took anything out of a pack-bag, that set of bags was immediately balanced and buckled up again. I used to set the bread-dough last thing at night, knock it back in the morning, and by the time we got to the next camp and got a fire going, the dough was ready to shape into loaves and bake.

What with the cooking and the horse-tailing and the night-watching, by the time we delivered the cattle at Bulliwallah in the Clermont area, I was buggered for want of a decent night's sleep. Four of us had been watching the cattle for five months.

The horses were worn out. We were worn out. Yet Jack wanted to take delivery of a fresh mob of cattle. I told him I was pulling out and that I'd got a job on Bulliwallah. Jack tried to get Manpower to take action against me for leaving him because during the war Manpower had control over who worked where. But I was still working in the cattle industry so that was that. I swore then that that would be my last droving trip.

I stayed nine years on Bulliwallah, seven of them as head stockman. My young brother, Kevin, came and worked with me on Bulli – as we used to call it. Kevin was such a fine horseman that Fred King once remarked to me that it was worth pulling up just to watch him galloping through the scrub. From a man of Fred

King's experience that was a recommendation to be proud of. Fred King was a very fine man, a man of honour, and I was proud to work for him. He used to lend me books. I had to look after them but I valued them as much as he did himself. Bulliwallah was a highly respected property. At Christmas time Kev and I would be invited up to the house for Christmas dinner with the family.

Hector Moody beside the grave of his grandson Ben on Square Post station, Mingela.

The finest horse I ever had anything to do with was a stallion I bought from Fred King named King's Regiment. He had a head and neck and a stance on him like those old paintings you see. Then the head stockman got sick and left so I bought his horses. Then Mary King, Mrs. Goodenough, left home, and I bought her mares and put King's Regiment with them. With foals I had about twenty head.

Bulliwallah had a good class of stock-horse. Murray Prior had left his good mares when he sold the place to the King family and old Mr King must have known a good horse. He bought a registered stallion, Kingsmond. Bulli horses would carry you all day. They were natural at working cattle. They might give a few bucks early in the morning but then they would settle down.

There were a lot of brumbies on Bulliwallah. They were a problem when mustering, galloping through the cattle. Horse hair was worth good money so Fred King lent me a .303 and I shot a lot of them out.

I have broken in about sixty or eighty horses in my time. I like to give each of them a name that suits them; Brunette, Sympathy, Marzipan, Venus and so on with the record of each of them in a note-book. Gentleness in breaking-in will do as much good as this horse-whispering they go on about. An American 'horse whisperer' took my son Graham and his mate and the rest of the audience for twenty-five dollars each, but one horse put him out of the yard! Why didn't he 'whisper' to him! When I was young I was told of breakers hypnotizing a young horse by rubbing a finger over the eyeball. But I was also told that the next fellow needed to watch out! I talk all the time to my horses. One time, my brother Kevin was taking a yearling colt of mine from Bulliwallah to Herveys Range and I thought it might go lame. So I caught him up in the D-crush and prepared a set of shoes, front feet. I tacked the shoes on, talking to the colt all the time – just a load of tommy-rot - but he seemed to like it and to understand. Horses know you for the man you are.

By Cobb & Co, Cloncurry to Hughenden –1900

By 'Basalt'

Introduction

I found this story – an article from the North Queensland Register dated Monday, July 9, 1900, in the British National Newspaper Archive at Colindale, north of London. And what a find! Outside it was dark and cold. Blue-black clouds threatened sleet. Inside, at my allocated desk, I found myself transported by the power of long-ago written word to the road between Cloncurry and Hughenden, through country in the iron grip of drought. I was home again.

Any one who has driven from Cloncurry to Hughenden will recognize the land described by 'Basalt'. The road may have changed; been upgraded from black-soil bog in the wet to modern all-weather bitumen and concrete, but the country has changed little. When you get through those first twenty-five miles of bony red Cloncurry hills and emerge on to the downs it is still to enter another dimension. The sky still heaves itself to a pale dome overhead capable of reducing the human ego to less vaunted stature. No matter what the speedometer on the dashboard reads, the horizon is still something you strive towards but seem never to attain. Distances of sun and heat drain the eyes. You would still be foolish to travel without a water-bag – or, more likely, these days, an Esky – and a shovel. It is a land where it pays to be circumspect and just a little bit humble.

And what of 'Basalt' ? – (great nom-de-plume!) Seemingly a man of some education, familiar with the writings of Mark Twain and his 'Mississippi riverboat pilot', he is an interested traveller, keeping notes of arrival times and departures and of the cleanliness or otherwise of establishments, though do we detect the onset of a certain travel-ennui, a discernible diminution of note-making zeal as the days trundle past? Day One is eagerly recounted. I trust the reader will enjoy the vertiginous moment of descent through the ranges; 'the horses appearing almost underneath us'. But Days Two, Three and Four are sketched with waning enthusiasm. After four days' lurching and jolting, arrival at the destination, Hughenden, is recorded tersely; 'covered the 280 miles in up to time'. Four days! Today it would take little more than four hours. We Moderns do not know we have been born!

It comes as something of a surprise to find in the epilogue, obviously written after a couple of days' Rest and Recuperation, for the drought has now broken and 'rain is falling steadily,' that sheep were being trucked on agistment by rail at this relatively early stage, though the rail link between Townsville and Charters Towers had been established by 1882 and the high level bridge over the Burdekin in 1896. But it is saddening to realize how doomed were 'Basalt's' hopes that 'the next cycle of drought will not be till the distant future'. The year 1901 would see the onset of one of the worst droughts in Australia's recorded history, one which would break the hearts and cripple the fortunes, of many an outback settler and traveller.

Cobb & Co. coach leaving Cloncurry Christmas, 1900.

Chapter 11...

BY COBB & CO FROM CLONCURRY TO HUGHENDEN

By 'Basalt'

'We leave the town at 5.50 a.m. The night is dark and as we shoot the gullies of the first fifteen miles the pace does not seem safe, but we come out of it alright. We pass by a stony hill and the next minute the horses appear almost underneath us in the dim light. As daylight appears at about 6.30 or a little later, we see shafts put down for copper here and there. To the left, about eighteen miles from the town we see a high mountain and the smoke of a fire where there is a well and a camp. Water may be obtained almost anywhere in wells about here. Grass is scarce but at the Eighteen Mile there is some dry last years's grass, which is carted into town for hay. A sawpit always shows that there is some marketable timber to be obtained.

Shortly after, we cross Flah's Creek and get on to the downs country. There the grass is slightly better but the cattle look poor. Our horses also show signs of failing, but by dint of whip use we arrive at the Williams River, where there is a mail change, at 10 a.m.

After a meal, served very cleanly, we start at 1.45 p.m. for the next stage, with a pair of greys, to go to Box Tank, where there is another change. Before we get there we stay at Leilavale and have a cup of tea and give the horses a spell, which makes it 4.45 p.m. for 51 miles. We then go on to Box Tank which we reach at 7.15. After getting a change, four horses this time, we start for the Gilliat River Hotel. Being dark we see but little; but the smells we experience a good many times tell us that cattle are having a bad time. Then, as we approach the Gilliat, we see the river timber, looming darkly before us. We have eight channels to cross, and it is pitch dark. It does not look too good. The break (sic) tells us we are to go down a bank, and just as we think we are into a large gum, we glide smoothly along on the level ground again. This is repeated eight times, and the driver tells his mate, who is to go on this line in future, of the banks and dangers as we pass them. We see nothing, but the driver, Foster, is like Mark Twain's Mississippi pilot, and knows every tree and bank ahead of him, and as the turns to avoid banks, stumps etc are pretty frequent, the knowledge this man has for locality is remarkable. We arrive at the Gilliat Hotel at 9.35 and again bear witness to the neat, clean place it is. Next morning after breakfast we start again and arrive at Eddington, where a store has started, at 9 a.m. Mr Inglis informs me something of his losses and seeing the state of the country the wonder is that any stock are alive at all.

The whole road is desolate; grass is only known as a reminiscence of a former good season. Between Cloncurry and Coobiaby we see the tracks of the camels who have lately been travelling between Cloncurry and Hughenden the whole way. The only teams we meet are piled with horse feed and we also pass some light four-horse wagons with feed and water on them. The only green seen on the whole two hundred and eighty miles is the green of the tree leaves. Desolation and devastation everywhere.

At 12.30 we arrive at the Julia Creek Hotel. There is a large tank of water which is now filled with water from an Eddington bore and run-off will fill the creek for a considerable distance. At 6.oo p.m. we arrive at Coobiaby and thanks to host Ashes' enterprise, we have a good meal. Here he has a garden and its produce must be a godsend to the traveller who passes.

Next morning we are up at four and start about an hour later for Richmond. At noon we are at the Camp Hotel and at 6.20 p.m. at Richmond. The same early rising is repeated next morning and after sitting behind good teams the whole way we arrive at Hughenden at dusk, having covered the two hundred and eighty miles up to time.[1]

Now, as I write, the scene changes. Rain is falling steadily. Falls have been recorded at Richmond, Winton, McKinlay, Hughenden, Tangorin, Muttaburra and elsewhere, and the back of the worst drought that the North-west has ever yet experienced appears to have been broken. Telegrams of congratulations are flying everywhere. One from a town which has suffered badly in its neighbourhood, reads, 'Two inches of rain. Everyone drunk.' Pithy, but expressive.

Sheep have jumped fifty percent against the day before yesterday. One seller had 27 000 off shears; prospective buyer dubious on account of drought. Rain comes just as the buyer cries off. Today the sheep are not for sale. Such are the chances of the North-west. This year over 800 000 sheep have been trucked from or through the Hughenden district – many never to return. Trains have been booked to take sheep away to the coastal waters. After this rain the exodus will be the other way. Now the bookings will be just as far ahead to return. The Hughenden – Winton line has done credit to the officials, and the squatters are grateful to the traffic manager and give him the credit due to him for his energy and resourcefulness in the most trying time the North-west has ever experienced. Hope springs eternal in the human breast and the hope now is that when the cycle for another drought comes round it will be in the distant future.'

1 K. A. Austen in The Lights of Cobb and Co., records that the average speed of Cobb and Co.'s coach services in Victoria was ten mile per hour, that the stages were twenty miles apart and that upon arrival at each stage the stable hands had the change-horses harnessed ready to hook up for the change over, the passengers did not disembark, the driver seldom left the seat and the reins were handed up to him to continue the journey. 'Basalt's' journey from Cloncurry to Hughenden seems to have been in rather less pressured mode possibly because of the conditions of the roads and of the creek crossings involved. The run from Cloncurry averaged five and a half miles per hour and took four days to cover the two hundred and eighty miles. One can only wonder about the Comfort needs of the passengers involved in the brisker southern journeys and if, in the north, they followed the down-to-earth Outback dictum of 'Righto! Men to the left; Ladies to the right.'

Tiddley Triffid

Tiddley Triffid on Millungera station

INTRODUCTION

Tiddley Triffid, another of the North's noted old-time stockmen and drovers, lives in pleasant retirement in Charters Towers, with a large adjacent paddock where his two taffy horses, Gem and the inestimable Lyndon, '...the best horse I ever owned', live in even sleeker retirement, concerned only to remind Tiddley, by nickering at the fence, that it is time for their dinner-feed and for him to hurry up about it. That Tiddley has them trained to balance elegantly on all four hoof, like circus stars, on a specially padded drum, is something they are prepared stoically to accept. In fact they seem to enjoy the challenge, feeling round delicately with back hoofs before mounting aloft and shaking their well-groomed heads as though acknowledging the applause. While the performance takes place, Tiddley's sulphur-crested cockatoo who has spent the afternoon making scathing comments on interviewers and interviewees alike, from his aviary under the yellow-bell tree, shrieks with jealous rage.

At the beginning of recording the audio-tapes that went into making this story, I sensed Tiddley was uneasy about talking of himself. 'Ah! I don't want to be blowing m'own bags!' he protested. I tried to convince him of the importance to Queensland's history of recording something of the droving days as he had known them before road-trains brought the era to an end. At such moments it is handy to be able to relax into easy chat about my own time on Chatsworth station at Cloncurry, on Banka Banka at Tennant Creek and to establish that, Yes, there were people Tiddley and I had both known and places we had both been; Mick O'Neill on Chatsworth. 'Great cattleman! Could sink a Black Label or two, eh!' and Mary Ward, at Banka Banka. 'Strict with those girls of hers! Kept them under lock and key at night!' and Sandy Gabongie, old fencer on Baloothara! 'That tractor of his reared over on him and pinned him. Poor bugger!' Sandy's little dog had kept the crows of his face for a week. I had known Sandy well on Chatsworth. He had seen the Min Min light come to his camp and thought it was the station vehicle. Suddenly Tiddley and I were on a wave length. When we got on to the topic of Tiddley's having been a spare-boy for his father's horse-team, we were away! The memories came flooding. Memories are like that. One incident will trigger another and before long you are looking for an extra tape so as not to miss a moment of it.

As a little boy, it had been Tiddley's job to harness his father's thirty-eight draft horses each morning; 'hames' 'collars' 'tugs', 'shafters,' 'pins', 'leaders'. Here was a man who could use such words as others might speak a foreign language, with fluency and ease. Such moments are the joys of oral history, to slip back through time into the chilly-fingered dawns of some far-off decade to be present as the Narrator goes about a humble task, the skills and technicalities of which are long forgotten, and the recording of which so valuable for our heritage.

When I asked, in all innocence, in the discussion of killing for fresh meat on long droving trips, 'How did you pick your killer?' there was a longish pause. Ray Fryer, who as an old mate of Tidley's was present, and Tiddley himself, both gave a bit of a grin, then one of them- I can't remember which - said with a laugh, 'It just depends on where you are!' And they both laughed, complicitously. I understood. I also understood that this was a drovers' joke that other drovers would enjoy, even though trusty Jack Sherwin of Millungera, in his grave on the banks of the far-off Flinders might have stirred a little uneasily in his long sleep.

The recording session done, I helped Tiddley feed the horses, had the good sense to knock back the offer of a ride on the younger of the two, especially bareback, as it seemed a little inclined to a happy-go-lucky pig-root or two even with Tiddley, and was enormously pleased when, before our departure, Tiddley presented me with a beautifully plaited miniature whip to wear as a hat-band on my Akubra. I will cherish it.

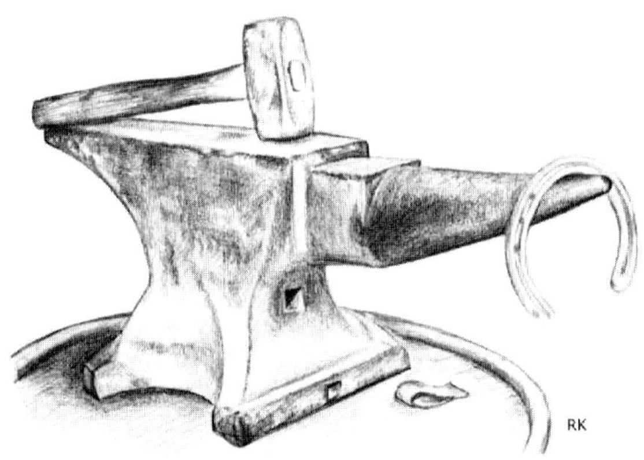

Chapter 12...

THE BETTER THE MAN, THE BETTER THE CATTLE

Tidley Triffid – Stockman and Drover

I was born in Rockhampton because there was no hospital in Julia Creek in them days. 1930. The family came from Croydon. Mum was born at The Cumberland, out between Georgetown and Croydon; a little gold-mining place. There's nothing left of it now. Just the chimney and a dam. Her Old Fellow was from Tasmania. Mum and Dad worked for Tom Quilty[1] and when he took up Euroka Springs, up from Julia Creek, they all shifted over with him. It was better country, all open. The family worked for Quilties on Euroka Springs for a good few years and then they shifted into Julia Creek. The Old Fellow had a blacksmith's shop there in town. There was plenty of work for a blacksmith, doing wagon's up, and station vehicles, for the bush people.

There was twelve in the family; there was Evelyn, Bill, Ted, Lil, George, Les, Sheila, Irene, Dorrie, Althenia, and Gladys. And me. My proper name is Cyril. I don't know where I got 'Tiddley' from. But I've always been 'Tiddley'. I'm the last one; the only one left now. I didn't get much spoiling. No-one got spoilt them days. You all had to pull your own weight. I pumped the bellows for the Old Fellow and done a lot of striking for him. But as soon as he went out the back somewhere I'd be out the door and gone. I'd catch it then. He was a tough old fellow. In them days you were working from a kid. Dad had horse-teams and I left school about eleven, working with the teams, spare-boy for m'Dad and out in the stock-camp when the mustering started.[2]

I was looking after the horses. He was fire-ploughing, building fire-breaks on stations. I was off-siding for him from about twelve. You start off after the Wet when the country's starting drying out; mid-April; early April. You couldn't plough boggy ground or the dirt'd roll up. The blade had a nose in the front. You'd go right through to probably September, October; then the storms'd start. From station to station you'd go, putting in fire-breaks. Ten foot wide they were, like a road, or a track. Thirty-eight horses. You'd start off just thirty-two, thirty-four and when they get a bit tired you put fresher ones in. Most of them horses would go all season, but then you might get sore-shouldered horses from your collars and you didn't work 'em. You always had to have fresh horses.

1 See also Buchanan, Bobbie; *Keep the Branding Iron Hot*; CQU Press; 2002

2 See also 'All Chinee Apples and Lagoons' in the author's *Barefoot Through the Bindies'*, CQU Press, in which Henry Brown recounts starting work at twelve as spare-boy for his teamster father on the Georgetown Road.

Tiddley Triffid at Crowfells, an outstation of Millungera, 1949.

At night, no hobbles, just bells on 'em. They wouldn't go far, a quarter of a mile from the camp, sometimes a mile or two. But if you got homesick buggers, you'd find them back at the furtherest fence. It was my job to get 'em every morning. We always had a night horse tied up. We had about ten or twelve saddle horses in the plant. As soon as you got 'em together and got 'em on camp you'd winker 'em. Then every horse had his right place where he had to go. They knew their places. You had your leaders, your shafters, your pin horses; Every horse had to have his right collar. If you put a collar on a horse and it's too big for him, that's where you get sore shoulders. The same horse goes to the same place every day. You yoke 'em up. I'd get up on a box or a tin, if I got a high horse, to collar him. Then you put the hames on 'em; then the harness, you slide it over his backside. Mainly, when you pick a set of harness up, the leather part, you grab the spreader and chuck it on. But the pin-horses', that was heavy. The closest horses to the shaft, they were the pin horses, heavy horses; heavy harness. Then it gets lighter up to the lead. The leaders have lighter harness. Then you do the tugs up. There's always a method in things.

Some horses, if they weren't pulling their weight on the job, Dad'd liven them up! Oh, yeah! He had a whip with a big handle on. They'd dance in the collar a bit! One old teamster-chap we knew used a stick with a light bit of chain on it. That'd move his lot along! Old Flogger Bill was his name.

You'd camp at night where the team could get water, on a water-hole or a bore-drain. You'd throw a swag out on the ground. Where we were ploughing was all full of bores, south of Julia Creek. And later in the year you'd go over on the northern side. There was bore-drains everywhere in those days. We'd get about ten mile a day done, average. But then if you seen a good camp with plenty of grass you'd unyoke and give them a spell. And we'd have a spell for a day; do a bit of cooking. The Old Fellow was a great man to make curries and he'd heat it up for dinner while you take the horses away to water when you unyoked. You water 'em like cattle. If you watered and fed your horses properly they never went away. Same as you if you watered and fed your cattle you never had rushes.

On dinner camp you never unyoked 'em. They just stood in the chains. And the Old Fellow, he always had an old ship-tank of water. He had a trailer behind the plough to carry your gear. And he'd have a bucket and he'd water his leaders. His leaders were his pets. Old Toby! And Old Toby wouldn't do without his drink. But if you were stuck, and you had a tight pull, he'd knuckle down and that was it! He'd get you out.

The Old Fellow ploughed that forest country on Millungera for ten years or more. Then after the war, tractors come in and the station people bought their own tractors and they'd do their own fire-breaks. But they were still ploughing 'em on Millungera with horses until the mid-fifties. At one time the Old Fellow had a big steam tractor; drove by cutting wood all the time. It's still on a property, High Vallum, out from Julia Creek where he left it.

Then I went droving with Bill, the oldest boy. That was in the war when there was no men. Droving was protected because of the war. The country had to have the meat. Bill was a boss drover for years. He drove from Dalgonally to Millungera. He drove from Oakland Park outside Croydon to Euroka Springs for old Quilty. One trip with fifteen hundred spayed cows and bullocks from Esmeralda to Brighton Downs on the Diamantina, they rushed and he done the lot. He was six weeks mustering to get 'em back. Got the majority of 'em. And old Jack Gunn, he was an old poet, he wrote a poem;

If you want to beat Bill Triffid's rush,
You got to do more than you got.
He done the lot.

The next year a fellow called Harry Cain, he come through and he done the lot plus all of his horses, so he beat Bill Triffid's rush! See, they talk about the Murranji, but that forest from Croydon to Bunda, it's worse than the bloody Murranji! It's all full of scrub. Yeah! Then when you get to Bunda you get on the open downs country on the Saxby River.

I done my first trip with Bill when I was eleven; from Glenore to Winton. No pay. Just getting the experience. The mob was about twelve hundred. There was Bill and me and a cook and two blackboys, old Kurumba George and a fellow named George. Real good men. Old Kurumba George was about sixty but in them days you addressed them as 'boys'. You cut their tucker off and give it to them and they made their camp away from you a bit with their own fire. They'd pull their swag off the pack and take it away a bit. You never spoke to a 'boy', only when you told him something. And if you caught a white fellow talking to a black fellow you'd put him in the camp with them, too. They were the hard days.

So I was ploughing the fire-breaks with the Old Fellow and in between times I'd go back to Millungera into the stock camp; go back to m'brothers. They were contract mustering there when the war finished. Millungera was full of clean-skins that had never been mustered. They had no men. We had some real smart Yellafellas there. Two of them were by Quilty. He bred his own men. My brother tells the story that old Mrs. Quilty was hard on the boys. She used to lock the young gins up of a night. But one of the young fellows climbed up on the roof and took two sheets of iron off. So he was right.

In the mustering camps on Millungra they had about eight or ten big drafting yards. But we did a lot of broncoing there. Any horse that rooted, you bronchoed with him. That steadied him. When he had a big bull on the end of the rope! A big bull, you put two horses on to him. One fellow'd throw the rope and catch him and pull him up. The other fellow'd throw a rope to pull him back so he don't charge you. We bronchoed with good clumpers. They bred good clumpers there. When you're breaking them in you broke 'em in to ride.

We took a mob of horses over to Bradshaw on the Victoria. Bill used to take horses over every year for old Quilty off Euroka Springs. We'd pick the horses up at Kajabbi, mares and geldings, and go the old stock route, down the Camooweal road, out on the Barkly, across to the Murranji, up through to Timber Creek and across the Victoria to Bradshaw. Bradshaw is about forty mile north of Timber Creek. We'd have seven hundred in the mob. You'd have a lot of men; six or seven of Quilty's blackfellas. Horses was like cattle; you never got out of the lead. Horses will get a fright and take off and you'd never know where you're going to get 'em again. You're up on the wing close to the lead and if they started to walk a bit quicker you got in 'em, rode in with them. With horses you never got out of the lead. Never! You'd do your stages, eighteen, twenty-odd mile a day. He'd sell 'em when we'd get 'em over there. Might keep two or three hundred for his own use and he'd sell the rest. Everyone would want to buy horses. Two years was a good season for horses out there; they die with walkabout disease. Two or three years and they'd die. But the brumby horses in that country didn't seem to get it. That would be about the early 'forties. I was just a kid. We had a rubber-tyred wagonette made out of an old truck. I rode on that most of the time. I done a couple of trips like that.

I find with brumbies they're just as good as bloody station-bred horses. Mainly what brumbies you got were young bucks hunted out of their mob. The old stallion would hunt 'em and wouldn't let 'em in! They'd get the smell of a mare and come into your station mob. You'd break 'em in. I've broke in brumbies quieter than station horses. Those Millungera horses, they had a bad name. They were a bad breed, out of a stallion called Vallig Knight. All his descendants, four or five generations back, would come at you. Millungera would get a good stallion every couple of years, but mainly them other Australian Estates places, Chatsworth, Burleigh, Liston Downs, Dagworth, whatever horses they didn't break-in, they sent 'em to Millungera. Old Bruce Hudson was manager a good few years and he knew a good horse. Every year he'd take in horses to Sedan Dip[3] . And Merv Royes, he was managing thirteen years, he had some good race horses.

I broke in a lot of horses on Millungera. The book was full of me. During the Wet before I went droving. I'd do the cowboying and kill and make ropes and mess around with the hides and do the breaking-in. I learned off Ted and he was an old Jimmy Wilson man; throw the rope on 'em and put a half-hitch on their nose and put a black blindfold on 'em. There's all different ways of breaking in. A lot of people put a colt in the yard on his own and throw a rope on him and choke him down. In our time, if you went into a yard without a breaking-in horse, you

3 A celebrated picnic race meeting at Sedan Dip station.

got the sack. You caught him off another horse in a little round yard, put the halter on him, and put the hobbles on him, and rubbed him down and lunged him so you could get near him; pull him from side to side. That's half the mouthing of a horse; bending their heads back. And when you done that you'd catch another. Say you did four. You'd keep working on the ones you'd caught and when you got the tackling on 'em, you caught the other two and worked on them. In them days you only rode a horse once in the yard and twice out. And if he was good enough you handed him over. I got ten bob a head and station wages; three pounds seventeen and six - about seven dollars in today's money, but it bought you a lot more. That's back in the 'forties. Now they get eight or nine hundred dollars and take six weeks to break 'em in.

I learned plaiting from when I was a kid, ten or twelve, off an old Quilty Yellafella there on Millungera. And I learned off another fellow to make twisted ropes. They used to reckon I was one of the best twisted-rope makers about, barring old Harry Hinch that had taught all them. There's an art in making a twisted rope. To make a rope properly you gotta have each strand the same. If you get one strand tighter than the other two, that's how a rope breaks.

We were branding about fourteen thousand a year on Millungera. They'd send off around the ten thousand mark of steers and bullocks. For a long time they didn't spey cows. They mostly had Brahmans from about '32. Then they went back into shorthorn and then into the Santas. They got a bull off Risdon Stud down at Warwick. I went in to Julia Creek and got him off the train; took a few cows in and walked him back. No such thing as transport. The outstation where I was, Crowfells, was only forty miles from Julia Creek.

Conditions on Millungera were rough, really rough, them days. They traded under Mereth and Menzies, the two old English fellows that owned it, but it was run by Australian Estates. They never even had ringers' quarters. When you came to the station in the Wet you just camped out on the bore-drain. All they had was a two-room hut for the cowboy and the handy man. Old Woodhouse was managing there. I think he was there for about twenty-two, twenty-three years. He wasn't hard. He just never give them anything. When he got a case of jam, all you got was the bloody apple jelly. All the good jam went up to the house. The best tucker you ever got there was old Mrs. Crossley. She was cook there. Old Woodhouse's wife died real young and he had four sons, Neville and Ralphie and Colin and Bill. Mrs. Crossley sort of reared them and she was a good cook.

Old Jack Sherwin, he was head stockman on Millungera for forty years. A great man he was, too! A big old fellow, with a big mo. And his hat, he always folded it under like a pirate so that as soon as he

Jack Sherwin, head stockman of Millungera for forty years.

went after a mob of cattle, there was no going back looking for his hat. He was the most honest! He would never let you kill a stranger. You kill another fellow's calf and you'd soon see how you got on! He never sacked a man in his life and he made it hard for them to go. He worked day and night. He didn't care where night hit him. He could find his way anywhere, day or night. He'd go out eight or nine days away just on his own – no tucker - with just an old saddle-bag. You'd never know where he was. And he never left the place. Never went into town. Day and night he worked. He was a real hero. He died of cancer in hospital in Townsville 8th August 1956. The company buried him at Savannah, an out-station of Millungera, where he loved, with a little tombstone, 'Forty years loyal service'.

When stockman Jim McGoffin of Etta Plains went missing, search parties from nearby stations rode out along the flooded Flinders.

Jim McGoffin was a fellow who drowned on Etta Plains on the Flinders. They had VRD bullocks on agistment there, and he was looking after these bull's head bullocks [4] and this give-and-take[5] where the Flinders went through, the fence crossed and went around about a mile on the Kalmeta boundary, and he was camped there. And this fellow called Jim Alzeimer went down to his camp to see him. And he seen he'd just gone. The coals in his fire was still going. And Jim Alziemer waited all day to see him and he never come home, so he stacked his set of billy-cans up so's he'd know when he come back. Every Sunday the mail used to come from Julia Creek and Jim McGoffin used to go into the station and collect his mail and this Sunday he never come in.

And Jim Alzeimer went back out to his camp and the billy-cans was still in the same place. So they notified the police and they checked all the other places, Dalgonally and Kalmeta where he might have been, and then they got a search party. Three of us, Jim, Rex Allan and me, we went to the Flinders. It was about ten mile over. The police constable, Sam Henry, and the rest went the Cloncurry side. The river was still running, and Jim and I swum over, and as soon as we got to the other side I picked up his stirrup-iron and leather. So we went around this give-and-take fence. It only went about a mile around. And we got his horse with the saddle under his gut. The surcingle had cut into his wither. And we crossed Jim McGoffin's tracks where he'd come out of the river. He'd had his dinner there.

4 Bullocks from Victoria River Downs with a symbol-brand of a bull's skull with horns.

5 Give-and-take; a section of boundary fencing where, because of difficult terrain, for example rocks or swamp, the official fence-line is slightly altered by mutual agreement between the owners of both properties.

And we rode back and we met this other fellow, Rex Allan; he'd rode up the river. We said, 'We got the horse.' He said. 'Yeah. I got the body down there.' In those days your trousers had cuffs and a little twig of tea-tree had caught his cuff as he'd gone down the river. If he'd gone another hundred yards he would have been out in Kalmeta country and they'd have never found him. And the fish had ate all his face away, head down in the water like that. The police constable that was there went into the homestead at Haddington, twelve mile up, and rung the Sergeant at Julia Creek and the sergeant said he wanted him brought in but he told him he was too far gone. So we buried him there near a big old mulga. And years later I seen a letter in the paper of people that wanted to know any information about him, some nieces of his. So I got in contact with them; said I could take them to the place that we'd buried him. And they come out and put a tombstone for him there near the mulga.

I had me own plant of horses from when I was a young fellow. I drove for years off Millungera and Iffley on the Saxby. In those days you could get horses for nothing. Anything that rooted they'd give 'em to you. You could work 'em up and quieten them and get a plant together. And where you worked they would know your ability and the boss would say when there was a mob of fats to go into town, 'You'd better get your horses together and take these in.' You had your own men.

The longest droving trips I done was twelve weeks; with twelve-fifty [6]. I'd have two men and a horse-tailer. See, Dalgonally fats were steady. They were walked up from Canobie as weaners. Dalgonally was a bullock depot and Canobie'd walk their weaners up, so they were broke-in cattle – educated, you might say - and fattened when you took them away on the stock route. You could take a mob of Dalgonallies and the first day they'd be settled down; walk along nice and steady. One man could watch 'em. But Millungera cattle, they'd jump all night. Never settled down for about a week. Millungera weaners, when you branded them today, tomorrow you'd take them out to their paddock and bush 'em. You never seen them again until they grew up. They grew up bloody mad as March-bloody hares!

And in them days there were a lot of reserves on them stock routes; a mile-square paddock with water in it. And if the grass was good you'd have a day there. Just let your cattle go of a day-time. Put 'em together at night. And away you'd go again next day. First, I had pack-horses but when I got a bit of money together I got a truck. A truck was easier. You could put anyone on the cooking, see. When you had pack-horses, you had to have a good reliable man to pack the horses. If you put one pack heavier and the other pack rolled, the horse'd go bush and kick the bloody guts out of them. You had to have a good man to pack 'em balanced.

With a truck you could pack easy. With a truck you carry plenty of water; two forty-four gallon drums of water. And a drum of petrol. You could carry more stores. You got better tucker with a truck. Plenty of potatoes and onions and pumpkin. The pumpkin wouldn't last long. And plenty of course salt. Your main diet was plenty of bullets and a good gun, salt, spuds and onions, and flour. Tea and a bit of sugar. They were your main diets. And, see, in them contracts on a big trip they give you a killer every ten days. But, well, you never know. A stranger

6 A mob of twelve hundred and fifty.

might wander into the mob along the track, or something like that. Then you'd have fresh meat for a couple of days and you salted the rest. And you could carry plenty of corned beef. You'd have corned beef curry, corned beef stews, Burdekin duck[7]. You never had puddin'. You never had time to eat puddin'! I had good cooks. Old George Milward; died not long back; was with me a long time. He was a good cook. But I mainly had a Yellafella; Frank Douglas, one of them Quilty fellows. He was a good man; he had his own plant. I had him for years. He could knock up a good feed. Died two or three year ago of sugar.

If your cattle rush, you go to the fire. A fire will split the cattle. See, if you put a torch on a beast's eyes he can't do nothing. There was a rush on Thorntonia two or three year ago. They put the cattle in the brake and they rushed. And this young fellow told me he climbed a tree. And I laughed. He said to me, 'Well, what would you do?' I told him, 'I'd go for a night-horse.' He said 'They had no horses tied up!' Christ Almighty! No night-horses! They lost a hundred and ninety that night! But when they rush you go to the fire. That splits 'em. But if there was a spare horse, you go for a horse!

I done a twelve-week trip from Dalgonally to a place called Nardoo down in the Springsure country. It's called Tandera now. Australian Estates bought it off old Russel Squires. Good trips. Through to Julia Creek, then Winton, Longreach, down through Blackall and you cut across that route that goes by Springsure to Tambo on the Nogoa River. At Julia Creek you knew that Kynuna was another seventy mile on. And Winton was a hundred mile on further. And Longreach a hundred and twenty. You knew all them places to get your stores. Nowadays all these stock routes are given to the stations they're on. See, they were a mile-wide stock route; and they couldn't hunt you on. But now, if you don't do your stage they'll hunt you; keep you going. They want all the grass for theirselves. Yeah!

There'd be some days you might have to do a dry day. See, with a dry day you worked it that you'd water your cattle about one o'clock and you'd go out as far as you can; might do seven or eight mile that afternoon. Gen'ally you go about two or three mile after dinner. You do your main stage in the morning. But then when you get a dry day you go as far as you could and you do a good day next day and you hit the water the next day. That's what they call a dry day. Oh, Yeah!

They smell water for miles. And then all they want to do is walk. They're thirsty and they want to walk out. See, if you've got your cattle full of water they want to feed. But if they've got their gut dried up they want to walk to water. Them government fellows put down the bores and troughs. And when you're coming on to water, say there was three of you, two of you keep in the lead to hold the mob back. The more men in the lead the better. Then the tail follows. You'd have one man back to keep his eye on the tail and the rest of you would be in the lead. About a mile back from the trough you'd cut about a hundred and fifty – all depends on the length of the trough – and let them in to water. Then when they're full you'd hunt them and let another hundred and fifty come in. You keep cutting them out like that. If a big mob of cattle hit the trough at once they'd be on top of each other and the trough'd be dry. See, while you're driving that first lot a couple of hundred

7 Corned beef patties fried in dripping.

yards away it gives the trough time to fill up. The man in the lead of the mob, he'll just ride in when he reckons the other lot is through and cut out another one-fifty and let 'em come in and block the rest. It might take four, five hours to water the mob.

I never had dogs. They jam your cattle together and bite them. See, the better the man the better the cattle.

If you seen a beast standing back eating a bit of grass you never went and hunted him along. You stood off and let him walk up himself. The men you get today they'll trot him back up to the mob. You'd never trot a beast for nothing. You break their toes and then you got crippled cattle. You never yarded cattle. If you were going to dip, you watched 'em back from the yards and brought 'em in and yarded early in the morning. See, cattle on their feet all night in a yard are jumping one another and crippling them. You put a mob of cattle on camp and they'll lay there all night; get up in the middle of the night and have a pee and lay down again. But if you yard 'em they're on their feet all night. These bloody brakes [8] they use today! I tell you; there were no bloody brakes in our time! You watched your cattle at night. Went round them, singing. And after you got your cattle broke in they'd lay down there all night. Yeah. Twelve weeks, the trip. And then to bring the plant back; a month back. If you seen a good water-hole you'd have a spell there; hobble your horses out for a feed and maybe do a bit of fishing for a coupla days. Oh, Yeah!

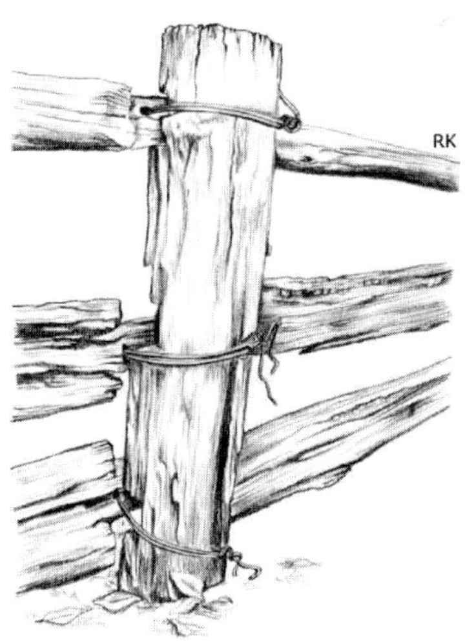

8 Brake: Electric fencing run off a portable battery, erected to hold cattle overnight. Round brakes are believed to be better with stirry cattle but most drovers opt for square brakes because they are easier to erect. The brake should be just big enough to let the cattle lie down, with star-pickets about fifteen paces apart.

Mary Ada Core

Mary Ada Core (nee McDowall) taken shortly before her wedding in 1914.

INTRODUCTION

This remarkable document, the early recollections of Mary Ada Core, was given to me by Mrs. Jennifer Roberts of Townsville, the daughter of noted North Queensland pastoralist, the late Mac Core of Blue Range station and later Mount Full Stop station. Mary Ada Core was Mac Core's mother. Mary Ada and her sisters and brothers grew up before the end of the nineteenth century, on some of the best known cattle properties of the north, including Greenvale, Christmas Creek and Cashmere, all owned by Mary's father, William McDowall.

There will be few readers who will not be lost in admiration of the exploits of Mary and her favourite sister Lizzie - Mary recalls, 'We were never apart' - the running of brumbies, the wild night rides after scrubber cattle, fraught with danger but undertaken by them with zestful enthusiasm and astonishing horsemanship. The sternness of the children's father, William McDowell, of whom they lived in great awe, must be considered in the light of the onerous task he faced in pioneering isolated wilderness areas of the North which were, in the late eighteen hundreds, still prone to attack by hostile tribes defending their traditional hunting lands.

The Mount Fox Track of which Mary Ada speaks is still, in sections, an unnerving road to the unwary traveller. It crosses the wild, rain-forest-clad Seaview Range west of Ingham to connect eventually with the Lynd Highway near Greenvale. In places the road is so narrow that vehicles must pull over, or back up, to allow one another to pass. Passengers are uncomfortably aware that the foliage beneath their window is in fact the crown of the forest canopy below.

Mount Fox, a 560,000 year old pyroclastic cone is one of the youngest volcanoes in Australia. It lies on basalt lava flows that are 23.6 million years old. Covered only in guinea grass, Mount Fox can be climbed easily in half an hour. At the summit there is a bowl-shaped depression, the remains of the ancient volcanic throat. A lava flows extends away from the southern base of the mountain and to the west, exposed basalt pavements in creek beds are evidence of the lava flows of long ago.

Few readers will not feel some sense of regret at the passing of the wild, free innocence and exuberant vitality of the period depicted in this story. But we can be grateful that the fearless and spirited girl who would in time become the mother of one of the North's most eminent cattlemen, Mac Core, has left us this vivid account, presented here verbatim, of her remarkable, long-ago girlhood.

Chapter 13...

A FAST AND SPLENDID RIDE

MARY ADA CORE

I was born at Lake Lucy cattle station, in the Ingham district, in the year 1885. My father was William McDowall, of Scottish descent. My mother, before she was married, was Elizabeth Schumaker. She was a great-aunt of Mel Schumaker, the jockey. I had two brothers and three sisters.

One of the first recollections I have of my life at Lake Lucy, is gazing through the fence at a big black stallion named Boom, loaned to my father by Scott Brothers of Valley of Lagoons station, and wishing I could ride him. I stood there for hour after hour. Then one day, my hero and friend, Jim Costigan, came over to see us from the Valley, where he worked. Taking Jim by the hand I led him over to the stallion and asked him if I could ride him. 'Sure.' said Jim, 'You run in and get your riding cushion and I'll saddle him.' So away we went, me perched in front of Jim, but only at a walk. 'Make him gallop, Jim,' said I. Boom must have been a very quiet horse and a good hack, for we set off at a canter and I kept Boom and Jim at it until I developed a stitch in my side. But I said, 'Never mind the pain. Mumma will give me some ginger-tea when we get home. So let us keep galloping.' Jim used to tease me about this as I grew older and that is how I remember it so well.

When I was about seven I went to the Ingham Show, with all the family riding on horseback from Lake Lucy. It was the first town and the first show that I can remember seeing. The last night before getting to Ingham, we camped at a station called Cold Water, which was managed by Ted Blackman. He was schooling his horses ready for the Show and as it was early afternoon we joined in the fun. Fred, my brother, who was always my tutor and adviser, said to me, 'Come, Mary! Put Masher over those jumps.' I never disobeyed Fred - well, hardly ever. I had ridden Masher all day and he was a baulker but Fred handed me a whip, so I knew by that what to do. I gave Masher a few good cuts to liven him up and he cleared the jumps like winking. So then it was decided; 'Let Mary ride Masher in the Show tomorrow!'

I was really bewildered when I got into the show-ring. I was afraid Masher would baulk and throw me over the hurdle instead of jumping it himself. But I was armed with the whip and Fred's advice to 'hit whim hard when he comes to the jump and make him take off'. It was a wild ride but I didn't let him baulk and got the first prize. When the judge put the ribbon on Masher's neck the crowd threw their hats in the air and cheered, and I said to Fred, who was holding Masher, 'What are they

The Upper Burdekin, which would have been familiar to Mary Ada and her favourite sister Lizzi. It forms the boundary of Lucky Downs, one of William McDowall's properties.

doing that for?' And so ended the first, but not the last, of my rides in the show-ring.

This is one of the rare occasions that I disobeyed Fred. He took me as a gooseberry[1] when he took our governess for a Sunday ride. We got to the creek and he said to me, 'Now you wait here until we get back. We are going round the bend there.' So I waited and waited, looking at the sun and thinking it must be dinner time and that they must have got bushed. So, finally, I went home and was peacefully eating my dinner when Fred walked in. He took off his belt, grabbed me by the neck and I got one of the best hidings of my life. All the time, Fred kept saying, 'When I tell you to wait, I mean it. You wait there. Wait, I say! Wait! Even if you die there!' So I learned to wait when left (even if I died there!) But I never lost faith in Fred. He was one of the kindest and most generous persons I have ever known. In those days we seldom 'went to town'. And if Fred went, he always brought something back for us, even if was only a bag of lollies.

One morning I went with Fred who had a goat-team of five wethers, carting firewood. Fred loaded the cart and said, 'You stop here. I'm taking this load home, and, don't, I say, don't touch that axe!' As soon as he had gone I picked up the axe and put my foot on a log, and, bang! It came down on my big toe and split it almost in half. I ran all the way home, fascinated by watching the blood spurt from my toe. When I got home they could not stop the bleeding. So my mother saddled her horse, took me up in front of her, and rode twenty-five miles to Walters Plains where my father was camped out mustering. I amused myself on the journey by watching the blood from my toe run down the horse's shoulder. When we got to the camp they were yarding a big mob of cattle, and the cattle 'rung up' [2] and somehow we got into the middle of the ring, and were pushed around, but somehow the horse kept on his feet, and all was quite okay. My mother wanted Father to take me to Herberton to a doctor, but he sent the men hunting for cobwebs and bound my toe up with spider webs and flour, which partly stopped the bleeding. The next day we were sent back home; it was 'not necessary' to take me to the doctor. I still have a deep scar the length of my toe and halfway up my foot, the full length of the axe blade.

1 Gooseberry; a friend or relative of an unmarried female who accompanies her as chaperone when she is escorted by a suitor, in order to preserve proprieties.

2 rung up; milling in a circle, especially when being yarded

In the year 1890 my father took some bullocks to the Herberton Show and won a silver cup, which the family still have. It is inscribed, 'Herberton, M.P. and A. Association, 1890. For best pen of 5 fat bullocks. Special regard to quality. Presented by W. McLeod, Esq. Tirrabella station. Won by W. McDowall Esq. Lake Lucy station.'

While we were at Lake Lucy, Fred, who was the eldest of the family, was sent away to boarding school in Herberton. He ran away from the school after a few months. It was during a heavy wet season. He walked to the nearest property, swimming a creek on the way, borrowed a horse from them and rode it to the next station, swimming more creeks and so on, until he got home. Unseen, he let his horse go and hid in the saddle-room, where we found him, being afraid of what my father would say and do. So we had to get Mother, and after a long discussion between all of us, she was sent to 'bell the cat'[3]. Things were not so bad as we had expected for Fred was not thrashed, as he had expected, nor was he sent back to school. He was an exceptionally good rough-rider and old hands always said he and Fred Kepple were the best riders in the district.

Just before we left Lake Lucy I was invited by Mrs. Fenwick, then staying at the Valley[4] which was then owned by Fenwick and Ramsden, to go to the Valley. Gone were the Costigans, to my sorrow. For some reason Mrs. Fenwick had taken a fancy to me and wanted me as her riding companion. She went for a ride every afternoon on a groomed horse, which had shining buckles on her saddle, etc, and galloped all the time, bringing her horse back white with foam. This went against my grain and I didn't like her very much for it. I tagged along behind and nursed my horse, taking short cuts. At nights she would sing and dance for us, and she could dance too; all sorts of fancy dancing. One night she broke her pearls and they were scattered all over the floor. The room was locked and I was the one on my hands and knees all over the floor, next morning, picking up her pearls.

I didn't like staying there, and fretted for my family. I didn't eat my 'nice food' as my sisters and brothers couldn't share it. I wouldn't drink their 'rain water' for the same reason, and used to take a cup and go down to the lake and drink the lake water – as my sisters and brothers only had lake water to drink. So, finally, I was 'taken home'. Evidently Mrs. Fenwick's 'riding companion' had failed her. But I was happy to get home, even though we ate off tin plates and drank lake water, and used 'fat lamps' not kerosene glass lamps like the Valley. My mother was a good cook and we always had plenty to eat. We were a very happy family.

We all slept in a home-made galvanized-iron shed divided into three rooms. We girls had one room. One night, just after getting into bed, and lying awake, we saw a man lying along one of the rafters high up in the unsealed roof. We never stirred, but Cissie called out in a loud voice, 'Father! Bring your gun! There is something up in the rafters!' The man was down and out of the room like a shot. Father was miles away, camped out, but Mother brought the gun and let off a few shots, just

3 To bell the cat; an expression derived from the nursery story of mice who agreed that if one of them were bold enough to fix a bell to the collar of the cat while she was sleeping then all their lives would be made safer. The unanimous decision having been taken, the next thing was to decide who among them would the heroic one to actually put the bell on the cat.

4 Valley of Lagoons station

to let him know we had a gun. A few nights after that, we were all in bed and had been asleep, when Hetty woke and saw, leaning over the end of her bed, the head of our old white donkey which had wandered in looking for bread. That frightened us all more than the man in the roof.

About this time of the man in the roof, Father had to go to Brisbane on business and he told Mother to always have the gun handy. He gave Fred a whip handle weighted with lead and told him to keep it by the door and to use it if the occasion warranted it. At that time we had a governess, Miss Hamilton, who was obviously a bit silly, who planned a 'joke', not letting anyone, not even Mother, know of it. She told us all, just about sundown, that she had seen a man standing up on the ridge and when he saw her he had ducked behind a tree and hid. So after supper she went and blackened her face, and put on a dirty old pair of trousers and a shirt that Father had been killing in. She walked into the dining-room, where we all were, with a tomahawk in her hand. Fred jumped straight for his whip handle and gave this 'man' a good hit on the side of the head. 'He' dropped like a stone. Mother had run into the next room and hidden the baby under the bed, thinking the blacks had come to kill us. When she came out we all crowded round to look at the dead black-fellow. But Fred cried out, 'Good God! I've killed Miss Hamilton!' But a bucket of cold water brought her round and she didn't get any sympathy from any of us.

When she had come into the room, Sambo, a little four year old black orphan boy Mother was bringing up, ran to the fire-place and tried to climb up the chimney - no fire luckily - calling, 'Masser! Holy Sailor! Come home! Quick! Black-fellow come to kill us!' After that we youngsters nick-named him, 'Holy Sailor', as he used to say it as often as he could. Father stopped us calling him that as he said it was not suitable. When Sambo grew older he used to go with Father droving, and he always asked for the middle watch as he said 'that way I get two sleeps.'

We lived at Lake Lucy until I was about eight years old and it was there that I saw my first cattle tick. Our old Aboriginal boy, when milking the cows, got one off a cow. He gave it to me and told me to take it down and show it to my father. My father, who must have been a keen businessman, then swapped Lake Lucy for Kangaroo Hills station, as the ticks had been through that place and were only just coming to Lake Lucy.

Leaving Lake Lucy was quite a performance. We had a five-horse dray on which was loaded our piano. We were a musical family and the piano was my mother's prize possession. There were also her hand-operated sewing-machine and all our bits and pieces. We all rode horse-back, my mother side-saddle and carrying my youngest sister. Each one was carrying something – a cat, a hen, a parrot, a box with chickens in it, and I was carrying a pup. My pony objected to the pup and he bolted with me. I lost my hat, but held on to the pup and rode all the way to Kangaroo Hills for two days without a hat. No wonder I had freckles.

Kangaroo Hills was a straggledy rough bit of country with lots of clean-skins and wild cattle in the scrub-oaks around Mount Fox. Father and Fred were good cattlemen and after many exciting adventures they had Kangaroo Hills cleaned up. Bull Hill is named after a wild clean-skin who used to run there but was eventually thrown and yarded. All that country was mustered from the old Mount Fox out-yards and hut and many a night we kids camped there. It was notorious for fleas which bred in the ground there and feasted on us at night. Mac's Creek was named after my father, who was always called Mac, short for McDowall.

One day my younger brother Bob and I were sent to tail some horses about two miles away. We found this monotonous and decided to have a race, picking a dead tree some distance away as the winning post. Away we went, and both hit the winning post together, knocking it and our horses down. The horses ran away. I got up but failed to catch one. Bob lay very still. I dragged him into the shade and ran all the way home. By the time we got back Bob was gone from where I had left him. So we had some tracking to do. Fred, who was an expert tracker, being taught by a half-caste, Charlie Burdekin, to track on the oak-leaves of Mount Fox, found Bob quite a distance away and walking down a creek quite unconscious of where he was or what had happened. I don't remember what happened to the two saddle-horses or to the tailers. Someone must have seen to them.

Once we lost our flock of goats and Charlie Burdekin and Fred were sent to track them. They rode, taking a split-bag of food with them, and were gone two days, bringing the goats back with them. My father gave Charlie five pounds, all in silver shillings, which thrilled him no end, and he'd tip the coins out of the bag and poke and prod them around by hand or sometimes he'd tip them on the floor and move them about with his bare feet.

On another occasion there was a good looking brumby which had been seen at the Two Mile. Fred was determined to run him in. He fed our old racehorse, Apple Jack, and he and I went to get the brumby. I was given all sorts of instructions. I had never been running brumbies before and Fred decided that I was so light that I was to ride Apple Jack and do the wheeling and he would manoeuvre the coachers[5]. We spotted what we thought were the brumbies and I went as instructed to 'work wide' but as the horses moved away, Apple Jack set off after them. The pace was so fast and I evidently didn't have a 'Ted Sloan' seat, as the wind got between me and the saddle, and my legs and the flaps of the saddle were flying out. All I could do was to hang on to the pommel like a monkey. Old Apple Jack galloped slap bang into the horses, which luckily were some drovers' horses, tired and quiet and heading for home. I got a terrible scolding and was pulled off Apple Jack, as 'not being fit to ride a decent horse.' But, I'll never forget that ride. It was a thriller! Though I didn't appreciate it as such then. Some weeks later we did run the brumby in. But this time Fred was on Apple Jack and I handled the coachers.

While at Kangaroo Hills we young ones were invited to the wedding of Mary Johnstone, the eldest of the Johnstone girls of Stoneleigh station. She was marrying someone who was taking her on a honeymoon around the world. We rode down in one day taking our 'wedding togs' in a valise which was strapped to the front of the saddle. We each caught and saddled our own horses in the dark, and Hetty my sister, who was always most particular about her appearance, discovered when daylight broke and we were miles on our way, that she still had her yard boots on,

5 Coachers; in this instance used of a mob of quiet, well-behaved horses into which the wild horse, by herd instinct, would run when cut out from the brumby mob. Similarly used of cattle.

and the ones she intended to wear were nicely polished and still on the verandah at home. History doesn't relate what she actually did wear at the wedding, but there were a few tears shed on the way down.

It was about this time that I started riding in shows. I trained and rode horses of our own. I also rode for the Alston brothers of Ingham; also for Reg Boyd, the son of one of the pioneers of Ripple Creek sugar mill, the first mill in the Ingham district. Reg had a team of three; Brilliant, a perfect lady's hack, a lovely easy and smooth jumper, with a mouth like silk; Stephen, a big dappled grey Gentleman's Hack and my favourite, Donald, a big strong brown gelding and a bold jumper. In his youth he had been a baulker, but after some of the Masher treatment, and once he and I got to know one another, he was a thrill to ride, and felt strong and sure under you. I rode with girls like Meg Cameron who was the Queen of the Show Rings in those days. One of her stunts was to drive a horse ahead of her in reins, make him jump and then jump her own horse after him. She was killed in a show ring and a monument was erected in her memory as one of the greatest show-riders of the day.

While we were at Kangaroo Hills I was sent to boarding school in Townsville. My bed in the dormitory was next to a girl named Violet Black who became Mrs. Joe Allingham.[6] We became firm friends. At Christmas I went home for the holidays. We left Townsville, travelling by ship to Lucinda Point, I being sea-sick all the way. We went to Ingham by train[7] and then out to Mr. Pappin's farm, where Father had left the horses. They had brought a freshly broken-in grey filly for me. I was always partial to greys. But when I got on her, next morning, she bucked and threw me. Father was very annoyed with me. I hurt my back and hip but was afraid to say so. So riding from there to home for two days was a nightmare.

We all hated boarding school, and we persuaded Mother to take a house in Townsville so we could go as day girls. So my father bought Ellersleigh, a lovely old home in the Aitkenvale area. There was a small paddock at the back of the house and we soon had our favourite horses there. We worked to erect a show-ring and jumps to school the horses. It was great fun riding the bush horses through the town, and not satisfied with that, we would put the horses into the sulky and drive them through town. One day I took Stepper, a new arrival, and when we got into the main street he bolted, and as there are no brakes on a sulky, I had to let him go. We went down Flinders street and past the Queen's Hotel along the Strand and home by way of the German's Gardens.[8] It was a wild drive but before we got home Stepper had settled for a trot. In those days the traffic was very light, so no cars, and only horse-drawn vehicles to get out of our way.

When Kangaroo Hills was properly cleaned up, my father got itchy feet and sold it and bought Greenvale and we all moved over there. These were the days before motor-cars, gramophone or wireless and it was at Greenvale that we formed our own

6 Two noted North Queensland pioneering families. See also Two Days into Charters Towers in Barefoot Through the Bindies, CQU Press, 1992.

7 Not a standard gauge passenger train but a narrow-gauge sugar train which took raw sugar to the wharf at Lucinda Point to be loaded on to steamers for the refinery at Cairns. The sugar-train was the only viable means of transport in an area of crocodile infested swamps and creeks, for farmers and their families.

8 The original name of Belgian Gardens. The name was changed during World War One.

band. Fred played the violin by ear. Billy Wade also played a violin by ear; Cissy, my sister played the piano, a friend played the oboe and Mother the accordion. My mother had a particularly good singing voice; Fred had a good baritone and Cissy a soprano. Mrs. Ramsden, of Fenwick and Ramsden, more or less offered to adopt Cissy and take her to London to have her voice properly trained. She believed there was a fortune in it. But Father would not give his consent, much to Cissie's disappointment.

The wild range county which Mary knew so well.

When we first went to Greenvale there was a mob of about twenty Timor ponies running about the junction of Porphry Creek. The proper name of it is Palfrey, meaning a pony. They were brought to Greenvale by Albie Lyall, who at one time had owned Greenvale. But they were let run wild and their numbers accumulated. We had great fun with these ponies. We would get some of them in and break them in, to both saddle and harness, and they would become very quiet when broken-in and handled. They were too small to be of any real use, and we even had some as pets. They were pretty little things. They finally died out as my father gelded all the stallions and colts.

It was while we were at Greenvale that Lizzie and I were with father one day driving along that ridgy country about Doughboy. Father was driving, four-in-hand. Lizzie and I were in the front seat. We went over a bad rut and father's foot must have slipped off the brake. You drove it mostly with your foot right on the brake. However he took a header out of the buggy, taking the reins with him and both Lizzie and I jumped to our feet with an exclamation unprintable. I, being on the outside, grabbed the near-side poler's trace with my right hand and worked my way up to his collar, where the leader's reins ran through the hames. I gradually pulled them to one side, and with Lizzie's help, for she had followed me, got them to a stop. Luckily, it was near changing time and the horses were tired, and only going at a slow jog. Father, at this stage, caught us up, gathered up the reins, climbed back on to the seat, and no-one spoke a word, then at or any time later, for we dared not put father at a disadvantage. I'm sure no-one ever knew of that little incident. But the next day Father was busy in the blacksmith's shop welding a bar on the outside of the brake, to prevent a foot slipping off it again.

One day at Greenvale, Bob and I were supposed to be tailing the goats, but instead we were on the roof of the shed, playing. At about 9a.m. we suddenly saw

Father riding home and we both took fright. Bob was jumping up and down on the roof, saying, 'Quick! Quick! What will we do now! Here he comes!' I said, 'Jump down and go for your life after the goats!' So away we went without any dinner or even any matches to cook a goanna. We dared not bring the goats back before sundown.

While we still owned Greenvale, Father bought Cashmere station[9], and we girls moved over there, Fred remaining at Greenvale while Father and Mother moved between the two places. One night, when we three girls were alone at Cashmere someone threw a stone, a big one, about six pounds, through our bedroom window. We jumped up and barricaded ourselves in but we could hear him walking about outside and trying all the doors. He was gone in the morning and we never found out who, or what, he was. Probably a swagman.

It was while we were at Cashmere that we made friends with the Garbutt girls of Tirrabella station, fifteen miles away and our nearest neighbours. They were a big family and we spent many happy times together, visiting them and going to Mt. Garnet, the Hot Springs and up to Herberton Show or wherever there was any fun to be had. We formed a party once and went to Dunk Island for a week. We went by boat from the mouth of the Tully River and were all sea-sick on the way. Ernest Garbutt, one of the younger of the boys, was my very first boy friend and my brothers escorted the Garbutt girls of which there were four, and there were four boys, so we had plenty to pick from but we never married any of them. We had advanced to a buckboard-buggy and four in hand in those days and many a mile I drove that buggy and four horses.

Father eventually sold Cashmere and Greenvale and we moved to Christmas Creek. Father was a great one for giving you something to do that he thought, perhaps, you couldn't quite manage. One day, at Christmas Creek – we were then in our middle teens – he said to Lizzie and I - we were never one without the other - 'I have bought a thoroughbred mare. She was bred at Maryvale and been run in from a brumby mob. She is now in the Clarke River paddock and said to have been roughly broken in. If you can ride her home from the Clarke you can have her.' Lizzie and I gave this some thought and made a few plans. We rode down to the Clarke next morning and yarded the mare. She could strike like lightning and was very touchy, but in due course, we caught her and got her saddled.

There was no question as to who would ride her. Lizzie was a really good rough rider and could beat me any day. I have only seen her thrown once. When Lizzie finally got on to the mare, she couldn't buck, but pig-jumped, and raced around the yard, striking at the bit, and had no mouth at all. So we had to have another confab and a smoke and a drink of water. We finally decided for me to drive them home. We put Paul, the horse Lizzie had ridden, in the yard, and Lizzie got on. We made the mare follow Paul. Paul knew where home was and set off at a smart canter. Luckily the mare followed him with me bringing up the rear. I could hardly keep them in sight, for the faster I went the faster the mare went ahead of Paul and didn't need any excuse to make the pace. It was really a wild ride and a fast one. Paul kept

9 For a further account of the early days of Cashmere station see 'A Hardier Breed' in Barefoot through the Bindies, C.Q.U. Press, Outback Books.

to the road and went straight home. I blocked them up in a corner, got the rails down, and we were safe in the home paddock. Paul went straight to his mates and I yarded a dozen or so horses, with Lizzie still on the mare. She was really a nice mare, a bright chestnut with markings, and looked every inch a thoroughbred.

We called her Quality. She really had very little vice and had only been half-broken-in when she got away on the Clarke. We put her straight to breeding, as we had Braw Laddie, a five-furlong Brisbane record-breaker at the time, and she had many foals. There were; Grey Quality, Bay Quality, Big Quality and Young Quality, all good useful mares. They broke in quietly and were all good-lookers.

Father eventually sold Cashmere and Greenvale and bought Curruchan on the coast and we moved there, taking our flock of goats and my pet emu, who used to run with the goats. Curruchan was a nice home, right on the very bank of Kennedy Creek, which was always running with lovely crystal-clear water. We had plenty of social life there as it was near Cardwell and there were lots of farms and stations around. We girls and boys used to drive the buckboard to Cardwell, twelve miles away, for the Saturday night dance, then drive twelve miles home again at daylight to milk the cows and cook breakfast. The Henrys, of Bellenden Plains were our friends and neighbours. They were a family of three boys and two girls all about our age, so we never seemed to lack for company. It was nothing to canter off, or drive, twenty miles to visit friends.

Curruchan was only a small property with about a thousand head of cattle, half of which were scrubbers and had never been branded. It was a network of scrub-lined creeks and these cattle ran under the range on the western boundary. Fred and some of our boys from Christmas Creek cut roads through these scrubs and fenced on each side. We used to then moonlight the wild cattle by sneaking between them and their hiding places in the range. When daylight broke we were all nicely placed, having left coachers near the first creek. There was always a rush of hooves. Cattle would split off and break but we could always get some of them and finally we got them all. Some of those bullocks went 1 000 pounds weight and had been getting away for years. We would take them straight into the butchers in Cardwell, selling everything except weaners, which we paddocked. I always used to ride a piebald called Thunderbolt and always joined in the moonlight rides or raids which I enjoyed. I would leave my dog, a good one, with the coachers and many a beast she brought in out of the scrub.

At some time before I was born my father was head stockman cum manager of the Valley, which was then called Pelican Lakes, the head-station being at Glen Dhu, where they were trying run sheep, but the wild blacks killed all the sheep, also the shepherds. So, finally they gave sheep away. The machinery in the wool shed was removed and dumped in the deep waterhole near the crossing at Glen Dhu Creek on the road to Herberton. When the water settles and is quite clear it can still be seen to this day.

One night while my father was away at Glen Dhu, and only my mother and a gin were at Pelican Lakes, a half-civilized black boy came into the gin's hut and told her that at daybreak the wild blacks were coming to kill her and my mother. She went and told Mother and they barricaded themselves into one room with a gun and a revolver each, and waited, hoping and praying that father would come home.

Meanwhile Father had a premonition during the day that something was wrong so instead of going to bed that night, he caught a fresh horse and rode all the way to Pelican Lakes, arriving there an hour or so before dawn. So they were ready for the attack. Father shot the first black-fellow to show up, with mother and the gin letting off gun-fire as well. The rest of the blacks scattered and fled, thinking, I suppose, that all the men were at home. In those days one never went out without a revolver strapped to your saddle, and when you came home, a thorough inspection was made of hut and surroundings for tracks or signs of wild blacks. Most of the huts were built on a rise or a clear piece of ground for a better view of anyone sneaking up, for the wild blacks were adept at sneaking from tree to tree. Both Father and Mother could tell hair-raising tales of those days when the blacks were wild and really dangerous.

My father owned and re-sold thirteen properties in his lifetime. He would buy a place, improve it and always sold at a profit. Abingdon Downs was bought and sold next day at a profit of a thousand pounds. These were the days of no sales tax. The stations owned at some time by my father were; Welcome Downs, Lake Lucy, Kangaroo Hills, Greenvale, Cashmere, Pandanas Creek, Lucky Downs, Abingdon Downs, Southwick, Christmas Creek, Curruchan, Woolco, which adjoined Curruchan on the northern boundary, and The Grange, near Trebonne outside Ingham.

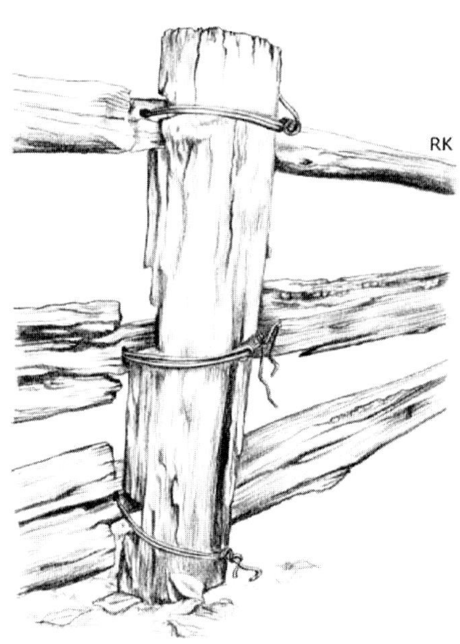

Jock Chiverton – Saddler and Whip-maker

Nineteen year old Jock Chiverton, newly enlisted to fight in New Guinea.

INTRODUCTION

I met Jock Chiverton at Camooweal in August 2005. Jock and his devoted companion, Marie, had towed their caravan from their grain and cattle property, Brazil, on Queensland's Darling Downs, to be in at Camooweal for the Drovers' Camp Festival.

Jock would be one of the most cheerful-hearted men I have ever come across, with a fund of outrageous stories, enough to keep any gathering of friends shouting with laughter late into the night;... 'Y'know old Gough! Well he's down the Cross one time and this prostitute approaches him. Gough asks, 'How much?' She says, 'A hundred dollars.' Gough says, 'I've only got a dollar on me.' She says, 'You don't get much for a dollar, y'know!' So that night, Gough and Margaret are in the restaurant and this prostitute comes in and she spots him. She takes a bit of a squiz at Margaret and she bends over and whispers in his ear, 'I told you you wouldn't get much for a dollar, didn't I!'

Or; 'Prince Charles, he's driving into Buckingham Palace one time and he skittles one of the Queen's corgis. He gets out and he's trying to hide the body under the hedge when up pops this genie and says, 'Mighty Prince! I will grant you one wish! What is your heart's desire?' Charlie thinks, 'Here's a go!' He says to the genie, 'Well, look. I've made a bit of a mess of Mum's corgi. Can you bring it back to life?' The genie tells him, 'Oh, Mighty Prince, not even with my great power can I perform such a miracle. What other longing of the heart can I grant unto you?' Charlie says, 'Oh, well. Do you reckon you could make Camilla a little bit younger and prettier?' The genie looks thoughtful and he says, 'I reckon we'd better have another look at that corgi.'

And; 'There's this padre and he's baptizing some young recruits in the river. And, up a bit, under a tree, there's this old sergeant and he's a bit the worse for the grog. The padre, he finishes dunking these young blokes and he spots the old serg. So he goes up to him and he says, 'Would you like to find God?' The serg, he gives it a bit of thought and he says, 'Yeah. I've finished all me grog and there's nothing else doing. Might as well give it a go.' So they go down to the river and the padre pushes the sergeant under. When he comes up the padre says, 'Did you find God?' The old serg says, 'No, I can't say I did.' So the padre shoves him under again. He comes up and he's spluttering. The padre says, 'Did you find God?' And the sergeant says, 'No, I can't say I did.' The padre shoves him under, again. Serg comes up and he's shaking the water out of his ears and coughing. The padre says, 'Well, did you find God this time?' The sergeant, 'No. I can't say I did. Are you sure this is where he fell in?'

A gentle, sweet-tempered man, Jock Chiverton is automatically loved by everyone who meets him. It is only when you have got to know him better that you notice that Jock walks with a limp, and you learn that on his twenty-first birthday Jock's right leg was shot away in a Japanese ambush in New Guinea . You can well imagine Jock livening the spirits of the entire ward at Greenslopes Military Repatriation Hospital during the long months of rehabilitation.

Jock holds no bitterness towards the old enemy. 'They were just soldiers like us,' he says. 'It's governments that are to blame for wars.' Then, his voice close to breaking, he added, 'Funny thing, you know. I never talked about these things before. I have never told this story to anyone.' I felt truly honoured.

Chapter 14...

COMPLAINING DON'T GROW LEGS

Jock Chiverton – Saddler and Whip-maker

My father was a professional soldier. He went all through World War One – India, Italy and France – in a Britisih artillery regiment without getting a scratch, and then at the very end he got injured. Kicked by a mule! That's how life goes.

In our family there were four of us, three boys and a girl. I was the youngest but our mother died of a carbuncle in her throat when I was fifteen months old. We lived at a little place called Nagoorin, south of Rocky. It wasn't much of a place, just a cream-loading siding. We used to have to walk barefoot, a fair way, about four mile, to Lake View school. There were big swamps and the cattle would leave tracks in the mud. After rain they would be full of water and if you slipped into them they would go squelch and up would come the mud all over your clothes. One time the teacher made me take my shirt off to get it dry and even though I was only little, I was embarrassed having no shirt on in front of all the school, like that.

I left school when I was thirteen and went to work on a dairy farm at Inglewood. It was tough. They were milking about thirty or forty cows by hand. And in winter, cold! Up before daylight and going till after dark. No boots or anything. Working overtime all the time. I got ten bob - about a dollar - a week, and my keep. I used to have to carry two kerosene tins of milk through the cow-yard and I wasn't much higher than the tins myself. I had to take the dray and this old horse, Thunderbolt, out bush and cut logs for firewood for the dairy. One time I cut the turn at the gate a bit too sharp and wiped out the gate and half the fence. I only went into Inglewood once in the nineteen months I was there and that was to get my first pair of boots.

Then I wanted to go out west. The west had a sense of adventure about it; something new. It was where I had always wanted to be. I went out on the western mail to Quilpie and then forty-odd mile on the mail truck to Pinkilla station, owned by the Tully's. The agent had given me the ticket and a meal voucher and if you stayed for so long they paid, but if not you had to pay them back.

Pinkilla was a sheep place, fairly big. It had ninety miles of bore drain. That was my first job droving, bringing stock back from the sales to the property. But most of the time I was the cowboy; milking the house cows – and those cows were running in a hundred square mile paddock; that was my first job every morning, to get them in. They were just ordinary station cattle, and some kicking ones amongst them. I had to break them in to being milked. Then it was cut the wood for the big kitchen, look after the chooks and the garden; take orders from the manager's wife mostly - once you do one job for them they just mount them up - and doing the killing and butchering on killing day.

Part of the cowboy's job was to do the killing. When you're picking your killer from the pen you feel around his tail. If he's got plenty of fat around the tail then he's good. To cut his throat you get him on his rump and pull his head backwards over your knee and cut the artery. And then you bleed him. There was a gallows, a long rail on a fork and there was a hook on it like a gantry, and that goes between the hamstrings. Then you hang him up and skin him and open him up and throw all the insides away. Some of that would go to the dogs. I'd carry a sixty pound wether up to the butcher's shop on m'shoulder. One killer a week, or more, depending who was at the station at the time. They told me, before I came, the boss said to Jackie, 'Better kill a sheep today, Jackie. We got visitors coming.' So Jackie takes the meat up to the house. Afterwards the boss says to him, 'That was a good killer you got, Jackie.' Jackie says to him, 'Me no kill'im, Boss! He dead already!'

Meals were up at the kitchen of the big house; plain tucker, nothing fancy. The jackeroo ate with the family. There were a couple of coloured blokes there. They didn't have quarters. They had a camp away a bit by themselves and they ate by themselves

You got Saturday afternoon off to wash your clothes and clean up your room in the quarters. Everybody had some sort of instrument and tried to play. Harold Donavan used to play the gum-leaf. I tried many a time. I nearly stripped all the trees around the quarters bare but I couldn't get the knack. I had a mouth organ and a button accordion. I was earning ten bob a week but I was sending eight bob a week home. It was Depression times. You don't do a lot on two bob. But I never felt I was missing out on anything. Never give girls a thought. I just loved the bush. Loved the life.

They had twenty or thirty dogs, good quality working dogs, sheep dogs, on the place. They had to put boots on the working dogs because of the thorns and the stones; it was bad country for burrs. The dog-boots were just a piece of leather wrapped round with toe holes in, to cover the pad of the feet, then laced around. I never ever heard any of the dogs complain. They seemed to understand they didn't have to keep stopping to pull thorns out of their feet. All those dogs ever thought about was work. Some of them, they'd almost be lying on their backs with their paws up to get those work-boots on! The same as when we were young, we shifted that many times it got that way, when the truck come, the chooks used to lie on their backs to get their legs tied up.

When I left Pilkilla I bought a couple of horses and my first new saddle and headed up north, with a spare horse on a lead, just camping out of a night. I'd have been about sixteen at the time. The spare horse was a pretty heavy sort of build and when I got to Gin Gin one fellow asked me what race I was entering him in the next day. I had to cross the Burnett River at Wallaville and it was full of quicksand. There weren't that many people on the road, but I knew it was how Sir Sydney Kidman had started out in life. I had the idea of getting up to Munduburra, where my brother was on Redcliffe station, but war broke out and he'd ridden a push-bike to Brisbane to join the RAAF.

Then, 1940, I was on Granville station outside Jericho, and I did a lot of rough-riding, but not by choice. They had bad horses. One little blue mare, oh, she was dirty. One time we were shifting cattle out the back and one beast broke. Well, of course, I took off after him on this little blue, and I'm over her neck, like you do, and she just dropped her head and, of course, I speared right through her ears. You could ride her all day and then, coming home, you'd get off at the gate to open it, and go to get on her again and she'd rear! Rear right over. I can't recall her name; but I called her a few!

And they had house-cows there and I used to use a push-bike to bring them up into the yard. And this time the bloody old bull they had turned on me. As soon as I saw him coming I dropped the bike and left! He put his foot through the spokes of the bike and that give me a bit of time. He shook the bike off his foot and come after me! And I looked back over my shoulder and I could see the tips of his horns right behind. So I dodged in behind this big ironbark tree, and waited till he got so far around, and I scooted off. In them days I could run. I run real good, that time! I beat him to the fence!

Christmastime, I left to go down and join up. It was just the natural thing to do. I didn't like the idea of the Japs taking the place over. I enlisted in Brisbane and that's where I made my mistake. I should have enlisted in Jericho. Because all the country fellows got Comforts Fund parcels from their home towns; knitted socks and chocolate and cigarettes. I didn't smoke but it would have been nice to get a parcel. So then all us young fellows, us rookies, camped at the Exhibition grounds in Brisbane, were marched down to the quarter-master's store to get our gear, and there'd be all these yells of 'Youse'll be sorry!' One of our fellows yells back, 'So was your sister when I left her!' And these overcoats they give you! There was only two sizes; big ones and whoppers! And there were ladies there doing your sewing and they'd look at me –knee-high to a grass-hopper - my pants turned up to m' knees, m' pockets hanging down, hat over m'eyes! A real smart soldier!

So then it was route marching at Redbank and to Canungra for jungle-training and up north to Selheim and then from Cairns to Port Moresby to join the Second Seventh Battalion. Then to get over that big mountain range you had to be at Ward Air-strip at 2 o'clock in the morning to get through the gap in the mountains before the clouds came down.

The Japs were holding Wau and you came under fire as soon as you landed. One of our blokes, he got off the plane and he said, 'Where are these bloody Japs!' and the next thing he's being loaded back on the plane, shot. We were under fire from the word go.

From Wau we moved up to Mubo and were out on patrol all the time. We all got malaria and very little medical attention. One patrol, I finished up carrying me mate's rifle as well as me own; we were all that crook, just staggering along. We slid down into this ravine where there was a creek at the bottom and tried to drink it dry, we were that burning up. You just can't get enough water. And you're shivering with cold and yet you're burning hot and got a raging temperature. They put us on a plane and took us back to Moresby. I had scrub typhus as well. You get it from the fleas in the kunai grass.

After a bit of a spell in a rest camp we rejoined our unit outside Salamaua. To get there you had to climb this mountain so steep you had to have ropes to get up it. The top of that ridge was so narrow you couldn't have driven a truck along it. There was a big shell hole and we dug little bits of fox-holes for ourselves out from it. And when you're digging in like that you keep pretty close to the ground because you'd hear these sniper's bullets; crack! And you don't know where they're coming from.

Every afternoon, four o'clock, down would come the rain. You were never dry. You never changed your clothes. No hot food. Just dog-biscuits and bully-beef. Blokes with false teeth used to soak those biscuits in water to soften them or make a sort of porridge they called 'burgoo'. As for a cuppa tea. You never got one. And the mossies! You'd just wipe them off your arms by the fistful. They give us Atebrin tablets for the malaria. And of a night-time, you'd do an hour on watch and an hour off. And while you're on, you're dying to sleep. And when you get your hour off, you can't get to sleep because you're worried in case your mate does! But there was no whingeing. We took it as it come.

We got shelled all the time. Two of our fellows were buried there and they both got blown out of their graves. I got hit in the temple with a bit of shrapnel. It dropped me like a bullock. I never even reported it or they'd have sent me out. I didn't want to leave my mates. I couldn't eat for a week. I was living on powdered milk and giving my rations to the other fellows.

On patrol we used to go round the native villages, right round the mountains. There'd be about eight of us; the scout up ahead. It was a full day's going, checking if there were Japs in the area. The villagers didn't like the Japs because when they brought in prisoners they'd bring them in like a pig tied to a pole and just drop them on the ground. The natives used to say, 'E no kai-kai' – 'Him not food'.

We knew the Japs were there and we were sent forward to rout them out. We were the first ones in; Number One Section, A Company. We'd crossed the Kombiatum-Bobjubi track and were just crossing the Frisco River and we run slap-bang into a Jap ambush. We were sitting ducks. We never saw them at all. You don't see them. They're in the scrub. Me mate on the left, Jimmy Hill, got hit in the head. The lieutenant, Lieutenant Smith, got hit. Seven of us got hit. I was the last one to go down. But I was lucky. I got the worst shot in the Japanese army. He got me in the knee with a machine-gun bullet. It blew all the bone away. I laid there and I heard Lieutenant Smith ask me if I was hit. He needed a bit of help. I left me Bren gun and crawled over to him and did what I could for him. He'd been hit in the spine and he couldn't move. I straightened his legs out for him as best I could. Then I crawled back to me gun and laid there all day. I wasn't game to do too much moving in case the Japs finished me off. I've never been so lonely in my life, lying out there like that; being classed as dead and gone.

When it was getting on for dark I thought, 'This is no bloody good! I'd better get back. They've left us here for dead.' The lieutenant had died; poor bugger. I started crawling back and I was just crossing the river and the doctor saw me and come in and dragged me out. He tied a tourniquet on m'leg; said he didn't know how I hadn't bled to death. I hadn't even looked!

All the other wounded blokes had been got away, but they rustled up these fuzzy wuzzies to carry me out on a stretcher. When we got to the dressing station one of me mates, Eric Chelman, from Mackay, come and he said, 'Cigarette, Mate?' and offered me a smoke. He knew I didn', but you don't get mates anywhere in the world like you get in the army. You rely on each other. You put faith in each other. You'd do anything for each other. So then they put a plaster dressing on m'leg. I was taken back to Mubo. The little plane that was the evacuation plane had been shot down just before, so I was there ten days; just lying out on the ground on the stretcher. They didn't think I was going to make it. Never had a wash. I asked for water but they were too busy to give me water. Then they came and cut the plaster off and pulled it. And I was hairy legs and all! That was murder.

Then the Fuzzy Wuzzy Angels - and they were angels - carried me over those bloody mountains in relays. They'd take it in turns. But, sure-footed! They dropped me once but caught me before I hit the ground. Those mountains, you've got to see them to believe them! They're straight up and down!

They were putting us wounded on a Yankee barge at Morobe and a siren went and three planes came in low over the point. Even I could see they had the Yankee star on the side of them plain as daylight, but the Yankee gunners all opened fire on them! On their own planes! Then they took us down to Salananda, and that's where they amputated the leg. I was down to just bones. They'd give me up for dead a few times. And one morning I woke up and the orderly brought me water and I was just going to have a wash and I noticed the bed was full of blood. The artery had broken. So they pumped gallons of blood into me. I was that close to finish my eyes glazed over and I couldn't see. They called the priest. I'm not a Catholic but he was the only sort they had. He read the last rites over me. But, oh, well! I out-smarted him!

I was so crook I couldn't eat so the doctor said I was to have a beer a day. But the orderlies used to get into the beer. They thought I wasn't going to make it and it would just be wasted on me. From there they flew me to Port Moresby and things got a bit better. One sister, Sister Burke, she looked after me, real good. And from there they flew me to Atherton. Doctor Brown asked me, 'How old are you?' And I told him, 'Twenty-one. I got hit on me twenty-first birthday.' He said, 'No. I mean your real age.' He thought I was having him on; that I'd put me age up to join up. He did a pinch-graft on me. They pinch up the skin on the back of your thigh and cut it off. After that I knew what it was like to be skinned alive.

On the train going down to Brisbane, Lady Blamey[1] was there and she wanted me to be in a photo with her. When we got to Greenslopes Hospital it was very early in the morning and my Dad was in the army and he just happened to be in hospital there too. And he went to get a leave pass and the orderly said to him, 'You come in this morning?' That was how Dad found out I was there. They hadn't notified him.

1 Wife of General Blamey, Commander in Chief of the Australian military forces.

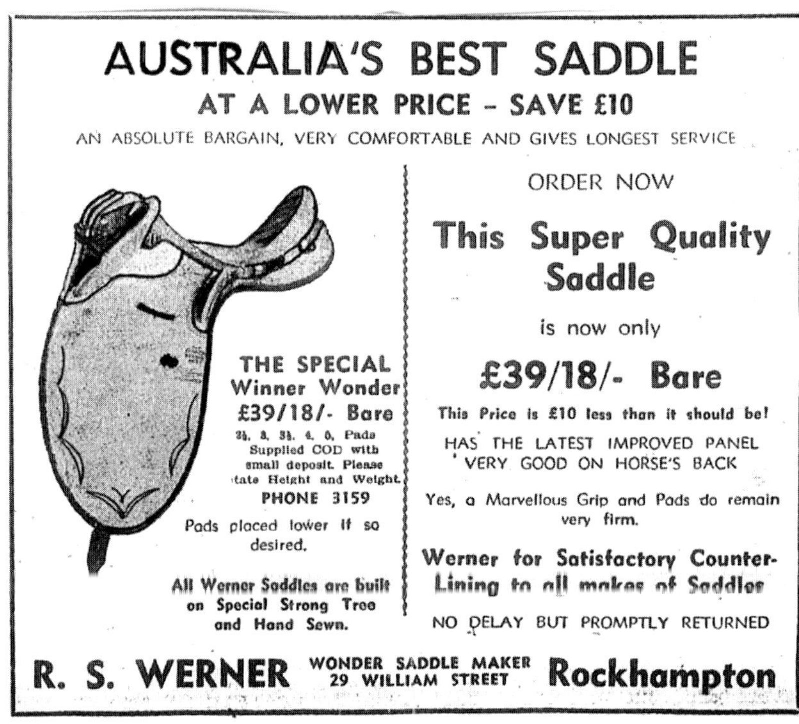

I was in Greenslopes and then Lady Chelmer Rest Home, where the wounded were sent to recuperate, ten months all told. And though Repatriation were very good, they didn't tell you much. You had to find things out for yourself. When you were discharged from hospital they give you six pounds to get a suit made and thirty shillings a week pension. And after that you were on your own. A lot of the disabled soldiers became lift-drivers, but I didn't want anything to do with cities. I decided I could take up saddling and, that way, I could still stay in the bush. I never done saddling before, but I knew a bit about saddles and to be saddler appealed to me. I started at Edward Butlers, in Brisbane. Harold Worthington was the foreman and he was a very, very good saddler. I had to learn from the start.

To make a saddle, you get a 'tree' and dress it down; the tree is timber with a steel lining. Then you've got to cut the flaps out and the seat and set the knee-pads. The knee-pads are solid, packed with waste leather. You skive them, pare them, until you get a nice shape. At first it's all tacked together. For the stuffing you use horse-hair. First you have to tease it. You get a brace – not a brace and bit, just the brace, with a hook on it, and twist the hair into big skeins. Then you boil it. Then you dry it out and tease it some more and that gives it the spring. That's your stuffing, that and flock – which is cotton waste, very soft. You put a skirt which has slots where the knee-pads fit through. Then it's all sewn. About a week's work goes into to making a saddle. We used to sell them for nineteen guineas, fully mounted. They are round about three-thousand dollars now.

When I was qualified I bought a thirteen hundredweight Chev truck and went on the road as a station saddler, going from station to station repairing saddles, doing any counter-lining, any repairs to straps and gear, making hobbles. Stations would get in touch and want me to come. I had a mate with me, Charlie Mitchell, that had been in the army with me. We decided to go to Exmoor station outside Collinsville to see the mother of a mate, Les Bailey, that was killed at Salamaua.

On the way to Exmoor, there had just been a storm, and we came to a fork in the road. One track was blazed and the other one went straight ahead, so we took it, and next thing we got bogged crossing a muddy gully, so we started to walk. I was just getting used to my leg. I wasn't using crutches or a walking stick in those days. We walked twelve mile and never got to anywhere. We camped by the track overnight, nothing to eat, not even a billy to boil. Next morning we started to head back. Charlie said he'd go on ahead and try to get the truck out. He managed to get it out and came back and picked me up. Next morning we took the blazed track and got to Exmoor. The wet season set in and we were there six weeks. They were wonderful to us. All the ringers had gone for Christmas and so it was just family. Exmoor was an outstanding sort of homestead, very modern, with beautiful big rooms and bathrooms. It had belonged to Dr. Dalrymple.[2] Mr and Mrs Bailey couldn't do enough for me because I'd been a mate of their son Les before he got killed.

From Exmoor I moved on to Scartwater station that the Cunninghams of Strathmore gave to the RSL to pay for Legacy kids' education. Then on to Yaccamunda. Yaccamunda means 'Hard yakka for your tucker'. If they ran out of grog they used to get into the metho. They'd come over to me where I'd be working in the shed and say, 'You got any carmi?' That was what they called metho, 'carmi'. They'd strain it through a half a loaf of bread to purify it a bit. Some of them reckoned straining it through burnt toast was better. Then I went on to Strathfield, owned by Fred Williams. He was a terrific fellow. He said, 'Make yourself at home! If you spit on the floor at home, spit on the floor here!'

From there I went to Strathmore station, near Collinsville. I met this fellow there who had a tin mine up at Chillagoe and he wanted a partner with a truck to go into it with him, so I thought I'd give it a go. The mine was on Blackdown station near Mungana. We got the shaft down to 84 feet with just a ladder made out of bush-timber to get up and down. But the worst part of it was hoisting those bloody buckets of stone up. With one leg you can't get the purchase you need for the job. Then the seam cut out. It was thirty inches wide but there was no tin in it so we gave it away. In any case, I didn't like being down a shaft all day and living rough and not being able to getting cleaned up at the end of the day's work.

Then I went cooking on Rookwood station for George Fergusson. I used to scrub that place out! George said to me once, 'You mightn't be the best cook in the world but you've got to be the cleanest!' From there I moved to Rutland Plains up in the Peninsula.

2 Readers familiar with The Letters of Rachel Henning (Angus and Robertson; 1963; David Adams, editor) will greet this mention of Rachel's much loved Exmoor with delight. The present-day 'outstanding sort of a homestead' at which Jock and Charlie were made so welcome is some distance from the original bush homestead built by Biddulph to accommodate his spinster sisters in 1862.

I done the saddling at Rutlands and then the cook left, so I took on the cooking; cooking for the house and the men and the Aboriginals and making twelve to thirteen loaves of bread a day; sending some out to the camp. I put the Wet in there. Rutland Plains was a very nice station, everything neat and in order. The Aboriginals had a proper dining-room, though they never used it. They seemed to prefer just to eat outside. And, cooking for them, you'd have to ring the bell for an old gin to bring all the dixies over. And one of the old fellows would walk over with his dixie and he'd have to put it down on the track and turn around. Then the gin could pick it up. She couldn't 'look' at him, because he was 'poison uncle' to her. Some sort of taboo, they had.[3]

And one day when the musterers were heading out, one of the Aboriginal stockmen was on this big horse and it kept throwing him. The boss, Fred Kreideman, told him, 'Don't let him beat you! Get back up on him!' But this blackfella reckoned, 'No, Boss. More better me ride along you on foot!' There was a place near Rutland called Lochnagar, a run-down, derelict sort of an out-station, and one time the fellow there had a yard full of horses and the police came out to arrest him for cattle-duffing and took him away to gaol. All the horses that were left in the yard perished.

Rutland is all salt-pan, tea tree country; a lot of billabongs and creeks running into the Mitchell. Very good fishing. When the Aborigines were hunting ducks on the lagoons, they would put some leaves around their heads and just float down on the ducks and pull them under by their legs. They weren't worried about crocodiles, but there were plenty about. There were a couple there I saw that would have been over sixteen foot. And a blackfella at Kowanyama Mission, he had a big bend in his head where a croc had hit him with his tail. And one bloke, Ted Young, got into a lot of trouble. He came across a croc's nest and collected the eggs and they started to hatch. As soon as one came out of its shell it bit his wife on the leg. He was giving these baby crocs away. The DPI got to hear about it and didn't they go crook! You couldn't touch a croc's nest. There were buffalo about in the scrub. One time Fred Kreideman shot this big old buff in the swamp. It took two of us with a sapling to lift the hide on to the truck. The skin around a buff's neck is like armour-plating; it's inches thick.

Next Christmas I got the idea I'd go out to Camooweal and set up a saddlery shop. I got to Camooweal just after a big hotel robbery at the Post Office Hotel. Someone had pinched the safe out of the pub and got about seven thousand pounds out of it; big money then. The Mount Isa police came out but they never caught up with who done it. And, funny thing, years later, they found the safe over the back of the air-strip, blasted wide open and rusted out.

Camooweal was the centre for a lot of droving in those days. The drovers made their homes there for their families and they'd run their horses on the common. Then at the start of the droving season they'd head off over the Barkly Tableland for

3 See also the author's Red Dust Rising, CQU Press, in which Ray Fryer describes a similar practice among the Aborigines of Urapunga station in the Northern Territory, where members of one tribal moity, or 'skin group' could not 'look' at certain members of other groups.

places like VRD and Brunette and Anthony's to pick up their mobs. It was a lively little town and I set up my shop at the old pub.

There was plenty of work for a saddler and I did alright. If there were pack-saddles needing new counter-lining I'd get the straw beer-bottle wrappers from the pub and use them for the stuffing. What stood me in good was that if I told a man I'd have his saddle ready by such-and-such a day, I'd stay up all night if necessary, to see it was finished. I always reckoned once you give your word on a thing you stuck by it. I was paying a pound a week for the rent of the shop and boarding at the pub; three meals a day and a room.

'Then, as now, Freckleton's Store, was a feature of Camooweal life.

Freckleton's store was the hub of the town. There was one old chap there, Billy Walker, an old ringer; always on the grog. That was all those old ringer-fellows done when they come into town. They'd slap their cheque on the bar and cut it out in grog. When they'd run out of money they'd go across to Freckleton's store to get a bit more cash from Mrs. Freckleton. Once they got back out to the station they'd send a cheque in to her to wipe the slate clean. One day Billy went to Mrs. Freckleton's but she said, 'Oh, I don't know, Billy. You're a long way behind on the slate.' Old Billy laughs. He tells her, 'Hell, no! I'm way in front! You're the one that's behind!' That's how the town was. Nobody saw anybody stuck for a feed or a beer.

But by 1951 I'd decided to go back to Dalby and get married to a girl I'd known there. We bought a cropping and cattle place outside Monto. The first fortnight we were there a bushfire went through and burnt the place out. Not the house but all the paddocks and crops and fencing, bar two posts. No insurance, so things were tough. To re-fence I cut new fence-posts out of the scrub with a cross-cut saw and split them with a maul and wedges. My brother came and give me a hand. My wife was a country girl and a great worker. She stuck by me. We had our family there, four boys and a girl. We battled on for nine years.

My wife's family were on the Downs and they wanted us to move down there so we bought a place called Brazil, outside Irvingdale; a nice place, grain and cattle. See, I was lucky it was my right leg gone; I was still able to swing up into a saddle with the left. When we were first there I rode a young horse thirty-two mile from the father-in-law's place, picked up a mob of cattle and took them back home, sixty odd mile, on my own, in the one day. That wasn't droving. It was driving!

Jock on his property Brazil, on the Darling Downs. He says, 'I was lucky it was my right leg gone. I was still able to swing up into a saddle with my left.'

Actually, horses gave me the least trouble. Now cattle, they'll go you. I've had a few near misses in the yards with cattle. We had mob in the yard one day when the buyer was coming and this steer charged me. I dodged but he hit a railing of the fence and it swung out and flattened me. I was a bit sore for a while. Another time we were drafting and I went to step back out of the way and tripped. I put my arm down to save myself and did my shoulder in. That put me out of action for a while. Without your arm you can't get about on your crutches! But most of the time things run pretty smooth

We had twelve years of drought when we first went there and I was cutting tree-pear for fodder with a chain saw. The place next door was infested with pear; so thick you couldn't have opened your pocket-knife in it. They reckon one old piker bull lived inside a patch of prickly-pear for a couple of years, just eating round and round in a circle, before they went in with a grader to clear it and found him.

I love lucerne and I always liked growing it. There's a lot of skill in growing good lucerne. We used to stook it until it was dry and then cart it in and make stacks. That takes a bit of skill, too, You have to cap each stack, like a thatch, so that it sheds any rain. You can cut lucerne every few weeks for a while so you might make three or four stacks for the year.

One time, the solenoid on the tractor was crook - a big John Deere - and those tractors were built so that if you've got the gear leavers in gear, you can't start it. And this time, I got up and turned the key and nothing happened. So I got down and went round the front to short the terminals across to get it going. But unbeknowns to me, as soon as I done that, I by-passed the safety on the gears, so the tractor sprang into action and starts coming towards me and I'm right in front the wheel. And I can't do much in the way of running! I was just dumb-founded for a bit! I couldn't make out why it was moving, but it's coming, coming! It runs over a forty-four drum of paint, knocked the bench down and it was half-way though the shed wall before I could get round, reach in and turn the key off. I had a few nightmares about that for a while because not long before another fellow had done the same thing and the wheel just flattened him out like pastry. But see, that's why I'm a friendly bloke. I can't fight and I can't run!

And another time I had a six hundred pound drum of molasses, and I'd put it on a cradle I'd made, but the bung wasn't the right way round for the tap. So I put a chain around it and got on the tractor to hoist it, then got down to turn it round so it would fit. And it slipped out of the chain. It brushed past me and jammed my artificial leg up against the fence. I wasn't hurt but I couldn't get out because of me leg. So the only thing I could do was take off all me clothes, take off me leg and all the harness, hop around, get back on the tractor, shift it, get back down again, hop around, put me harness and leg back on and get dressed again. It was just as well the Jehovah Witness ladies didn't turn up just then!

And another time I was putting the chooks away with me little dog Bonnie, and I looked down and there's this big black snake with his head flattened out and he's chewing on me leg! I don't know how long I'd been standing on him. He must have been thinking, 'Why won't this bastard die!' But in a reflex action I brought the walking stick down, and that settled him!

I never let m'leg stop me from doing a job once I'd made up my mind to get it done, but I find the biggest disadvantage of having the one leg is getting a shower. Your shower is one of the best things in your day but for us amputee blokes it's one of the most difficult. And a shower over a bathtub is a death trap! So at our place I built a solar shower outside. One time I'm having a shower and I'm just reaching to hang the towel up and I see this black snake, and he's all wet, so he must have been under the shower with me. There's not much you can do when you're standing on one leg and your crutches are over in the corner. So I hop over and grab them and give him a couple of smart jabs as he slithers out under the wall. I thought no more of it. And that night, I felt sort of scratchy on my stomach and I thought I must have had a bit of wood-shaving in my singlet from my wood-turning - which is my hobby. And the next night this scratchy feeling is still there and there's a bit of a lump so I had a look and there's two fang marks. The bugger must have got me when I was bending over to pick up the soap. So I went to the doctor and he said it was a wonder I didn't die. He said, 'What saved you must have been that he bit you through the towel.' I said, 'Well, he could've. It was hanging pretty limp next morning.'

My other hobby is whip-making. One year I went to Farm Fest and I saw a bloke, Jimmy the Whip, doing a whip-plaiting demonstration. I decided I wanted to learn. There was an old fellow, Alf Reimers – he was ninety-two – lived about forty miles away from our place, a very good whip-maker, and I said to him, 'I'd like to learn to make whips. Could you teach me?' and he said, 'Yeah. Come over.' So I used to go over to his place at Hayden and he showed me how to cut out a kangaroo hide and the plaiting of it. Whip-makers are very open, very friendly. If you admire something, they would show you how to do it

The main things about a good whip are taper, shape and weight. You start off with a kangaroo skin and you cut eight strands, right around, until you've got twelve foot. To judge cutting the strands, a lot of fellows just use their thumb-nail, but I'd rather use a cutter to get all the strands even. We've all got our own method but I use the hole in a toothbrush handle to run the strands through and that makes all the laces the same thickness. Otherwise they will show up as uneven in the whip when it is made. The secret is to have a nice taper all the way through. The fall is about twenty inches. Kangaroo hide is too thin to make a fall. It has got to be red hide – that is, tanned – or green-hide. And on the end of the fall you put the cracker. The cracker is what makes the noise. It's the super-sonic boom of air being displaced. To crack a whip you throw it out as if you're throwing a stick for a dog. Use your wrist. Get it going in a big hoop that gets smaller and smaller and smaller until, crack! Keep looking straight at what you're aiming at, a leaf or a bit of dirt, and your hand will follow your eye. A lot of blokes can kill a snake with their whip.

I used to do a lot of contract harvesting and contract grader-work, putting down sileage pits for people. Those pits would have been sixty feet long and eighteen feet deep. With sileage there is very little waste. Once you fill the pit you put a layer of soil over the top and pack it down and that seals it. I have put pits down for people that lasted fifteen years and when they have dug them the feed is still beautiful. The cattle love it. Once you open a pit it will last you two or three months, depending on how many cattle you are feeding. It won't spoil with any rain because it is too solid for water to penetrate it.

That Downs country is good country though the dingoes were bad. I've seen as many as thirteen at one go getting among the sheep. I put in a six foot dog-fence round the boundary; cut the posts, dug the holes myself. I also built two silos, concreted and reinforced. I painted the house, except for the roof. I put in any number of fruit trees; oranges, lemons, mandarins, nectarines, a plum tree, a lemonade tree – lemonade is a cross between an orange and a lemon; makes beautiful drinks – and grapes; we give grapes away by the bucketful - a macadamia tree and two bunya pines. We're only fifty-six kilometres from the Bunya Mountains. Bunya nuts, you roast them, and they taste something like roast potato. The Aboriginals used to come from all over to hold big bunya nut feasts in the old days.

Brazil has been a good property to us. We raised a family and always lived well. I don't owe anybody a penny. It's taken work, but the motto of our family crest was 'Unconquered by fatigue' and I've stuck by that. My son Don brought a mate home from school once and this kid hurt his arm. Don told him. 'Don't worry! Even if you broke your arm, Dad would still let you work!' The things I have managed to get done around the place have amazed some people, but I always reckoned it was no good complaining. Complaining don't grow legs. You might as well keep smiling and get on with the job.

APPENDIX A

Extract from Commando; From Tidal River to Tarakan; The Story of the 2/4th Australian Independent Company by G.E. Lambert

Survivors' Accounts of the Loss of the LST off Milne Bay;

(1) The weather was beautiful. It did not seem as if there was a war on. The sea was like a mirror with landing craft strung out in convoy and the sub-chasers slipping in and out amongst them. We lay on the deck, playing cards or two up and looking lazily at the sea.

It was on the last afternoon before we landed that the alarms rang and the ack-ack opened up. The Japanese planes came in diving very low. We could see their bombs fall away from under them and the pilot looking back over his shoulder as he pulled out of his dive. Then we were told to go below deck into our compartments. The American sailors locked the doors between each compartment, locking us in.' (Cpl Ken Bloomfield)

(2) Japanese bombers screamed down to spill their loads on the convoy. Orders came through for all troops to go below and then all watertight doors and bulkheads were closed and locked. It was very traumatic being locked up in there. I wanted very much to be on deck in daylight and fresh air. Then came a blast followed by a monstrous detonation. I thought, 'God! I'm going to die without firing a shot. Without a chance to fight back.' (Jim Rae)

(3) When the raid started we were down below in the sailors' quarters. For some unknown reason I said to my mate George Squires, 'Let's get over into that corner by the steps.' Next thing, she hit. The explosion rolled the deck right up. George was slumped against the lockers. All the bunks – those wire-mesh things – were squashed in a tangled heap of metal. I scrambled up on top. I said to George, 'Come on!' He said, 'I can't move!' His back was broken. I went back to him and tried to pull the poor bugger up over the tangle of steel. Alan Kelso was lying there. I yelled, 'For God's sake help me with Squizzy!' But he couldn't. His leg was broken. But as far as I was concerned we only had one option; to get out of where we were in a hurry. The water was right below us. The back part of the ship was gone.

A barge that had landed its troops came back and hooked on to the side of ours and towed us into Morobe. They sorted out the casualties and gave us a feed. They put those of us who were fit to go on to another barge and took us off to the landing on Red Beach. Of those from our company who were on the barge that was torpedoed, only five of us were fit to carry on. No.3 Section was effectively wiped out.' (Keith Talbot)

APPENDIX B

Extract from *The Diaries of Joseph and William Hann.*

Joseph Hann and Family; Settlement in North Queensland

November 30, 1861

Left Sandridge Pier this day for Queensland.

March 27, 1862

Left camp 6.45 a.m. Travelled over very rough, broken country, steep range to a deep creek running north, for dinner. Crossed the same class of country to the Burdekin Jack and Mr. James went down to the river. They saw a blackfellow.

March 28th, 1862

Left camp at 7 a.m. Ran up the Burdekin 2 miles. Came to the Clarke River, crossed at the junction. Ran up the Clarke 13 miles. Came to some very high ranges and broken country. Jack shot a native companion.

March 29, 1862.

Shoeing horses. Crossed over some good patches of country. Came to a mountain running into the Clarke. We had some trouble getting the horses under it. Travelled fourteen miles.

March 30th, 1862.

Bill and Mr. James went on a mountain. Saw some fine country. Left camp at 9 a.m. Crossed the Clarke. Went up a range on a fine table country. 15 miles to a stony creek with waterholes. Beautiful country. Weather fine. 16 miles.

March 31, 1862.

Bill and Anning went and found a beautiful valley with waterholes running through it. They killed two emus. Jack and I went up junction (sic) creek, 6 miles. Saw beautiful country. Went over to the valley.

April 14, 1862.

Left camp 8 a.m. Fine morning. Went down the Burdekin. Very rangy and stony. Dinner on the Burdekin and went down twelve miles. Divided the country over into the Valley. Mr. James 3 blocks. Jack 3 blocks. Bill 3 blocks. Anning 4 blocks. I have 4 blocks on Negor Creek, Red Bluff. Good.

APPENDIX C

Notes from ***A Brief History of the Queensland Primary Correspondence School*** by C.E.Bedford

The Queensland Primary Correspondence School was established in 1922 for children living in places so far from existing schools that they could not attend them and for those children unable to attend school owing to some physical disability. In order to be eligible a child had to live three or more miles, not across paddocks or by other short-cuts, from a State or Provisional School. The first name entered on the register was that of Robert Cecil Hoddinott, aged eight, of Clifton Farm, Benaraby, on the North coast Line. By the end of 1922, 796 children had been enrolled.

Children were enrolled from the age of five years and upwards. During the war years lessons were also sent to all children who were, owing to war precautions, debarred from attending school in the Cairns and Townsville areas. Pupils were graded according to the information given on the enrolment form, each child being put into a grade for which it was considered he or she was most fitted. Each child's regular mail day was also marked on the form. The child was allotted to a teacher who noted any necessary information such as physical disabilities, reason for absences, left handedness, weak eyes, etc.

All work set was carefully graded to cover the work required in corresponding grades in State Schools for a similar period. A week's work was sent for every pupil for every week. The books of each grade had their own particular colour. A complete school-year's work consisted of 42 sets of papers. Pupils were asked to work at their papers on the five school days of each week for from three to five hours in each day, according to age and grade, but not necessarily under the home supervisor all the time. The finished weekly work was returned to the school by the first available mail. The teacher checked, marked and annotated each set of returned exercise books, giving merits or special merits for work well done and scolding that carelessly done. Teachers came to know their pupils as though they were in daily contact with them. Personal letters were exchanged with each child.

From its early days the school forwarded a gift book to all its pupils at Christmas time. During the war the children gave up their precious books so that the money could go to provide two mobile canteens for servicemen in New Guinea. Each canteen had the school badge on the side and the inscription 'A gift from the children of the Primary Correspondence School of Queensland.' The school's active branch of the Australian Comforts Fund sent parcels to past pupils serving in the forces. In 1939 The Mail Way, the magazine of the Primary Correspondence School was first published. Contributions of stories, poems, snapshots and drawings sent in by the pupils together with articles by well-known people on topics of interest, made up the contents.

Children taught by the Primary Correspondence School were well able to hold their own with children from ordinary schools. Teachers felt that their writing was definitely superior and their application to study and their self-reliance of a higher degree.

The Primary Correspondence School is now known as The School of Distance Learning and using the technological advances of the twenty-first century continues to educate isolated children to a very high standard of primary education.

APPENDIX D

Making a Greenhide Rope

Charlie Rayment – Eildon Park, Winton

Choose a hide off a freshly butchered beast, peg out tightly on the ground with at least eight pegs and clean off as much meat and fat as possible. It is impossible to cut the strands evenly without proper cleaning first. A hide from a white or roan shorthorn will often twist into the softest rope.

Commence cutting the strand from the middle of the hide. Depending on whether the hide is from a bullock, cow or calf determines the width of the strand. About ¾ of an inch from a three year old bullock is about right. Cut a six inch diameter hole in the centre and start from there. For a head-rope of about thirty ft length you would need to cut the single strand to about 120ft. A small bullock hide will cut this length easily without using the thin flanks of the hide. Next cut the strand into three even lengths and soak in a 5 gallon container in very salty water for 12 hours until the hide is quite soft.

Find a post or tree and attach three swivel hobble chains to it about six inches apart. Find a suitable weight for the other end. A coil or two of plain fencing wire does. Attach a strand to each hobble chain and the other end to the weight. When attaching the wet strands, put a small split in the end, tie an overhand knot and insert a small peg – a three inch piece of wire does – through the slit to stop the knot pulling out. For the top and bottom strands it is easier to tie them on to a small s-shaped hook so as to transfer them to the middle chain after twisting, before the final reverse twist.

Insert a short stick through the hobble ring and twist separately each of the strands, clockwise. When you think each strand is twisted enough, undo the top and bottom strands and attach to the centre chain that holds the other strand. Now twist the three strands anti-clockwise. You will find the weight at the other end creeping up as the twist gets tighter. The shorter the twist the stronger the rope, as the twist tends to stretch out with a heavy animal on the other end.

Depending on the weather, leave the rope on the twister for about ten days. New rope needs the twist tightened several times a day for the first three days as the moisture dries out. It is better to make ropes during the winter as they do not dry out so hard. It is important to keep the rope stretched out tight until it is dry enough to cut off the twister.

Now drag the rope for about twenty miles or so behind a vehicle to remove the hair. This is easier than scraping it off with a knife. Next the rings need to be put on. I generally use one which is heavier than a hobble ring, on either end of the rope. Some prefer a leather ring or a keeper instead of a steel ring. I put the rings on with a Turk's Head knot, sometimes known as a Double Wall and Crown. Use the finished rope as soon as possible so that it will soften up. The more use a greenhide rope gets the softer it will become. Keep stretched tight in the shed when not in use. I do not ever grease a rope as I understand this causes it to rot.

GLOSSARY

Bag down; to rub soothingly a horse that is being broken in, with an old bag or piece of hessian, in order to get it used to being handled and saddled.

Bit of a blow; rest

Brake; temporary paddock of electric fencing run off a portable battery.

Broncho; branding without the use of a cradle. A horse trained especially to pull the calf to be branded into position; heavy harness used for the purpose.

Broncoing; branding calves in open paddock without using a crush. The calf is cut out of the mob and roped by a horseman on a bronco-horse, a horse of heavier build, and dragged to the bronco-panel, a set of rails designed so that the rope slides into a slot between two upright posts, enabling the calf to be grabbed by 'front leg' and 'back leg' members of the team, thrown to the ground, castrated, ear-marked and branded. It is then allowed to run back into the mob to suckle on its mother to promote healing. Bronco branding has become a popular team sport in the west, during which paint is used to brand the calves instead of heated irons. Points are awarded for skill and timing.

Camp; the men of a mustering team

Choked-down; of a male drinker, completely drunk; of horses, brought to complete submission by having a rope tightened around its neck.

Clumper; a horse of sturdy build usually with a degree of draught animal in its breeding, suitable for pack work or for bronchoing.

Coachers; a small mob quiet stock, either horses or cattle but usually the latter, into which wild stock being mustered are likely to run by herd instinct for security.

Cowboy; on a Queensland station, odd-job man or rouse-about

Fats; cattle of weight and size suitable for sale to the meat works.

Fly; a sheet of canvas drawn over the ridge pole of a tent to form a second roof for coolness, but more often, and especially in the Outback, used as a shelter without a tent underneath.

Flying fox; a cable across a river or gorge underneath which is suspended a box capable of transporting goods or one or two passengers.

'have a lend of'; take advantage of

Pack; (verb) to carry by pack-horse; (noun) pack-horse

Plant; the horses and equipment that make up a mustering team

Pleuro; pleuropneumonia, a virulent bovine disease caused by viral infection, against which cattle can now be vaccinated but which were formerly inoculated.

Purse; male genitalia

Root; to buck with head down and stiffened legs.

Rousie; odd-job man; especially in a shearing-shed

Rung; ringing (of cattle); occurs when the leaders of a mob circle back into the mob setting up a spiral effect that can lead to stock losses through crushing and trampling.

Sheath; bull's genitalia

Side-line; to hobble a horse front leg to back leg

Split-bag; a bag of hessian previously used for stores such as sugar or flour, put to secondary use by being cut across one side so that it can be thrown across a horse to carry other goods.

Stage; the distance cattle travel on an average day on a stock route, usually about eight to ten miles. It was etiquette among drovers to 'do their stage', i.e. not to linger, so as to leave sufficient grass for the mobs coming behind.

Stranger; a beast belonging to another property.

Tailers; stock being watched by a mounted rider or riders when no paddock is available to hold them.

'thirteen fifty'; 'thirteen hundred and fifty ', colloquial usage among drovers for the size of a mob of cattle, especially if in their charge.

Turkey nest; a dam constructed with a circular earth wall and filled by means of a pump from a windmill or bore.

Yellafella; person of part-Aboriginal extraction

BIBLIOGRAPHY

Adams, David (ed), *The Letters of Rachael Henning*, Angus and Robertson, 1963

Bedford, C.E; *The Queensland Correspondence School;* Shell House Journal; 1946.

Buchanan, Bobbie; *Keep the Branding Iron Hot;* Central Queensland University Press, Rockhampton, 2002

Callinan, Bernard J, D.S.O., M.C.; *Independent Company, The 2/2 and 2/4 Australian Independent Companies in Portuguese Timor, 1941-1943;* William Heinemann, London.

Clarke, Harry, (1) *Joseph Hann and Family; Settlement in North Queensland* (2)William Hann; *Expedition of Exploration to the Endeavour River Cape York Peninsula, 1872; Reconstructed from Their Diaries and Two Notebooks.*

De Vries, Suzanne & Jake, *Historic Brisbane, Convict Settlement to River City;* Pandanus Press, Brisbane, 1998

Durack, Mary, *Kings in Grass Castles;* Constable and Company, London, 1957

Eastgate, Marion et al. *Directory of Moreton Bay Region 1852/53; Queensland Family History Association, 1984;*

Gibson, Dorothy and Bruce; *A Pattern of Pubs, Hotels of Townsville, 1864- 1914; JCU Press; 1988*

Houldsworth, Marion; *Barefoot Through the Bindies; Growing up in North Queensland in the Early 1900s;* CQU Press; Rockhampton; 2002

Houldsworth, Marion; *Red Dust Rising; The Story of Ray Fryer of Urapunga;* CQU Press, Rockhampton; 2004

Kent, Nancy; edited by Lorraine Nott; *The House That Jack Built;* Boolarong Press, Brisbane, 1985

Lambert, G.E, *Commando, From Tidal River to Tarakan; The Story of 2/4th Australian Independent Company, A.I.F; 1941-45;*

Miller, Ada; *The Border and Beyond – Camooweal since 1884*

National Library of Australia, Canberra; *Australian Collections; Oral History; Ethel Donnellan;* Interviewed by Bill Gammage and Bruce Simpson.

North Queensland Register, Charters Towers, July, 1900.

Penzig, Edgar, *Fast Squatters, Gents and Gamblers;* Tranter Enterprises, Katoomba. 1996

Perkins, Di; *Outback Insights; A Social History of North West Queensland,* 1925 -1950; Mount Isa Historical Society; Merino Press; 1996

Petrie, Constance Campbell; *Tom Petrie's Reminiscences of Early Queensland; UQU Press;* 1992

Rayment, Charlie. *Making a Greenhide Rope;* Longreach Leader; September, 2000

Rayment; Pauline and Charlie, Winton; Personal Collection; Ethel Donnellan; Recollections of Davenport Downs and Winton.

Reynolds, Henry (ed); *Race Relations in North Queensland;* JCU Press; Townsville; 1992

Journals and Other Publications;

Shell House Journal; *July, 1946; The School That Went to Its Pupils; A Short History of the Queensland Primary Correspondence School;* Bedford, C.E.

Whitehead, P.J. and Stephenson, P.J ; James Cook Univesrity Press, 1998; *Lava Rise Ridges of the Toomba Basalt Flow, North Queensland.*

North Queensland Register, October 7th, 1999; *The Second Second Commandoes,* Larry Dalhunty.

Pettigrew, J.D. *The Min Min Light and the Fata Morgana; An Account of a Mysterious Optical Phenomenon.* www.uq.edu.au/jack/Min Min C.E.O.pdf

INDEX

V

W

Y

The Gulf To God Knows Where
Volume 2

Maybe It'll Be Rain Tomorrow
Marion Houldsworth

ISBN: 978 1 921920 81 3

RRP $29.95

List of Personalities Featured in Volume 2

Dale Appleton
Brian Beveridge
Mac Core
Lennie Forman
Reg Hart
Ross Leake
Tom Martel
Bob Masso
Wayne McCulloch
Estelle Moody
Toby Rogers
Clargie Saltmire
Tommy Saville
Ab Teece
Kate Darcy Teece
Jack 'Scrubber' Watson
Margaret Whelan
Brenda Wilson
George Westmacott

Other titles by Marion Houldsworth...

Barefoot Through the Bindies

Australian children of this new millennium take for granted a lifestyle that includes videos, T.V. soapies, DVDs, computer games, rock concerts, brand-name clothing and Mum's taxi service.

But the Australian children of a hundred years ago, the Federation era, had a different set of expectations. Many of them walked barefoot through the bindi-eyes to school. Their homes were bark-huts with ant-bed floors. They harnessed their billy-goat carts to fetch wood and water, and on starting work at thirteen, gave their pay-packets to mothers struggling to feed large families. Narrators of this book remember mothers who cooked on open fires and made bread, or damper, that staple of bush life, in camp-ovens. Evenings at home were lit, not by electricity but by kerosene-lanterns or candles. When times were hard they improvised with fat-lamps. This earlier generation of North Queenslanders lived with floods and droughts. They knew grinding poverty and they knew hard work. But they revelled in the freedom of the bush and the mateship it engendered. They were proud of their independence and self-reliance; of their resilience. It was the spirit that the boys of the period took with them to the heights of Gallipoli and the mud of France, and which came to embody all that was finest about their newly-formed nation, Australia.

And yet they recall their childhoods with intense love and joy. This is a deeply moving book about the way Australia used to be.
Prof. David Myers, CQU

The early history of North Queensland comes to life through these remembered stories.
Prof. Alistair Thomson

An important contribution to our understanding of earlier generations of North Queenslanders.
Dr Dorothy Sheridan, Sussex University

Poignant and captivating. A joy to read.
Prof. Kett Kennedy, JCU

Other titles by Marion Houldsworth...

Red Dust Rising

ISBN: 978 1 921920 16 5

Ray Fryer says of himself, "I always admired those old-time pioneers, the Duracks and the Buchanans. I wanted to do something like them; something worthwhile." So, when the government resumed the Fryer property for an army training reserve, Ray threw his swag into the back of his truck and headed off to the Northern Territory.

This is is the story of Ray's 'making something worthwhile' of Urapunga, a run-down property on the Roper River. After [illegible] of '[illegible] up to touch [illegible]', rough living and hard work, of learning to live in harmony with the tribal Aborigines, of coping with crocodiles in the rivers, diseases among his stock, and of being cut off in the Wet for months at a time, he could at last begin to feel he was 'getting his head above water'.

Then came the cattle crash of the 1970s. How Ray faced and overcame this challenge and succeeded in making Urapunga a valuable property is part of this gripping story of a man pitting physical strength, integrity and principles, against the odds.
Told with humour in Ray Fryer's own words, this is a great yarn.

'To the Aborigines of Urapunga station, Ray Fryer was not only 'Maluka', the Boss, an experienced cattleman, but also 'a good bloke'. If something went wrong in the camp, lack of food, sickness or death, it was to Ray they turned immediately . And Ray's help was always forthcoming. Urapunga was Ray's whole life for over three decades. This book is a great opportunity to sing the praises not only of Ray Fryer and the hospitality I enjoyed at Urapunga but the beautiful Roper River itself.'

Les Hiddins, 'Bush Tucker Man'; Townsville.

The Wild West in Australia and America by Jack Drake

ISBN 1876 780 66 5

The Australian Outback and the American Wild West were two of the last frontiers in the territorial conquest and expansions of the 19th century. These frontier territories were wild, lawless and extremely colourful.

The Outback vs The Wild West by Jack Drake

ISBN 1876 780 67 3

Famous pastoral explorers and drovers; poddy-dodgers and horse thieves; land-grabbers; colourful females on the frontier; Cobb and Co and puffing billies; rough riders and rodeos.

Colonel Lionel Rose by Trish Lonsdale

ISBN 1876 780 82 7

Colonel Rose AM OBE, after a very distinguished military career, solved the bovine pleuro-pneumonia problem and pioneered the live cattle export industry.

Kajirri: The Bush Missus by Alexa Simmons

ISBN 1876 780 75 4

In 1948 young Adelaide girl Lexie Simmons went to live on the great Victoria River Downs station in the remote outback of the Northern Territory. Before she knew it she was married to a head stockman & thrust into the role of 'bush missus'. It was sink or swim - she swam!

From the Gulf to God Knows Where by Marion Houldsworth

ISBN 1876 780 89 4

Features the life stories of pioneering bushies from the Gulf including Ann Brunner, Bob Forster, Bluey Ellis, Ethel Donnellan, Charlie and Pauline Rayment, Bill Petrie, Rob Whelan and more. Due: July 2006

Red Dust Rising: Ray Fryer of Urapunga by Marion Houldsworth

ISBN 1876 780 52 5

This is the inspiring story of a northern cattleman who built up the Urapunga cattle station from nothing. From the 1950s to the 1990s, he lived rough and worked hard. He worked closely with the tribal Aborigines, made Urapunga a dry station, coped with the many crocodiles in the Roper River, fought against cattle diseases, hunted buffalo, built himself a homestead and survived.

The Bush and the Never Never by Gerald Walsh

ISBN 1876 780 51 7

From Victoria River Downs to the Paroo, and from the Darling to the Murray, this book evokes the eccentric characters, the swagmen, the pioneers and the great bush entrepreneurs who built pastoral empires. It also evokes harrowing tales of babes lost in the bush, and historical treatments for snakebite.

On the Wallaby by Gerald Walsh

ISBN 1876 780 62 2

Continues to revisit and explore the largely neglected but important aspects of life in the Australian bush – the deeds of colourful pioneers, bizarre incidents and little known or forgotten facts about rural life.

Ten Thousand Campfires by Rex Ellis

ISBN 1876 780 65 7

Rex tells of his bush experiences leading safaris in the Outback over a period of more years than he cares to remember. But he also gives hilarious accounts of the down-to-earth tourist safaris that he led in Europe, Africa and India.

Mulga Madness by Rex Ellis

ISBN 1876 780 77 0

Rex Ellis made the first commercial tourism crossing of the Simpson Desert in 1971 and in 1974 was the only person to cross Lake Eyre by boat. He has been a jackaroo, a sheep station overseer and a safari guide from the Kimberley to the Simpson and the Gulf.

Victoria Downs by Mary Roberts

ISBN 1876 780 85 1

This is a book about a Merino Stud with a well deserved and very high reputation and this history is by implication an informal, social history of the merino industry in south-western Queensland.

Another Era by Helen Arnaboldi

ISBN 1876 780 73 8

This book is an inspiring account of the outback NSW and Queensland pioneers in merino sheep, the Mitchell family, from 1865 and especially of Jim Mitchell from 1897 to 1992.

Hauling the Loads by Malcolm J. Kennedy

ISBN 1876 780 63 0

This is the first book to explore in detail the vital roles played by our beasts of burden in the development of outback Australia. A comprehensive history of bullock and horse teams.